GIANTS
OF
JUSTICE

GIANTS
OF
JUSTICE

by ALBERT VORSPAN

Illustrations by ISMAR DAVID

Thomas Y. Crowell
New York

97176

Dedication

SO MANY AUTHORS THESE DAYS SEEM TO LAVISH praise upon their wives for their "frank and detailed criticism" of their work. This I cannot do. My wife uncritically acclaims everything I write. For her superior judgment, and for being not a critic but a loving wife and warm companion, this book is dedicated to Shirley, with heartfelt affection and gratitude.

Library of Congress Catalog Card Number: 60-9931

COPYRIGHT, 1960
UNION OF AMERICAN HEBREW CONGREGATIONS, NEW YORK
PRODUCED IN U. S. OF AMERICA

Introduction

WHAT ARE THE JEWS? A NATION, A RELIGION, A NATIONALITY, a culture, a civilization, a problem? None of these, or all of these? There have been countless answers—none of them fully satisfactory. This simple and perennial question has rocked the foundations of the State of Israel in a momentous debate. The reason is that the Jew defies all the pigeonholes of language and is, in the end, a unique animal, shaped by a glorious and miserable history into something different under the sun. Slavery, Mt. Sinai, the prophets, Christianity, the Talmud, the Crusades, the Inquisition, the French Revolution, America, Hitler, Israel—all have left their special prints upon this stiff-necked people and neither freedom nor democracy, nor science, nor suburbia have quite managed to wash out the uniqueness.

Whatever definition of the Jew is conjured up, one soon comes face to face with a characteristic which amounts almost to one of the stigmata of the Jew: a passion for justice. Judaism gave the world not only monotheism but *ethical* monotheism. All the major religions of the world, and democracy itself, have felt the impact of the sublime prophetic tradition. "Justice, justice shalt thou pursue"—this ancient injunction has weighed upon the shoulders of the Jew as a special yoke from God, the universal mission of the Jew through all of time. Jacques Maritain, noted Roman Catholic philosopher, described Judaism as "like an activating ferment injected into the mass, it teaches the world to be discontented and restless as long as the world has not God—it stimulates the movement of history."

It is a melancholy fact of our time, with all the busyness about religion and all the pretentious talk of revival, that many American Jews—like most other people—are hardly conscious, in their daily lives, of religion, or mission, or Covenant. Many Jews have strayed far from the fountainhead of Jewish religious faith and studiously avoid the synagogue. Yet they are, still, Jews. And, through some strange alchemy, the yearning for justice has left its brand upon these Jews, too. The messianic dream has become, for the Jew, a kind of incurable social disease. This dream permeates his literature, religious and secular. It motivates Jewish organizations in their work for brotherhood and democracy and social justice. It afflicts Jews with a painful sensitivity to social evil and a compulsive need to correct injustice. The People of the Book may have, in too large a measure, forgotten the Book, or even denied it. And, of course, not all Jews are just and fair and good. But the strange truth is that the world—both the Jewish and the non-Jewish—*expects* the Jew to maintain the highest moral standards.

The desire to build a better world has sunk deep into the chromosomes, the bones, the blood, the memory, and the soul of the Jew. An ancient tradition, which exalts this world and invests man with a spark of God, has been tested by centuries of persecution, and the totality of all this has made the Jew not only a barometer of civilization but also a symbol of divine discontent and a messenger of a brighter tomorrow.

Only in America (to borrow from Harry Golden) has the Jew in the modern world been free to express this social vision. Somebody has described the Jewish adventure in America as "history without tears." Here, where cultural and religious groups are encouraged to maintain their dis-

tinctive identities, here Jews have been able to contribute
the group values of their heritage to the building of a
great democracy. America is founded on basic concepts
which stem from the Bible and which undergird both
Judaism and Christianity: the equal dignity of all men
created in the image of God. It is no accident that Jews
and Judaism have flourished in America as in no other
place upon the globe. And, it is no accident that Jews have
contributed their full share of leaders in all walks of American life and that the greatest Jews in America have also
been among the greatest of Americans.

This book seeks to unfold the fascinating stories of some
of these giants of this century. Our focus is upon American Jews who have distinguished themselves as Jews in
the field of social justice and who contributed to America
and to humanity the fruits of their social vision and the
work of their hands. But whom to select? By what criteria?
If we cannot even answer the question, what is a Jew, how
can we expect to answer the question, what is a Jewish
giant? Let us, then, confess a certain amount of arbitrariness, even a bit of contrariness, in the selection. Yet, our
giants were picked so that, taken all together, they would
reveal the sweeping panorama of Jewish life in America
and, in a measure, of America itself. Because so much has
already been written of early American heroes, we have
selected mostly giants of the twentieth century, the third
century of Jewish life in this blessed land.

Whom would you include in a list of American Jewish
giants of justice? Would you include Justice Louis Brandeis,
who conspicuously avoided the synagogue and Jewish religious life throughout his amazing career as lawyer and
Supreme Court Justice, even during his leadership of American Zionism? Would you include Rabbi Henry Cohen of
Texas, who was an articulate anti-Zionist? Would you include David Dubinsky, the labor leader, who is neither

religionist nor Zionist but Jewish secularist? Would you call Rabbi Edward Israel a giant, although he died before he reached the prime of life and is, therefore, unknown even to most Jews? Would you list Dr. Abraham Cronbach, a humble professor at a seminary, who seemed to flounder in political quicksand when he ventured out of his ivory tower? What about Louis Marshall, who was a conservative, and Stephen Wise, a flaming liberal, two men who invariably stood in opposition to each other? Would you include them both? Does Herbert Lehman, who devoted his life to politics, rate as a Jewish giant? And does Henrietta Szold, who lived her most creative years in Palestine, qualify as an American giant? Does Albert Einstein, a German, who came to the U.S. only in his later years and then only because he was a political exile? What about Lillian Wald? And Henry Monsky? Rabbi Samuel Mayerberg? Or Simon Wolf, "the Court Jew"?

They are all giants—to me. They and their lives are the best answers to the question, What is a Jew? A Jew is a many-splendored thing. He defies category. He can cast off his faith; he is still a Jew. He can turn his back on Israel; he is still a Jew. Jewish life is like a mighty ocean, broad enough to encompass all the vagrant streams of Jewish thought. It is broad enough for all who regard themselves as Jews—for secularists and atheists, for Yiddishists and Reconstructionists, for Zionists and anti-Zionists, for Reform and Conservative and Orthodox, for Klal Yisroel, for all.

And now, may I introduce my friends. Through them, you will meet and come to know the fears and the nightmares, the hopes and the dreams of American Jewry—and, in no small measure, of America itself.

A.V.

Acknowledgments

GRATEFUL ACKNOWLEDGMENT IS MADE TO THE FOLLOWING persons for their helpful comments and suggestions upon individual chapters of the manuscript: Judge Justine Polier, Mr. Otto Nathan, Mr. James Lipsig, Rabbi Maurice Davis, Rabbi Joseph Klein, Mr. Emanuel Muravchik, Mrs. Henry Monsky, Mr. Charles Israel, Mr. Julius Edelstein, and Rabbi Erwin Herman.

I wish to thank the following members of the Commission on Social Action of Reform Judaism who served as readers of the entire manuscript: Rabbis Robert Goldburg and Sidney Ballon and Mr. I. Cyrus Gordon, chairman. Their criticisms were most constructive and helped to make this a better book.

For assistance above and beyond the call of duty—or of friendship, for that matter—I express my profound gratitude to two co-workers and colleagues, Rabbis Eugene B. Borowitz and Eugene J. Lipman. Their constant guidance and encouragement were indispensable in the carrying out of this project. My only regret is that other commitments made it necessary for Rabbi Lipman to temporarily withdraw from the literary partnership which both of us enjoyed so much in *Justice and Judaism* and other joint endeavors.

Although I have been helped immeasurably by these and many others, the views expressed in this book are my own —and so are any errors to be found in these pages.

My indebtedness is also expressed to those who labored with the manuscript and mastered my hieroglyphics. Mrs. Vivian Mendeles, Mrs. Ruth Leigh, and Miss Margery Kramer have been tireless in their preparation of the various drafts. I am grateful to Mr. Ralph Davis, production manager of the UAHC, for his usual excellent job in designing the volume, and to Miss Sylvia Schiff for her careful and conscientious reading of the typescript and the proofs.

And, lastly, a personal word of heartfelt appreciation to Rabbi Maurice N. Eisendrath who has been a source of inspiration to me as he has been to so many others. He came to leadership in American Judaism when the spark of social idealism was dying out in the synagogue. With bold courage and unremitting faith, he has fanned the spark into a bright, warming flame of the prophetic Jewish spirit in America.

A.V.

New York City, 1960

Contents

GIANTS
OF
JUSTICE

Simon Wolf

COURT JEW

S IMON WOLF died in 1923, but those who knew him will never forget the moving oratory, the magnetic presence, and the austerely distinguished demeanor which marked this dedicated gentleman to the very end of a remarkable life of eighty-seven years. Simon Wolf's sure hand and nimble spirit made their imprint upon the developing pattern of American Jewish life. Wolf was not altogether an appealing person and his defects of personality and philosophy perhaps make what he was less acceptable to our generation than to the many prior generations he served. But Wolf was a great man, a man of history. Through him and his life stands revealed an epochal and fascinating segment of Jewish history in America, stretching from Abraham Lincoln to Woodrow Wilson.

Frequently, in Jewish history, there arose a powerful leader in times of distress and persecution. He was usually not an elected leader, and his status resided largely in the influence which he had with the non-Jewish powers that be—whether king, or prince, or pope. A few such Jewish figures, such as Isaac Abravanel, Samuel Ha'Nagid, and

Moses Montefiore, actually lived in the king's court and served as his adviser. Simon Wolf lived his life in America, where monarchy had been replaced by democracy and where Jew and non-Jew stood alike before the law. Yet, Wolf too was a "Court Jew." His significance lies not in his own creations or prolific writings, but simply in this: he knew ten Presidents of the United States with considerable intimacy. To them, he was the representative of "the Jewish race." He had for half a century ready access to the ears of Presidents and to the gates of the throne where high policy was evolved.

Simon Wolf was born in Hinzweller, Bavaria, on October 28, 1836. His father, Levi Wolf, was an invalid who taught Hebrew when he could. Simon was born in a part of Germany which Napoleon had incorporated into the French Empire, bestowing citizenship in one stroke upon the Jews of that area. In the post-Napoleon period, however, reaction and anti-Semitism slowly stifled the promise of liberal revolutions. Hungry for freedom, Simon's family joined the "48'ers" who despaired of democratic progress in the Old World and turned their faces to the New. Brought to the United States at the age of twelve, Simon lived with his grandparents in Uhrichsville, Ohio. As a youngster, he clerked in a country store, made good grades at school, and picked the law for his career. Graduating from Law School in 1861, he put out his shingle first in Cleveland, then moved to Washington, D. C., in 1862, in the dark and critical days of the Civil War. He sought to enlist but was rejected because of his bad eyesight and fragile health. Still in his twenties, the intense and ambitious young attorney had already shown an acute interest in Jewish affairs and in politics. He had abandoned his previous attachment to the Democratic Party and was then—and would remain for the rest of his life—a loyal Republican.

In Washington, Wolf entered at once "upon the public

spirited and benevolent tasks ... winning the confidence of
leading men, broadening and strengthening his influence,
using all he gained for the service of his less fortunate fellows, making himself a new sort of tribune of the helpless
and needy in the departments of power, filling important
positions at home and abroad, enlarging the circle of his
friends till they included all sorts of men, and becoming in
his own way the typical man of his race in this country...."
Thus were Wolf's early years in Washington described by
Mr. Justice Wendell Phillips Stafford, of the Supreme
Court of the District of Columbia, in his foreword to Wolf's
The Presidents I Have Known.

Wolf was quick to establish himself, by virtue of his
obvious competence and ever-expanding influence, as the
"representative" of the Jews. If at first this was largely a
self-appointed role, Wolf filled it with such zeal, dedication,
and success that the Jewish organizations of the time had no
choice but to defer to him. From the beginning of his Washington days, Wolf worked with the Board of Delegates of
American Israelites, which had come into being in 1858, to
protest against the Mortara Affair in Italy. A Reform Jew,
he worked alongside Isaac Mayer Wise, the founder of the
Union of American Hebrew Congregations, in building the
institutions of Reform Judaism on the American scene. It
was always his boast that he had attended every Biennial
Council of the Union from its inception in 1873 to his death
(fifty years later) in 1923. Over two of the councils he
presided as chairman. For thirty-five years—from 1878,
when the Board of Delegates of American Israelites was
brought into the Union and became the Board of Delegates
on Civil and Religious Rights, until his death—he served as
chairman of that board. He was also extremely active with
the then-named Order of B'nai B'rith, repeatedly "representing" this organization as well in his Washington activity
and serving for a period as its president.

In his dealings with government officials, Wolf usually
acted on his own. A dramatic example occurred in the midst
of the Civil War. A Jewish soldier, unable to secure a fur-
lough to go to the side of his dying mother, had gone home
anyway. Thereafter, he was arrested, tried and sentenced to
be shot. Wolf was urged by friends of the boy to intercede
with President Lincoln. But the situation was hopeless on
the face of it, because it was common knowledge that the
Secretary of War needed every soldier at the front so
desperately that he had already threatened to quit if the
soft-hearted President would not cease pardoning deserters.
Knowing this, Wolf decided nonetheless to try. He called
Senator Corwin of Ohio, an intimate friend of the President,
and asked him to arrange an interview with the President.
Corwin sought to dissuade him, but Wolf was so importunate that the Senator asked the White House for an appointment. The word came back, "Later in the night."

It was 2:00 A.M. when Wolf and Corwin were admitted
to see the burdened President whose face "wore that gravity
of expression that has been so often described by his his-
torians and biographers." Even in the midst of the appalling
crisis of the Civil War, President Lincoln's sense of humor
served him well. He heard his visitors out and then replied,
smiling impishly, "Impossible to do anything. I have no influence with this Administration." Much as he regretted it,
however, the President felt he could do nothing in this
tragic case. As they were about to leave, Wolf turned to the
President and said, "Mr. President, will you pardon me for
a moment? What would you have done under similar circumstances? If your dying mother had summoned you to
her bedside to receive her last message before her soul would
be summoned to its Maker, would you have been a deserter
to her who gave you birth, rather than deserter in law, but
not in fact, to the flag to which you had sworn allegiance?"

The President paused, rang a bell which summoned his secretary, and ordered the execution stopped. Months later, the Jewish soldier was killed in action and Lincoln, upon hearing of it, told Wolf, "I thank God for having done what I did."

Of much broader significance to American Jewry (then numbering approximately 175,000) during Lincoln's presidency was the notorious Order No. 11 issued by General U. S. Grant. This incredible order, which excluded "Jews as a class" from Tennessee and other areas under Grant's control, stirred a storm of indignation. While Wolf joined in efforts to revoke this palpably undemocratic and unconstitutional order, it appears that Rabbi Isaac Mayer Wise, descending upon the White House in high dudgeon, was largely instrumental in persuading President Lincoln to revoke the order instantly.

During his own intimate association with Grant in the White House, Wolf became convinced that he bore nothing but the friendliest feelings toward Jews and that the offensive order was actually filled out by a bigoted underling of the general. However, in the light of Wolf's tendency to blind himself to the glaring faults of persons in high office who befriended him personally, it might be wise not to accept unreservedly the fervent apologia which Wolf rendered to Grant. One who could ignore the corruption and ineptness of the Grant regime and hail its leader as a man who "achieved greatness" and a "man sans peur, sans reproche" is not likely to label Ulysses S. Grant as the author of the most anti-Semitic document ever issued in the name of the United States Government.

President Grant and Simon Wolf were extremely close in their relationships, both official and informal. The President appointed him Recorder of Deeds for the District of Columbia, a position Wolf held for nine years. A busy, if not a weighty job, which he accepted mainly because there was some anti-Jewish opposition to him, it brought him into touch with Grant with great frequency. "No one during that time, except those immediately surrounding him or the members of his Cabinet, saw President Grant oftener than myself," Wolf recalled proudly years later.

But Wolf called also upon the President with great frequency on Jewish matters. Wolf always insisted that the actual behavior of President Grant while he was in office was the most striking possible refutation of allegations of anti-Semitism which had been directed at Grant as a result of Order No. 11. ". . . I here distinctly state," Wolf insisted many years later, "that during those years President Grant did more on and in behalf of American citizens of Jewish faith, at home and abroad, than all the Presidents of the United States prior thereto or since. This may seem almost incredible, but I speak by the card."

While the cynical may attribute this to the fact that Wolf had rendered effective service upon the hustings in Grant's behalf during the campaign, there can be no doubt that Simon Wolf was a powerful behind-the-scenes figure in Grant's Administration. When the Administration decided to sell arms to France, Wolf was called in to meet with the Cabinet about the possible effects of such an action upon German-Americans. When a Secretary of the American Legation in St. Petersburg, Russia, sent to the Department of State a crudely anti-Semitic defense of Russian pogroms, Wolf was shown the secret report. He subsequently blocked the appointment of the same man to an important government position. In 1876, when the Union of American Hebrew Congregations held its council in Washington, Wolf arranged for the President to receive the delegates personally at the White House. It is not surprising, in view of the warm cordiality between the President and Wolf, that Wolf named his own son, Grant, in honor of the President; and that President Grant, the proud godfather, sent a general rushing to the hospital to bring Mrs. Wolf a basket of flowers on the day of the baby's b'ris (circumcision).

In 1881 Wolf was appointed U.S. Consul-General to Egypt. As we look upon Egypt in mid-twentieth century as one of the chronic sore spots of American diplomacy, modern communications having pushed the Middle East and all the world into our back-yard, it is difficult to bring to mind the long-dead world of the 1880's. Wolf's appointment as Consul-General to Egypt was something of an honor; indeed, it was said to be the highest diplomatic post yet held by a "professing Jew." How did he get it and what were his qualifications? The answer illumines an era when oceans were not mere moats and the earth had not yet shrunk to a jumping-off point to the moon. "For some years," Wolf declared blandly in his reminiscences, "I had cherished the desire to visit Egypt, and some time after the election of Garfield to the presidency, during a conversation with my friend Carl Schurz, I told him that my health was somewhat impaired and that I would like to take a short vacation to the Orient. . . . Several days thereafter he informed me that he had no doubt that I would be appointed as Consul-General to Egypt." And so he was.

As Consul-General, Wolf handled the pleasant amenities of entertaining the pampered Egyptian Khedive, and the American's patronizing air seemed not to disturb, if it did not actually impress, the ineffectual Egyptian ruler. Wolf's duties were mostly minor and ceremonial. Their chief value was apparently the boost to the morale of Egyptian Jews who pictured Wolf as another "Joseph." If his brief career in the foreign service is remembered for anything, it is for an amusing incident which was circulated (mostly by Wolf) for many years. One day, while Wolf was having his coffee on the veranda of his hotel, the acting Consul-General of England rushed to his table and breathlessly announced, "My dear colleague, there is going to be an uprising among the natives tonight and they are going to slaughter all the Christians and Europeans." Wolf calmly continued to sip his coffee. The distraught Britisher repeated his dire warning. Wryly, Wolf inquired, "But how does that concern me? I am neither European nor Christian!"

In complete contrast to Wolf's brief fling in the foreign service was his constant concern as a private citizen, which he never hesitated to communicate to the government, about the fate of his co-religionists in Europe. When the new state of Rumania, representing the merger of two former Turkish provinces, launched a campaign of terror against its Jews, Wolf won the sympathetic ear of President Grant. News that the Rumanian regime was stopping Jews who sought to escape, and driving them into the Danube at bayonet point, outraged public opinion in America and throughout the civilized world. At Wolf's suggestion, Grant appointed Benjamin Peixotto to serve as U.S. Consul to Rumania. Peixotto was a Jew and the President named him to the position to give the Rumanian rulers a lesson in equality and justice.

Years later, during Theodore Roosevelt's administration, Wolf called upon the President repeatedly to discuss with him the barbaric pogroms which had taken place in Kishinef and elsewhere in Russia, as well as the continued discriminations against Jews in Rumania. The President showed genuine sensitivity to these problems and encouraged Wolf in a program to rally world opinion against these inhumane actions. Accordingly, Wolf, in 1903, initiated the Kishinef Petition which was distributed throughout the United States and was signed by prominent citizens of all religions

and walks of life. Although President Roosevelt had the
petition of private individuals transmitted to Russia via
official channels, the Russians refused to accept it. Despite
this rebuff, the petition served its purpose of awakening
wide-spread indignation against anti-Semitic practices in
Russia. Secretary of State John Hay declared, in accepting
the petition, "The archives of our government contain
nothing more precious, and the Jews of the world should
feel profoundly grateful for this great and enduring record." Nothing in his long life filled Wolf with more pride
than did the Kishinef Petition.

Russia's policies of anti-Semitism persisted. In addition
to continued persecution of Jews in Russia, the Czar invoked the U.S.-Russian Treaty of 1832 to justify his country's refusal to recognize the passports of American Jews.
Jewish leaders in the United States mounted a bitter attack
against this practice which they denounced as an infringement of the full rights of citizenship of American Jews.
Distinguished non-Jews, viewing the issue as fundamental
in its implications, joined and excoriated the American
government for acquiescing in such undemocratic discrimination. The issue had clearly come to a head by the time
William Howard Taft moved into the White House in
1909. Indeed, Taft came into office under a pledge, set down
in his party's platform, to take necessary action to protect
the rights of all Americans to full equality of citizenship.

For two years, the government contented itself with
mild protests to Russia. Neither Taft nor his Secretary of
State showed any disposition to abrogate the Treaty of
1832. But, fired by such Jewish leaders as Wolf and Louis
Marshall, the American people were becoming increasingly
disturbed by the indignities visited upon American citizens
of the Jewish faith.

President Taft, acting on a suggestion from Wolf,

arranged a conference with prominent Jewish leaders, including both Marshall and Wolf. To the utter consternation of the Jewish representatives, the President cut off all possibility of a frank discussion of the issue by launching immediately into the reading of a prepared document of his own conclusions. What they boiled down to was an exposition of why the United States could not abrogate the treaty. He cited the long history of the treaty, the hope that Russia would improve its treatment of the Jews, the $60,-000,000 of American capital at stake in Russia, and the danger that breaking off the treaty would dangerously accelerate the influx of Russian Jews to the United States. The Jewish leaders, straying from the protocol of presidential conferences, proceeded heatedly to challenge the President's arguments.

They rejected the implication that the integrity of American citizenship could be subordinated to business interests. They denied that this was a Jewish issue, insisting that this was a far-reaching American issue which cut to the core of American liberties. They argued that Russia had already vitiated the treaty by arbitrarily excluding American citizens of Jewish faith, in contravention of the terms of the treaty itself. They contended that the dignity of the United States Government and the sanctity of American citizenship had been besmirched by Russian arrogance, and that the time was now opportune to restore American honor by nullifying the Treaty of 1832. The conference ended on a sour note when the President showed his visitors a message from the American Ambassador at St. Petersburg. Incredibly, the message constituted a tortured rationalization of Russia's brutal methods of dealing with the Jewish problem.

The Jewish representatives had heard enough. Jacob Schiff, distinguished philanthropist and communal leader, minced no words with the President, ". . . Mr. President, you have said that you are not prepared to permit the commercial interests of ninety-eight million of the American people to suffer because two million feel that their rights as American citizens are being infringed upon. My own opinion has always been that it was the privilege of the head of this nation that, if only a single American citizen was made to suffer injury, the entire power of this great government should be exercised to procure redress for such injury; and now you tell us because some special interests who are trading with Russia might suffer if the abrogation of the treaty was carried into effect, you would not do anything to protect two million American citizens in the rights vouchsafed to them under our Constitution and laws. . . .

"We feel deeply mortified," Schiff continued, "that in this instance, Mr. President, you have failed us, and there is nothing left to us now but to put our case before the American people directly, who are certain to do justice. . . . In 1861 a small but in some respects potential minority claimed that it would be better to permit the slave states to go out of the Union instead of risking a Civil War, but public opinion insisted that the slave must be freed and the Union remain supreme at any cost; the war for the right was thereupon fought and won, even with all the sacrifice it necessitated. To this same public opinion, Mr. President, we shall now turn, and we have no fear of the results."

As the indignant leaders left the White House, Schiff muttered, "This means war!" Knowing that war, even a propaganda war, costs money, Schiff pledged $25,000 on the spot to go into a chest to spearhead an aggressive educational drive to bring about abrogation of the hated treaty.

The struggle for public opinion intensified throughout that year. Meetings were held in cities throughout the

United States. Petitions were circulated. Sermons were preached. Every Jewish organization threw its full resources into the fray. An extended series of conferences were held with Senators and Congressmen in their home districts. Newspaper editorials were solicited. By the fall of the year, public sentiment was clearly aroused and demanding abrogation of the treaty. On December 13, 1911, this sentiment was reflected in resolutions adopted in both Houses of Congress, urging the President to notify the government of Russia of our intention to terminate the Treaty of 1832 at the expiration of the one year's notice required under the treaty. Shortly thereafter, President Taft capitulated. Archly, he told Wolf that he would present him with a Christmas present by sending notice to Russia that the treaty was to be abrogated. He was true to his word.

The passport question is worth considering in some detail, not merely because it constitutes an illuminating episode in American Jewish history, but because it is so poignantly relevant to contemporary issues. Despite all the lessons of our own history, the United States entered into a treaty in 1952 with Saudi Arabia, by which the United States was given the right to build and maintain an air base at Dhahran. While all understood the heavy financial price which the United States was willing to pay to insure the use of this strategic base as a part of the world checkerboard of resistance to Soviet imperialism, few understood, at the beginning, the exorbitant moral price which the United States would be called upon to pay. In accordance with this treaty, since renewed, the United States acquiesced in the exclusion of American soldiers and civilian workers of the Jewish faith from our own air base in Dhahran. If anything, the current practice is even more evil than that which Simon Wolf and his colleagues fought against. Now, in our own time, the American government has permitted discrimination against its own citizens because of the accident of religious faith; the United States has indicated, by its deeds, that the full rights of citizenship may be qualified by considerations of political and military expediency; and the American government has demonstrated, by screening its own citizens to exclude Jews, that the rights of its citizens may be regarded not as ends in themselves but as expendable means to the much broader end of the foreign policy of the moment.

Another social evil which Wolf opposed diligently was the policy of restrictive immigration. Although, in 1890 there were only about 700,000 Jews in the United States, the stream of East European immigrants, which would soon become a flood, was already flowing into New York City. Poor, uneducated, Yiddish-speaking, clinging to their religious traditions, these East European Jews stirred doubts and fears which quickly made themselves felt in the government. Influential political leaders expressed alarm that America was about to be overwhelmed by a "swarm of undesirable Jews."

Senator William E. Chandler, of New Hampshire, typified a growing sentiment in the nation and, especially in the Congress. In a letter written to Simon Wolf in 1893, Chandler denounced all efforts to "encourage Jewish immigration of a character injurious to our people." The Senator complained that the influx of Russian Jews to the United States was not spontaneous; on the contrary, he charged, it was being "incited and promoted" by the Jews of the world. He pointed accusingly to the $10,000,000 fund which Baron DeHirsch had set aside to help Jewish refugees from Russia. "Public sentiment has not yet been strong enough to make it possible to pass a law making new exclusions. But shall we receive a whole nation of Jews as

Jews, who are not desirable citizens; and if we object and argue the question, shall we be vilified by you because we even venture to use the word 'Jew'?" While Chandler's anti-Semitic bias was too blatantly crude for many legislators, his purposes were shared by many. More subtle restrictionists began to talk about the factor of "assimilability to the American way of life," and of "racial stock." Freely translated, these slogans meant, keep those East European Jews out!

The wave of Jewish immigration to the U.S. had a profound impact also upon the American Jewish community. The first phase of Jewish immigration to the U.S. had been small, lasting until about 1825; it had consisted chiefly of Spanish immigrants. The second phase, beginning in about 1840 and continuing until around 1880, had been larger, but nonetheless moderate; it brought into the United States some 200,000 Jewish immigrants from Germany. By the end of the nineteenth century, the German Jews had assumed an ascendancy in the American Jewish community, efficiently organizing the institutions of philanthropy and social service, developing their synagogues and religious institutions in the light of the rather severe Reform Judaism they brought with them from Germany, rising to positions of economic power and political influence, and integrating themselves with remarkable success into the general American community. This comfortable pattern was shattered beyond recognition by the tidal wave of Jewish immigration to the United States from East European countries. More than 2,000,000 Jews swept into the United States between 1871 and 1910.

Simon Wolf, Louis Marshall, Judge Mayer Sulzberger, and other leading Jews—as well as the most potent Jewish organizations, such as the Union of American Hebrew Congregations, the American Jewish Committee (which was

organized in 1906), and the B'nai B'rith—did not exactly
welcome the Russian Jews with open arms. Some well-
established American Jews looked with revulsion upon the
tattered hordes of Jewish immigrants, garbed in old-world
kaftans and wearing their strange earlocks and yarmulkes,
speaking their guttural Yiddish. The German Jew, who regarded himself as completely Americanized, sensed in his
alien co-religionist a threat to his own psychological security and acceptance on the American scene. The fear turned
to alarm as the immigrants, by the tens of thousands,
huddled together in their common misery in New York
City's bursting East Side. Nor was it long before these
Jewish masses, fiercely Jewish in their loyalties and religious
traditions, were ready to challenge the "Uptown Daitch
bosses" in their tight control of the Jewish community of
America.

Simon Wolf and his colleagues did everything possible
to prevent the flood, to dam it up at the source, and, failing
that, to slow it down. As Wolf declared in his reply to
Chandler, "There is not an American citizen of Jewish faith
that has encouraged the emigration of the Russian Jews.
We were aware from the start that it was a great problem,
and that the solution thereof would fall on our shoulders,
as Jews. We tried in every way, by diplomacy and otherwise, to secure from Russia a mitigation of her laws, so as to
have gradual emigration and not a wholesale expulsion. The
whole financial world, concentrated in London, Paris, Berlin, and Vienna, tried its utmost and failed."

When they failed to persuade Russia to relax the grip of
persecution which was driving its Jews across the ocean,
some American Jewish leaders contrived desperately to
distribute the incoming immigrants throughout the United
States. Every effort was made to induce the immigrants to
go to farms, to settle in the South or the West, to leave the

teeming tenements of New York City. A grandiose relocation program was initiated; substantial funds were appro-
priated; the encouragement of the government was enlisted.
Indeed, a special Jewish office was established in Galveston,
Texas, and efforts were made to have boatloads of new
immigrants land there for relocation in the West. These
efforts, too, were foredoomed. It was like the proverbial
finger in the dike. The magnetic attraction of the large
eastern seaboard cities was irresistible to the insecure and
frightened "greenhorn," whose roots had been broken, and
who now wanted nothing more than to find the warmth and
comfort of his own relatives and townspeople.

While the Jewish community struggled to meet the overwhelming challenge of absorbing the immigrants, Simon
Wolf and others fought manfully against the rising demands
to end the traditional "open-door" policy of immigration.
Advocates of restrictive immigration seized upon the tactic
of the literacy test, hoping thus to admit those who descended from the same racial stock as old Americans and to
exclude eastern and southern Europeans. Wolf sensitized
Presidents Theodore Roosevelt and William Howard Taft
to the problem. When a new and popular restrictive immigration bill was pending during Taft's tenure in office, the
President summoned a large group of representative citizens
in the East Room of the White House and allotted each person one minute to express his argument. Wolf said, with
more accuracy of spirit than Talmudic knowledge, "One
of our ancient sages when confronted by a heathen with a
knife in his hand, who threatened to kill the sage unless he
could tell him what there was in religion while (the
heathen) was standing on one foot, gave as his answer,
'Love thy neighbor as thyself.'" The drastic immigration
bill was passed by a large majority but it was vetoed by
President Taft.

record of every Jew who fought in the Civil War so that he could demonstrate that Jews are patriotic and brave? And, as has been indicated, his thraldom at being admitted to the throne of the mighty blinded him to the mistakes, and even the evils, which history associates with some of them.

He was a great Jew, but limited in his vision. His motivations were philanthropic and benevolent; he was cold and remote from the burning currents of conviction which joined Jews throughout the world in peoplehood, Jews who hungered for Zion with all the passion of the Jewish soul, who were imbued with a compulsion to social justice which drove them forth to shake and change the world. He was a conservative, as American and Jew, and through the accident of temperament and history, he played the role of the Court Jew. Simon Wolf is gone, and so is the America and the Jewish community which would tolerate the position of "Court Jew" which he personified for three-quarters of a century. But in his time and in his way, he made a contribution to society of such magnitude to warrant including him among the giants of American Jewry.

Louis Brandeis

FROM ASSIMILATION TO ZION

Others will assess the measure of Brandeis's contribution to American life as a lawyer, as jurist, as social thinker. I can affirm, however, that since the days of Herzl, Brandeis was indisputably and incomparably our greatest Jew. I think not of his gifts as an economist or even his genius as a statesman, least of all of his boundless personal generosity. Rather do I think of the spirit he brought to our cause that I can best describe by using the Hebrew word K'dusho—holiness. I thank God for the fulness of his years and the richness of his days, for what he wrought and above all for what he was."

These glowing words of praise were spoken by Stephen Wise about Louis D. Brandeis. "Our greatest Jew!" How strange that such a superlative tribute could be evoked by a man who did not really become a Jew until he was more than fifty years old! For, although he was born a Jew (in 1856) and never sought to deny that he was a Jew, there was nothing Jewish about Brandeis's life, his contacts, or his interests until about 1910. Against this curious backdrop, one is hard put to explain the emergence of Louis Brandeis as ardent champion of Zionism, as spokesman for the Jewish people, and later, as the first Jewish justice of the United States Supreme Court.

Louis Brandeis was born in Louisville, Kentucky, one of the four children of Adolph and Frederika Dembitz Brandeis. His parents had come to America from Bohemia to escape from the reactionary consequences of the crushing of the European revolutions of 1848. Sensitive and intelligent, Mr. and Mrs. Brandeis were intoxicated with the wine of freedom. After a series of false starts, Mr. Brandeis struck roots in Louisville, where he established himself as a prosperous grain and produce merchant. Louis's first memories were of the turbulent days of the Civil War. "I remember helping my mother carry food and coffee to the men from the North," he recalled. "The streets seemed full of them always. But there were times when the rebels came so near that we could hear the firing. At one such time my father moved us across the river. Those were my first memories."

Louis raced through the Louisville schools with exceptional precocity. His cultured parents maintained a lively and loving home, full of intellectual stimulation. Formal religion, however, played no part in the life of the family. The Brandeises belonged to no synagogue. In her book, *Reminiscences*, Frederika Brandeis explained the religious philosophy in which she raised her children:

"I do not believe that sins can be expiated by going to divine service and observing this or that formula; I believe that only goodness and truth and conduct that is humane and self-sacrificing towards those who need us can bring God nearer to us, and that our errors can only be atoned for by acting in a more kindly spirit. Love, virtue, and truth are the foundation upon which the education of the child must be based. They endure forever. . . . And this is my

justification for bringing up my children without any definite religious belief: I wanted to give them something that
neither could be argued away nor would have to be given
up as untenable, namely, a pure spirit and the highest ideals
as to morals and love. God has blessed my endeavors."

When Louis was sixteen, the Brandeis family took a trip
to Europe which unexpectedly lasted three years, during
which Louis continued his studies in Germany. A discerning
observer, Louis took note of everything he saw and everyone he met. For example, a notation in his diary, describing
his fellow passengers on the return boat trip, revealed not
only a keen eye but perhaps even a faint suggestion of
adolescent anti-Jewish snobbery:

"The passengers of the second cabin are on the whole
rather unpleasant, very few interesting, very few fine, exceedingly many Jews. . . ."

Brandeis entered Harvard Law School in 1875 when he
was not yet nineteen. He loved Harvard from the very beginning, and he left the highest scholastic marks ever before
earned in the Law School. Nonetheless, Harvard was far
from being a breeze for the intense and brilliant young
student. His father's business had collapsed in the panic of
1873, and he was in no position to help his son through
Harvard. Louis was constrained to accept loans and to secure
a job as tutor to tide him over. More menacing than this,
however, was a serious eye strain which led his doctor to
warn him against any further reading and to advise him
against pursuing the law, which was Brandeis's one and only
chosen career. Brandeis overcame this difficulty by the ex-
pedient of having other students read to him and, also, by
following the advice: "Read less and think more."

Young Brandeis began his legal career in St. Louis. It was
an inauspicious beginning, and Brandeis longed for the more
congenial and culturally satisfying environment of Boston.

In April, 1897, he was invited to go into partnership with a brilliant classmate in Boston—and he accepted. In no time at all, the graceful and likable young bachelor was moving easily through circles composed of the "best" people in Boston: wealthy, sophisticated Yankee Brahmins, broadening his social and professional contacts. Oliver Wendell Holmes, Jr., who, with Brandeis, was destined to be a Great Dissenter, was one of the first of his new friends.

Success came easily to Brandeis, and his personal satisfaction was crowned by his marriage to Miss Alice Goldmark who was a source of strength to him through the balance of a long and hectic life. They were married by her brother-in-law, Felix Adler, powerful founder and leader of the Ethical Culture movement in New York City.

From the beginning, Brandeis knew what he wanted out of life and set a clear and consistent course. It was his plan to become financially independent as soon as possible because, as he put it, "in this age of millions, the man without some capital can only continue to slave and toil for others to the end of his days." But unlike other dedicated men, Brandeis had no intention of working himself into an early grave. He took time out of every day to spend with his wife and two daughters, and insisted upon a proper share of rest and vacations.

By 1890, Brandeis was one of the most eminent corporation lawyers in the East. He insisted upon dealing with the heads of corporations personally, refusing to act merely as the legal agent of a corporation. Moreover, his conception of his own role was such that he was approached by these titans of industry not merely for legal advice but for broad counseling on matters of business policy and judgment.

But, even as his lush practice flourished, Brandeis's high character responded to the ethical challenges of a changing society. When violence exploded between strikers and

armed Pinkerton strike-breakers at the Carnegie steel plant
in Homestead, Pennsylvania, in 1890, Brandeis was deeply
troubled. As he wrote later:

"I think it was the affair at Homestead which first set me
to thinking seriously about the labor problem. It took the
shock of that battle, where organized capital hired a private
army to shoot at organized labor for resisting an arbitrary
cut in wages, to turn my mind definitely toward a searching
study of the relations of labor to industry."*

The more Brandeis examined labor and industry, and the
relationship between the law and both, the more he set his
face toward public service. He became a reformer. The
lobbying activities of public utilities, the dizzy trend toward
monopoly, the intimidation of labor, the corruption in
political affairs—these and many other reflections of a too-
rapidly industrializing economy stirred the social conscience
of the restive Brandeis. Gradually, he took up his new role
as "The People's Lawyer." In an address delivered to the
Harvard Ethical Society in 1905, he declared:

"The leading lawyers of the United States have been engaged mainly in supporting the claims of the corporations;
often in endeavoring to evade or nullify the extremely crude
laws by which legislators sought to regulate the power or
curb the excesses of corporations. . . . Instead of holding a
position of independence, between the wealthy and the people, prepared to curb the excesses of either, able lawyers
have, to a large extent, allowed themselves to become ad-
juncts of great corporations and have neglected the obliga-
tions to use their powers for the protection of the people. . . .

"It is true that at the present time the lawyer does not
hold as high a position with the people as he held seventy-
five or indeed fifty years ago; but the reason is not lack of

---

* *Brandeis: A Free Man's Life*, Alpheus Thomas Mason, The Viking
Press, New York, 1946.

opportunity. . . . We hear much of the 'corporation lawyer,' and far too little of the 'people's lawyer.' The great opportunity of the American bar is and will be to stand again as it did in the past, ready to protect also the interests of the people."

Brandeis was describing the new role which was to shape the rest of his remarkable career: to protect the public interest, to save capitalism from itself, to channel the ferment of social change into constructive paths, to secure the rights of the laboring man, and to insure good government in Boston and in Washington. In this role, Brandeis turned his baleful eye here and there, leaping into one controversial issue after another, and—as he described it—"knocking heads right and left" in his tireless pursuit of the "trail of evil."

In 1910 Brandeis was asked to serve as chairman of the Arbitration Board in the garment workers' first general strike in New York City. In handling this delicate and volatile task, Brandeis found himself in close contact for the first time in his life with the Jewish masses and their problems. Unlike the comfortable, conservative Jews he had met in Boston, almost all of whom had left him cold, the intensely Jewish Jews he came to know in New York stirred in him a sense of spiritual kinship. Vital, aflame with a peculiarly Jewish zeal for social justice, and reflecting a deep sense of rootage to a Jewish tradition, these young Jewish men and women struck an immediate chord of sympathy in Louis Brandeis.

Brandeis, walking "on eggs" in the tense negotiations, helped to hammer out an agreement which ultimately led to a stable, responsible union and a model of industry-labor relations. But, beyond this, Brandeis found himself as a Jew. For the first time in his life, he began to probe the implications of his own Jewishness. He brought to bear on "the

Jewish problem" the same massive intellect, the fresh insights, and powers of analysis which had already distinguished his career in the law.

Brandeis came to the conclusion that only by expressing himself Jewishly could he and other Americans of the Jewish faith play their full part as Americans. This American, who had virtually surrendered his Jewish identity, came to the conviction in the fulness of his maturity that the Jew could and must contribute to the panoply of American life *as a Jew*—proudly, consciously, affirmatively Jewish.

"The twentieth century ideals of America," Brandeis wrote, "have been the ideals of the Jew for more than twenty centuries." It was the task of the Jew to help clothe these majestic principles with the flesh of reality, by ennobling American life with the Jewish reverence for social justice and the Jewish exaltation of the saga of the spirit. In short, Brandeis came to feel that a Jew in America could be genuinely and fully American only as he was fully and intensely a Jew. Brandeis repudiated the concept of the melting-pot in favor of a vital cultural pluralism. It was his Americanism which finally brought him to Jewish life.

But Brandeis was never an academic philosopher; he was, intrinsically, a man of action. His quick-developing association with Jewish life brought home to him the world-wide nature and magnitude of the Jewish problem. He sensed in the Jew a nostalgic homelessness, and he perceived the need for a Jewish national homeland. Thus did Brandeis, the assimilationist, who discovered his own Jewishness at the height of his career, set his feet upon the ground of Zionism.

Few mature adults have the plastic capacity for change and growth which characterized Louis Brandeis. Nothing in his background could have suggested a future leadership of the Jewish people. He had never had formal religious training. He had never been associated with any Jewish organization. Many members of his family, and his wife's also, had intermarried. He never attended religious services or practiced any religious observances. The full extent of his Jewish identification had been an occasional contribution to the Boston Jewish Charities.

In 1912 Brandeis met Jacob de Haas, a famous English Jew, who had been associated with Theodor Herzl, the founder of political Zionism. Brandeis was talking to de Haas about a problem unrelated to Jewish life. When their chat was over, Brandeis took de Haas to the railroad station. When the conversation turned to the fascinating experiences which de Haas had had as secretary to Herzl, Brandeis was so stimulated that he canceled his vacation plans and brought the Englishman home. Not long thereafter, Brandeis joined the Federation of American Zionists.

To Brandeis, Zionism became the best hope of the Jewish people. He was not primarily concerned with the return of the Jews to Palestine. To him, the chief purpose in Zionism rested in the spiritual and emotional effect which the restoration of a Jewish homeland would have upon Jews and Jewish life throughout the world. That the whole idea of Zionism was anathema to many of the most powerful Jews of the day, that the movement was at a dismally low ebb— these things did not deter Brandeis for a moment. Almost immediately after joining the Federation, Brandeis became a familiar figure on speakers' platforms all over the country, investing the cause of Zionism with a nobility of spirit which was a mirror of his own consecrated spirit.

Brandeis, who had deftly mastered the art of avoiding the public brickbats which had swirled about his head throughout most of his adult life, now had to contend with the special brand of internecine acrimony which always spices Jewish affairs. In 1915, for example, the *American Israelite,* founded by Isaac Mayer Wise, a mordant anti-Zionist, won-

dered out loud why such Zionists as Brandeis did not take
the first boat to Palestine. Said the *Israelite:* "But our good
Zionist friends prefer luxuries instead of privation. They believe that the Russian Jews should be experimented upon.
Mr. Editor, if Mr. Brandeis and one hundred prominent
Jews go to Palestine and live, then will their example cause
thousands of others to follow suit; will the Zionists accept
this challenge?"

With the outbreak of World War 1, the world headquarters of the Zionist movement had to be transferred to
New York. De Haas appealed to Brandeis to step forward
and take charge because, as he said, it was a matter affecting
not only the future of Zionism "but indeed the welfare
of seven-tenths of the Jewish race." Brandeis consented
and assumed the leadership of the Zionist movement in the
United States. He was elected unanimously as chairman of
the Provisional Executive Committee for General Zionist
Affairs.

Brandeis poured himself into the immense task with vast
energy. His speeches represented a magnificent synthesis of
Americanism and Zionism. Confessing that only four years
before he had conceived of Zionism as a wild vision of
forcing every Jew to live in Palestine, he defined Zionism in
these terms:

"It is not a movement to remove all the Jews compulsorily
to Palestine. In the first place, there are 14,000,000 Jews, and
Palestine would not accommodate more than one-fifth of
that number. In the second place, it is not a movement to
compel anyone to go to Palestine. It is essentially a movement to give to the Jews more, not less, freedom—it aims
to enable the Jews to exercise the same rights now exercised
by practically every other people in the world: to live at
their option in the land of their fathers or in some other
country; a right which members of small nations as well as

large—which Irish, Greek, Bulgarian, Serbian, or Belgian, may now exercise as fully as Germans or English."

Brandeis became a zealous supporter of the Congress idea, which was based on the concept that a representative conference of all major American Jewish organizations should be summoned to urge a Jewish Palestine upon the Great Powers in any negotiations following the end of the war. The Bourbons of the Jewish community struck back bitterly. Louis Marshall, chairman of the American Jewish Committee, declaimed that the very thought of the mass of Jews in America having a voice in the matter of deciding the welfare of the Jews in the world made him "shrink in horror."

Stephen Wise described this struggle as follows:

"Passionately unyielding democrat that he was all his life, he [Brandeis] found to his amazement and regret that little had been done by the first war democratically to organize American Jews. He deplored and resented the failure of the wealthy philanthropists in control of Jewish affairs to invite the judgment and participation of those whom, he rightly assumed, were no less qualified than the wealthy to conduct their affairs as Jews in American life. True it was that he saw that to organize American Jews democratically was to insure their effective support of Zionism. But he also felt that only through such instrumentality as the American Jewish Congress would Jews of America be free to use their own voice rather than be the echo of voices which spoke for them, free to reach their own decisions, to speak and act for themselves as Jews in the working out of their Jewish problems. Back of this understanding lay his recognition on the one hand of the contribution every racial and religious group could make to the democratic totality of American life, as well as his deep and unshakable faith in the worth and dignity as Jews as a people. He labored to the end that

American Jews might share such dignity and pride, and he knew that they could not be expected to do this as long as they as a body were treated as if they were incompetent to deal with, and, however blundering at times, to reach decisions with respect to their own affairs.

"He quickly won the honor of being vigorously opposed by those incurably distrustful of the democratic way of life. But Brandeis sounded the watchword of democracy with all the authority of a great personality and with the fearless vigor of one to whom democracy was not a party label but the one and only way of life. Once he had stood upon the American Jewish platform, the prestige of anti-democratic groups was lowered and their power of control limited."

But, thanks to the power of Brandeis's leadership, the Congress was created—and Marshall himself acquiesced.

Although Brandeis's public leadership of the Zionist cause was telescoped into a span of only seven years, they were critical years during which the Zionist movement was energized and great progress was made toward the ultimate goal of Jewish nationhood. Under Brandeis's leadership, President Wilson was approached, as were the British and French ambassadors, and verbal assurances were secured as to Allied policy on Palestine. Brandeis conferred with Lord Balfour, the British Foreign Minister, at a White House luncheon at which the basis for the Balfour Declaration was evolved. On November 2, 1917, the historic Declaration, pledging His Majesty's Government to the development of a national Jewish homeland in Palestine, was issued. President Wilson hailed the Declaration with great enthusiasm. A train of events was begun which, despite cruel delay and heartbreak, led ultimately to the final realization of that age-old yearning and modern miracle, the State of Israel. Brandeis was not to live to see that day.

Brandeis gave a significant part of his life to the Zionist cause. His lavish expenditures of time and energy were accompanied by equally generous financial contributions; no Zionist in his lifetime contributed as fulsomely of his financial resources as did Brandeis. It was as though he were seeking to make amends for his neglect of his people for so much of his life.

His period of leadership in the Zionist cause was not unmixed with pain, frustration, and despair. Particularly with the close of World War i, when a national mood of disillusionment permeated Zionist ranks as well, Brandeis tasted the bitter fruits of fratricidal conflict and rivalry within the Zionist movement. He and Chaim Weizmann, who had frequently clashed in international Zionist conferences, began a feud which had serious political implications and which polarized the movement. When the Weizmann forces succeeded in defeating the Brandeis Administration at the Cleveland convention of the Zionist Organization of America in 1921, Brandeis resigned as an active leader, although he continued to his death to be an unfailing supporter of Zionism and the cause of Palestine.

Brandeis's biographer, Alpheus Thomas Mason, in his *Brandeis: A Free Man's Life*, summed up in these words the meaning of Zionism in Brandeis's life:

"This cause, more than any other, fired Brandeis's imagination and captured his heart. It satisfied his love of adventure, brought to the surface his unflagging belief in the power of idealism. Zionism, inspiring as it did achievements of spiritual significance, gave him understanding and happiness, which even the compromising White Papers and Nazi barbarisms were unable to obliterate. Despite all trials, and throughout the lagging years, Zionism for him was no dream, but a beautiful reality."

IN JANUARY, 1916, while Brandeis was immersed in Zionist affairs, President Wilson dropped a bombshell with an announcement that he had appointed Louis D. Brandeis to succeed Joseph R. Lamar as an Associate Justice of the U.S. Supreme Court. The appointment surprised and shocked Washington, and it provoked a furor of press comment and debate all across the nation. Charges against Brandeis filled the air like Roman candles, and it was immediately evident that a bitter and lengthy struggle would unfold in the Senate Judiciary Committee, which had to confirm the nomination.

President Wilson was not unaware that his appointment would stir up the dogs of conflict. One year earlier, an uproar was evoked when Brandeis was proposed for membership in the exclusive Cosmos Club. Justice Hitz had written to President Wilson at that time that "several members of the club have started an opposition to Mr. Brandeis which bids fair to be successful unless his friends come strongly to his support. The grounds of opposition to Mr. Brandeis are stated to be that he is a reformer for revenue only; that he is a Jew; and that he would be a disturbing element in any club of gentlemen." On that occasion, the President had written to the admissions committee that he held Brandeis in "highest esteem" and that "his admission to the club would not only be an act of justice to him, but would add a member of very fine quality to its list."

In the Supreme Court fight, the "grounds of opposition" seemed to be about the same as in the Cosmos Club incident. But the stakes were obviously infinitely greater as the mounting controversy showed. Brandeis had made formidable enemies in his career. Privilege, which viewed the Supreme Court as its last great bastion, declared war. Such distinguished public citizens as A. Lawrence Lowell, president of Harvard, and former President William Howard Taft, joined in the opposition. The Judiciary Committee hearings, which more and more resembled a trial, droned on.

Spearheading the opposition seemed to be those powerful business interests in Boston whose practices Brandeis had excoriated. Alluding to these Bostonians, Walter Lippman, writing in the *New Republic* during the hearing, described Brandeis as "a rebellious and troublesome member of the most homogeneous, self-centered, and self-complacent community in the United States. It was a special community that had found Mr. Brandeis untrustworthy, the powerful but limited community which dominated the business and social life of Boston." A Bostonian, Charles Francis Adams, echoed Lippman's analysis, observing, "I have tried Boston socially on all sides. I have summered and wintered it, tried it drunk and tried it sober, and drunk or sober, there is nothing in it save Boston. . . . It is, so to speak, stationary—a world, a Boston world unto itself . . . and like all things stationary . . . it tends to stagnate."

In March, when it seemed the hearings had searched out every record and tracked down every false charge against him, Brandeis wrote his brother: "It is not as unpleasant to us as would seem to the outside. This attack continued throughout nine years has quite accustomed us to it and we are glad to have it out. At all events the country including Boston will know what I have been 'up against.' I suppose eighteen centuries of Jewish persecution must have enured me to such hardships and developed the like of a duck's back."

Two charges against Brandeis—the one pressed publicly and widely, the other muted and whispered—were true.

The first was that he was a liberal who had struggled to re-interpret the social law and who would, on the bench, seek to mold the law to social ends. Senator Walsh recognized the validity of this charge when he declared at the hearing, "The real crime of which this man is guilty is that he has exposed the iniquities of men in high places in our financial system. He has not stood in awe of the majesty of wealth. . . . He has been an iconoclast." The second valid charge was that Brandeis was a Jew.

The issue dragged into May, the fifth month, and predictions began to spread that the Republicans would stand solidly against the Brandeis appointment and that many Democrats were wavering as a result of testimony at the hearing. It was even rumored that Wilson did not really want Brandeis confirmed, that the Brandeis appointment had been a gesture to the liberals. On May 8, President Wilson scotched the latter rumor personally by writing a long and compelling letter, strongly urging confirmation. The crucial section of the letter said, "I perceived from the first that the charges were intrinsically incredible by anyone who had really known Mr. Brandeis. I have known him. I have tested him by seeking his advice upon some of the most difficult and perplexing public questions about which it was necessary for me to form a judgment. I have dealt with him in matters where nice questions of honor and fair play, as well as large questions of justice and public benefit, were involved. In every matter in which I have made test of his judgment and point of view, I have received from him counsel singularly enlightening, singularly clear-sighted and judicial and, above all, full of moral stimulation. He is a friend of all just men and a lover of the right; and he knows more than how to talk about the right—he knows how to set it forward in the face of his enemies. I knew from direct personal knowledge of the man what I was doing when I named him for the highest and most responsible tribunal of the nation."

The Brandeis nomination had simmered so long, stirring tension and conflict, that some influential Jews became anxious lest the protracted issue lead to a dangerous increase in anti-Semitism. One day President Wilson reportedly called in Mr. Josephus Daniels, Secretary of the Navy, who also happened to be Wilson's intimate friend. "What do you make of this?" the President asked. He displayed a petition signed by a number of "leading" American Jews, requesting the President to withdraw the nomination because the continued agitation would "hurt" the Jewish community.

"What do you make of this, Daniels? I know some of these people; they are good men," the President said. Describing this incident years later to Mr. Harry Golden, editor of the *Carolina Israelite*, Daniels recalled his reply, "Mr. President, of course these are good people, but we must be understanding and forgive them; the Jews are like any other minority which has had its ups and downs; their psychology involves always an element of fear, and the only way I can explain it to you is to tell you a story about another one of our minorities, the Negroes. It is a story about Mandy, who had spent all day fishing for crabs down there in my eastern North Carolina. Late in the afternoon Mandy put on her broad-brimmed straw hat; she had a whole basketful of crabs and she was through for the day. On the way home, she met her neighbor, Uncle Jim. Said Uncle Jim, 'Mandy, I see you've had a lot of luck with them crabs today, but you should have a lid for that basket. Ain't you afraid some of them crabs is gonna get out of that open basket?' And Mandy laughed and laughed. 'Lordy me, Jim, you know that ain't gonna happen; them crabs is like us colored folk; if one tries to get *out*, the rest of 'em is gonna pull him back.' "

The President laughed and ignored the petition. But the continuing crisis on Capitol Hill was no laughing matter, and Wilson exerted all his powers of leadership to drive the nomination through the Senate. On May 24, the Judiciary Committee voted; the decision was 10 to 8 for confirmation. The Senate, on June 1, broke the embittered impasse by voting 47 to 22 to confirm the nomination. "I never signed any commission," wrote Wilson, "with such satisfaction as I signed his." Louis Dembitz Brandeis was the first Jew to sit on the bench of the United States Supreme Court.

There is a legendary story that when President Wilson appointed Brandeis to the Court, somebody said to the President, "Isn't it a pity that a man as great as Mr. Justice Brandeis should be a Jew?" Replied President Wilson, "But he would not be Mr. Brandeis if he were not a Jew."

The record Brandeis wrote as a Justice on the highest court in the land is too vast to be discussed in any detail. Holmes is remembered as the Great Dissenter but, for both Brandeis and Holmes, this characterization is not quite accurate. Brandeis was usually in the majority. Four hundred and fifty-four of his five hundred and twenty-eight opinions were majority decisions.* But it may be said, with justice, that it was his dissenting opinions which blazed a trail of law "as it was yet to be." His "Brandeis-type" briefs made history, setting forth in microscopic detail pertinent social and economic data in addition to the technical legal arguments. His long career on the bench was a prophetic crusade for a better America where the "new freedom" would flourish; where monopoly would be checked and small business prosper; where trade unions would be protected so that they could spell decent living standards for workers; where human values would never be subordinated to property

---

* *The Social and Economic Views of Mr. Justice Brandeis,* Alfred Lief, Vanguard, New York, 1930.

values; where the government would not be a neutral observer but an eager buttress of social welfare; where man's right to think, to write, to exercise religious freedom, and to associate with like-minded persons, would be secured and reverenced; where the law would be a handmaiden of social progress; where the dreams which reflect the spirit of America would find the richness of fulfilment.

Not until his eighty-third year (1939) did the venerable Justice resign from the Court. President Roosevelt accepted his resignation, because "one must perforce accept the inevitable." But the old war horse was unwilling to rust away his last years in a rocking chair. There was still too much to do. Even before his retirement, the Nazi extermination of Jews had compelled him to break his customary judicial reserve and appeal to the President to do all in his power to prevent the impending termination of immigration to Palestine. He maintained close and vigorous contact with Zionist leaders, who leaned upon him as the elder statesman of the movement. When Great Britain issued its infamous White Paper of 1939, curtailing immigration to Palestine, Brandeis spoke out clearly and sharply. Even in the grim moments of Nazi butchery, he never despaired of the ultimate triumph of the democracies and of the imperishability of "Jewish ideals and aspirations."

On Sunday, October 5, 1941, at the age of eighty-four, Louis Brandeis died. He left to his wife and family, and to many public causes, a large legacy. He left to humanity an even richer, more permanent legacy. In his last letter to Brandeis, President Roosevelt had addressed him as "Dear Isaiah," using the name which the "inner circle" always applied to the Justice. It was an apt characterization. For Louis Dembitz Brandeis, whose rare spirit touched and quickened the heart of America, was, above all else, an American embodiment of the ancient prophet of Israel.

Louis Marshall

LAST OF THE GREAT SHTADLANIM

L OUIS MARSHALL was brilliant, autocratic, prodigiously energetic, fierce in combat, lustful for power but always intensely loyal to all things Jewish. Once he said, "I am something more than a Zionist or a non-Zionist, I am a Jew." But Louis Marshall was more than just a Jew. He was a towering Jewish figure who cast such a shadow of mildly despotic beneficence for so many decades as to evoke the sardonic comment that the American Jewish community existed "under Marshall Law."

For Marshall was the last of the great *shtadlanim* in American Jewish life. Until comparatively recently, the shtadlan was one of the most exalted figures in American Jewish life. It was the shtadlan who, having achieved the highest status in the non-Jewish community, acted as the intermediary between the Jewish community and the non-Jewish world. It was the shtadlan who served as the private foreign minister of the Jews to the Christian world, and especially to political leaders of the nation. By and large, the shtadlan was self-appointed but, by dint of his great influence, he served as the "spokesman" and "representative" of the masses of Jews.

And it must be said that frequently the quiet, behind-the-scenes influence-peddling of the shtadlanim resulted in significant, even historic, gains for the Jewish community.

The attitude of the shtadlan may be suggested by a current story, probably apocryphal, of a leading American businessman who was quietly reading his newspaper on the day that Charles Lindbergh completed his famous flight across the Atlantic. His wife, having heard the electrifying news on the radio, burst in to announce that "Lindbergh has just become the first person to fly the Atlantic alone." Without raising his eyes from the newspaper, the magnate replied, "I would be more impressed if he had done it with a committee." This is the motif of the shtadlan—and it was preeminently the attitude of Marshall: I can do it better and faster, so why bother with anybody else?

Suited as he was by temperament, philosophy, and great personal skill to the role of shtadlan, it was Marshall's fate to live in an era of dynamic change which ultimately forced him to bend to the winds of democracy which swept over the Jewish community as they swept over the entire American scene. Perhaps the greatest tribute that one can pay to this amazing man is to say, not that he was a great self-appointed leader of his people, but that his love for his people was so deep that he was, in the end, willing to subordinate his own temperamental and philosophical tendencies to the clearly expressed will of the Jewish community and to place his immense skills proudly at their command. While he was perhaps bowing to the inevitable, he did so with a grace and a dignity which reflected credit upon the last of the great American shtadlanim.

Marshall was born in Syracuse, New York, on December 14, 1856, the eldest of six children of German immigrant parents. His first language was German. His well-educated mother devoted many hours to reading classical literature

to her sons in German. As a boy, Louie helped out in his
father's hide and leather business, but this did not prevent
him from doing exceedingly well in both public and Hebrew school. A quick scholar, Louie spoke French, Latin,
Greek, and Hebrew as well as German and English by the
time he was graduated from Syracuse High in 1874.

The eager youngster had already set his eyes upon a
career in the law. After serving a two-year apprenticeship
in a Syracuse law firm, he enrolled in the Columbia Law
School in New York. The law school course was then a
two-year session. Marshall whipped through the course in
one year, taking his first-year classes in the afternoon and
the second-year classes in the morning, and leaving behind
him a reputation as a prodigious youngster with a phenome-
nally retentive memory.

Admitted to the bar, Louis returned to his native city
where he began an eminently successful legal career which
quickly brought him a partnership in the noted firm of
Ruger, Jenney, Brooks, French and Marshall. Between 1878
and 1894, the rising attorney carried more than one hundred
and fifty cases to the New York State Court of Appeals.
An indication of his growing eminence in the law was his
appointment by Governor Hill in 1890, when he was thirty-
four, to a special commission to revise the judiciary section
of the state constitution. A few years later, he was elected to
serve at the state constitutional convention where, again, he
earned praise for his energetic and constructive work.

Continuing to live with his parents until his marriage in
early middle life, Louis enjoyed the warm Jewish atmosphere which characterized the family life. His parents were
Orthodox, and Jewish rituals were cheerfully observed.
While Louis himself was no longer Orthodox in his attitude
toward doctrine and ritual, he derived great security and
satisfaction from the Sabbath candle-lighting, the Passover

Seder and other holiday observances, as well as from the family tradition of group Bible-reading. The family attended services at Temple Concord and Louis maintained, even as a young man, a wide variety of interests in Jewish organizations and causes.

Young Louis treasured these warm and sentimental bonds of family life, but he was to remember, also, the ugly experiences which his father recalled to him of anti-Semitism in his native Germany. The young man was always aware of the great contrast between the old-world antipathies, as he learned them from his father's memories, and the harmonious patterns of group relations in Syracuse, as he knew them, man and boy.

Standing at the pinnacle of his profession in Syracuse, Marshall, not yet forty, yielded to the irresistible magnetic pull of New York City, where broader opportunities awaited young men of talent. In 1894 he joined the firm of Guggenheimer, Untermyer and Marshall. The big city was throbbing with economic and cultural growth. Marshall gravitated quite naturally to a particular segment of Jewish society—primarily German in origin, men of success, wealth, and distinction.

Oscar Handlin, in his introduction to *Louis Marshall— Champion of Liberty*,* describes the group thus:

"The influence of this heritage was reflected in their religious attitude. The memory of ancestral suffering in the Old World was often with them, and also fear lest traces of prejudice intrude in the New. Their belief in Judaism was nonetheless strong and they were resolved to preserve and transmit their faith to their children. But, as Americans, they had broken with the older Orthodoxy of their parents

---

* *Louis Marshall—Champion of Liberty*, edited by Charles Reznikoff, Introduction by Oscar Handlin, Jewish Publication Society of America, Philadelphia, 1957.

and they were attempting to develop a reformation that would unite the values of their distinctive tradition with those of the nation of which they were a part. In doing so they grasped at the prophetic ideal of social justice, rooted in the Bible, yet comprehensible in twentieth century America. They made that ideal the center of their faith; for it justified their separateness as bearers of the message, yet asserted their identity with all men to whom the message was brought."

This was indeed a distinguished group—including Jacob Schiff, Adolph Ochs of the *New York Times,* Oscar Straus, Joseph Seligman, the banker, the Guggenheims, Cyrus Adler, later president of the Jewish Theological Seminary. But it may be supposed that what brought them together was, in addition to the vague promptings of some "prophetic ideals," the fact that their wealth made them upper class but their Jewishness excluded them from the upper crust of New York society, to which their wealth would otherwise have admitted them. Moreover, their dedication to social justice, profound as it was, reflected itself primarily in a rather defensive and insecure anxiety to prevent the anti-Semitism of the Old World from marring the bright vision of America.

Like his contemporary, Louis Brandeis, Marshall's fortunes in the law rose meteorically. Large and lucrative cases, including those brought by large corporations, flocked to him. His reputation and flourishing practice well established, Marshall, again like Brandeis, was able to turn his restless energies while still a comparatively young man to public issues and important causes. Like Brandeis also, Marshall was once seriously considered as a possible appointee to the U.S. Supreme Court. But unlike Brandeis, who received an appointment, Marshall was doomed to bitter disappointment in failing to achieve the only public office he had ever wanted. Had he won the appointment, he would have been a sound and conservative Justice.

Marshall did not marry until 1895 when he was thirty-nine years old. It was a happy marriage. His wife, the former Florence Lowenstein, presented him with a son a year later, and three more children joined the late-blooming household over the years. The family moved into an old brownstone house on East 72nd Street, and literature, art, the theater, and philanthropy were cultivated in the family circle. The greatest joy of the family, however, was their summer place on Saranac Lake in the Adirondacks, which they called "Knollwood." Throughout his life, Marshall was to indulge his passion for nature and to find surcease from the trials of leadership in this lovely retreat.

Politically, Marshall was a deep-dyed conservative. Revulsion for William Jennings Bryan and his emotional appeals to the masses pushed Marshall permanently into the Republican ranks. To Marshall, the law was the great conservator of values; he looked askance at those who saw the law as an instrument of social progress. Theodore Roosevelt and Woodrow Wilson stirred in him intuitive suspicion. He looked with horror upon such techniques as the direct primary and the referendum, which were advocated as measures to extend democracy. To Marshall, the law was the foundation, and one had to protect the law against the demands of the masses.

Marshall's political conservatism and his championship of liberty were closely connected. To him justice was possible only within an established framework of rules which limited the power of the state over persons and property. Thus, it was possible for Marshall to oppose federal legislation which would regulate child labor, suppress lynching, provide for minimum wages, or assist in housing. He objected to the broadening of centralized authority. But the same man who opposed social welfare legislation maintained a jealous commitment to individual liberty under the law. Equality for every American regardless of race or religion, full freedom of expression, undeviating respect for religious liberty—these were enshrined in the Constitution and the law of the land. They must be upheld regardless of the whims of public opinion and the accidents of time and place. Marshall was the true conservative—with all the strengths as well as the limitations of this position.

Marshall did not neglect his responsibilities to the Jewish community. He regarded the first of these responsibilities to be religious, believing that religion had always been "a vital force" in Jewish survival. Marshall had been a member of Temple Emanu-El since his arrival in New York City, and he rose to the position of president of this large and impressive "Cathedral Temple" of New York Jewry.

While serving as president of Temple Emanu-El, Marshall collided head-on with Rabbi Stephen Wise in a dramatic confrontation which was to have tremendous consequences for both antagonists. The pulpit having become vacant, the trustees had called young Rabbi Stephen Wise who had built a substantial reputation as an eloquent preacher and a vivid leader of Jewish life in the Pacific Northwest. But the marriage of Emanu-El and Wise, unlikely at best, was never consummated. Negotiations foundered on the rock of a basic issue: the freedom of the pulpit. Marshall quickly disabused the idealistic young rabbi of any notion that his pulpit would be free from control by the trustees, and Wise made it quite clear that he would never accept a "muzzled" pulpit. Thereafter, Wise formed the Free Synagogue in New York City, a cardinal principle of which was the freedom of the pulpit.

The conflict with Wise reinforced Marshall's instinctive uneasiness about rabbis, and especially those who, like Wise, had a prophetic bent which impelled them to speak out in appeals to public opinion. Marshall was always out of patience with those rabbis who, in his view, did not stick to "spiritual" matters and insisted upon meddling in public issues. For example, in a letter, he offered the following caustic comment on a recent sermon by a Rabbi Silverman:

"It is my personal opinion that Dr. Silverman's sermon was most unfortunate, untimely, and unnecessary. He should have foreseen that it could only result in needless irritation, and that, if misinterpreted, it was an inevitable consequence of his having said what he did in the sensational manner to which he resorted. Whenever a rabbi discusses the topics of the day in the pulpit and draws his texts from the daily newspapers instead of from Scripture, he is certain to get into deep waters and to create mischief, particularly when he has his mind on newspaper headlines and upon making a sensation."

The entire idea of a rabbi using the pulpit to communicate the truth about the issues of the day, subject only to his own conscience, was anathema to Marshall. It is ironic that his clash with Wise over this issue, and the resultant debate, did more to stiffen the American rabbinate to the utter necessity of a free and unfettered pulpit than did any other event. Today, the principle of freedom of the pulpit is almost universally acknowledged by the synagogues themselves. The Union of American Hebrew Congregations pledged itself to this principle in 1951 and other religious groups have taken the same position.

The ghastly outbreak of pogroms in Russia at the turn of the century had traumatic effect on American Jewry. This reversion to a barbarism, which the modern age of enlightenment was presumed to have left behind, was a vivid reminder that anti-Semitism was festering in many parts of Europe and, indeed, was far from being unknown in the

United States. A sense of urgency over these dark developments led Adler, Schiff, Marshall, and some of their friends to consider the formation of a national body for "those who have the welfare of Judaism at heart should come together, merely for the purpose of comparing notes, with a view of ascertaining whether or not there is a possibility of promulgating a plan which will be generally acceptable, and which will accomplish the objects which all of us have sincerely at heart." This group became the American Jewish Committee in 1906.

Originally, Marshall had conceived of the new organization as being representative of delegates elected by the synagogues. But this idea was abandoned in favor of a small and influential group of like-minded Jews who joined together to work for equality of Jewish rights and for integration of the Jews in the total American society. The method of operation was largely behind-the-scenes, orderly persuasion. Marshall and his colleagues had no desire to associate themselves with those Jews who were infused with Zionist ideals, or were dedicated to radical changes of the economic system, or who sought to achieve their ends through mass action and public activity. Marshall became president of the Committee in 1912.

A major issue confronted the new organization, as well as the entire Jewish community, in the first years of the twentieth century. Czarist Russia refused to allow American Jews to cross its border, except by special permission. The U.S. had from 1901 tacitly acquiesced in this religious discrimination between Jewish and non-Jewish citizens of the United States. Six years later, however, U.S. complicity in this discrimination was formalized through an order by Secretary of State Elihu Root, stating that American Jews would be denied passports unless they secured the prior permission of the Russian Ministry of the Interior.

Marshall led a strong attack on this infringement of the civil rights of American Jews. To high government officials, Marshall insisted that "nothing can be accomplished by treating this as a Jewish question, and until it is recognized as an American question, nothing can be accomplished." In a powerful address delivered to the delegates of the 22nd Council of the Union of American Hebrew Congregations in New York City on January 19, 1911, Marshall argued that the honor and integrity of the U.S. were at stake in the passport issue, ". . . Unless the virtue of manhood has deserted this republic, its citizens will no longer patiently witness the mockery of diplomatic procedure, but will insist on a complete abrogation of every treaty now existing between the United States and Russia."

Marshall's blistering indictment was supported by the entire Jewish community of America whose demands for abrogation of the Treaty of 1832 with Russia began to be echoed by powerful Christian leaders and important politicians. President Taft cited Marshall's UAHC speech in February of 1911. Private discussions were held in the White House and in the State Department. In December of that year, the long struggle ended victoriously. The United States announced to the world its unilateral renunciation of the Treaty of 1832.

One of Marshall's deep-seated convictions was that the glory of America rested in large part on its immigrants and that America could commit no greater folly than to slam the door on new immigration. He fought manfully against the restrictionists, and he recognized the undercurrent of anti-Semitism which ran just beneath the surface—and sometimes bubbled up to public view—in debates about the comparative desirability and assimilability of immigrants from various parts of Europe. He used all his prowess as a lawyer, as well as his well-developed access to proper channels, to seek to stem the rising tide of anti-alien sentiment which finally engulfed the Congress in 1924. This was a losing fight. Nor have his successors in Jewish leadership succeeded to this day in mobilizing American public opinion to the shame of an immigration policy which rests on the racist scheme of a national origins quota system and which, in its philosophy and mode of operation, mocks the sacred American tradition engraved upon the Statue of Liberty.

Few incidents of anti-Semitism, however trivial, escaped Louis Marshall. Few failed to move him to take pen in hand. His voluminous correspondence, part of which was published in 1957, indicates both a commendable vigilance and an irritating over-sensitivity. One of the most aggravated situations, in which Marshall played a part, was the tragic Leo M. Frank case which unfolded in Georgia in 1913. Leo Frank, a Jewish businessman in Atlanta, was charged with murdering a young girl who had been his employee. In an atmosphere charged with a feverish hysteria and which almost suggested an American Dreyfus case, Frank was tried, convicted, and sentenced to death. There were strong indications that the decision was the result of a frame-up at worst, and an incredible miscarriage of justice at the least.

While Frank awaited execution, Jews throughout the United States were aroused to a pitch of white heat. Mass meetings and protests were held across the country. Fervent letters to the editor were dispatched and passionate sermons filled the air. Marshall, characteristically, scorned and sought to stifle these resorts to emotion and utilized instead the familiar weapons which he had sharpened to a razor's edge over years of experience: the law and quiet persuasion. After the sentence was handed down, he became Frank's counsel and carried the appeal, unsuccessfully, to the U.S. Supreme Court. All else failing, he appealed to John M. Slaton, the governor of Georgia. History will enshrine Governor

Slaton as an American of rare and self-sacrificing courage, for it was Slaton who chose certain political suicide and barely escaped from a howling lynch mob himself for his decision to commute the Frank sentence to life imprisonment. But the blood-thirsty mob was not to be denied. Leo Frank was snatched from his prison and brutally lynched.

The outbreak of World War 1 confronted Marshall and other Jewish leaders with a host of new and complex problems. It was clear that European Jewry was in dire jeopardy, and American Jewry was quick to rise to its responsibilities. A unified approach to the program of relief was developed through the organization of the American Jewish Joint Distribution Committee which labored with diligence and effectiveness to bring succor to European Jews who fell victim of the war.

Resolving the thorny knot of political problems was an infinitely more difficult task. American Jews wanted not only to bind up the wounds of their co-religionists, but also, if humanly possible, to protect their rights in the post-war world through internationally guaranteed safeguards of their religious and civil rights. This would require Jewish representation at the Paris Peace Conference so that the nations at the peace table could be persuaded of the necessity and practicality of such provisions in the peace treaties. But who should represent the Jewish group? And precisely what should this representative plead for? Needless to say, Marshall had every confidence that he would be able to discharge this great obligation himself as he had done in other situations in the past. But the past was no more. The American Jewish community was undergoing a subtle but nonetheless real change in its essential character.

Jewish immigrants from Eastern Europe were no longer so insecure and uncertain of themselves and their part in America that they were willing to follow slavishly whatever the "bosses uptown" decided. Deeply Jewish, intensely moved by the fate of their European brethren, ardent in their Zionism, radical in their economic views, the Jewish masses demanded the right to play their proper role in the crucial decisions which had to be made. In Louis Brandeis, they found their champion. Brandeis urged the idea of an American Jewish Congress, which would include the elected delegates of all Jewish organizations in an over-all conference, whose twin objectives would be protecting Jewish rights in Europe and advancing Jewish interests in Palestine.

Marshall rebelled against the Congress idea, charging that it was the product "of juvenility and adolescence" and would merely "give to blatant and flamboyant orators an opportunity to make themselves conspicuous, irrespective of the permanent injury they might inflict." Moreover, Marshall was anti-Zionist and he viewed with distaste the possibility of collaboration with the Zionists, not to mention the laborites and socialists who now clamored for democratic representation. The American Jewish Committee fought hard to destroy the Congress idea. But it was evident that an aroused Jewish opinion was bringing the American Jewish Congress into fruition, with or without the American Jewish Committee. Besides, Marshall recognized the great harm which could result from conflicting Jewish delegations at the Peace Conference. Thus, he and his associates bowed to the inevitable and yielded to the proposal for a temporary emergency Congress.

Despite his disagreement with the whole idea of a Congress, and especially with its objective of furthering the Zionist program of a Jewish national homeland, Marshall not only pitched in with the work, but he became a leader. When the Congress dispatched a delegation to speak for American Jewry at the Peace Conference, one of the members of the delegation was Louis Marshall, president of the

American Jewish Committee. Some of his critics cynically
attributed this to the old political axiom: if you can't lick
'em, join 'em. Others said Marshall was at the mercy of his
own egomania. Both may have been right. But there is little
doubt that Marshall was also responding to an unshakable
loyalty to his people which made it impossible for him to
separate himself from the mainstream of Jewish life.

Thus did Marshall spend three years in intimate association with such Jewish leaders as Judge Julian Mack of the
Zionist Organization of America and Rabbi Stephen Wise,
Marshall's perennial antagonist. While Marshall never grew
zealous about the concept of a Jewish national homeland
in Palestine, he succeeded in working, with comparatively
little conflict, with these flaming Zionist spirits; indeed, the
war years, and especially the four months Marshall spent
in Paris in direct negotiations, seemed to mellow the aging
leader and to deepen his understanding of the importance
of Palestine for the Jewish people. He would never permit
himself to be identified as a Zionist, but neither would he
ever shirk from doing whatever he could for Palestine.

Marshall's strenuous labors in behalf of the Congress were
not in vain. He and his associates succeeded in securing the
minority provisions they sought which seemed, at that
hopeful hour, to offer genuine hope for a Jewish future in
Europe. Moreover, the enunciation of the Balfour Declaration seemed to Marshall and to the others a satisfactory
pledge that the great powers would move effectively to
assure a Jewish homeland in Palestine. Marshall returned
from Europe in high hopes.

But the glowing illusions were quickly dispelled by the
ominous realities of the post-war world. The visionary
hopes of a brave new world of international cooperation
were killed in the frost of post-war disillusionment. The
failure of U.S. support for the League of Nations, and for

the World Court, drained the minority provisions of needed
backing. Pogroms in Lithuania and elsewhere mocked the
high hopes which had been reposed in the minority provisions. At home, the stream of reaction was running swiftly.
Nationalist, anti-foreign, isolationist, and anti-Semitic prejudices found ready expression and easy targets. The Ku
Klux Klan by 1924 had enlisted four million Americans in
its anti-Jewish, anti-Catholic, and anti-Negro campaign.

These dire developments extinguished many of Marshall's
fondest dreams, but he never gave up the fight. Indeed,
during the last years of his life (he was then sixty-five), he
was catapulted into one of the bitterest of the issues which
commanded his interest. This was the dip of Henry Ford,
the powerful and famous automobile manufacturer, into
the troubled waters of anti-Semitism. Ford had allowed
himself to be persuaded of the truth of the grotesque
charges against the Jews which appeared in the ubiquitous
libel, *Protocols of the Elders of Zion*. The *Protocols*, which
had been circulated in Europe by the most vicious anti-
Semites, told a fantastic tale of an alleged plot hatched
jointly by Jewish capitalists and Communists to take over
the world. Ford swallowed this garbage whole and beamed
the infamous fiction all over America through the medium
of his *Dearborn Independent* and a book, *The International
Jew*.

American Jewry was in a panic. Henry Ford, idol of millions of Americans, was no mere crack-pot who could be
brushed aside as inconsequential. The damage he could do
was immense. Recognition of this fact led to demands in
the Jewish community for forceful action—a boycott, a
Congressional investigation, a court action, something. Following a familiar pattern, Marshall set to work, striving to
hold back the "extremists" while at the same time he took
steps to refute the fantastic charges and to establish personal

contact with Ford. Ultimately, Marshall was able to win a public retraction and apology in words written by Marshall and finally accepted by Ford. It was a signal and dramatic victory by the aging shtadlan.

In the ripeness of his later years, Marshall moved beyond the narrow negative defense against anti-Jewish attacks. He appreciated that Jewish security was interwoven with the status of democratic liberties for all Americans. Thus he fought the Ku Klux Klan and made clear that he would oppose it just as doggedly if it let up on the Jews and was only "against the Negroes or against any other part of our population." He became a director of the NAACP and spoke out against segregation. At the height of the "Red Scare," this arch conservative was not afraid to combat "anti-Bolshevik" measures which, in his view, violated the United States Constitution which he reverenced. The plight of the American Indians drew his sympathy, as did that of the Japanese-Americans who were denied the right to hold land under California law.

Similarly, Marshall was quick to defend the rights of all religious minorities. For example, Marshall made a distinctive contribution to American constitutional law through his challenge to the Oregon school laws, which, he argued, improperly denied to Catholics the right to maintain parochial schools. Marshall helped to persuade the U.S. Supreme Court to invalidate the Oregon law (Case of Pierce v. The Society of Sisters), thus affirming in a landmark decision the constitutional freedom of any religious group to maintain its own parochial schools.

Marshall continued to bear the heavy weight of Jewish leadership until his death on September 11, 1929, at the age of seventy-three. His death marked the passing of an era and of a special type of personal leadership. Though Marshall was a stubborn, blustering, egotistical, and self-

willed man to the very end, his contributions to America
and to the Jewish people were large. It may be true that
Marshall was more effective in his defensive role, as the
tireless watchdog of his people, than he was in creative and
positive planning and action. But he was always true to his
own description, "Nothing Jewish is alien to me." His wide-
ranging interests embraced the Jewish Theological Seminary (Conservative) and the Hebrew Union College
(Reform) and, in his over-arching Jewishness, could see no
reason why these two institutions could not be merged. Still
a non-Zionist (the kind of non-Zionist whom Chaim Weizmann once said was of more help to a Jewish Palestine than
an ardent Zionist like Brandeis), he was actively engaged
at his death in securing a broadening of the Jewish Agency
so that it would be made up of both Zionists and non-
Zionists alike, united in the program of rebuilding a Jewish
Palestine.

In the midst of his varied philanthropic, defense, communal, and other Jewish interests, Marshall recognized that
it was the religion of the Jew, above and beyond all other
elements, which had maintained the Jewish people through
the centuries. Unlike many of his associates and successors,
to whom Judaism was a foreign and obsolescent relic,
Marshall believed in the centrality of the synagogue: "It
should again become," he said, "the center of our life and
of our activities, as it was of yore." He was a Reform Jew
himself, but he was saddened by what he regarded as the
destructive excesses of the "Reformers" who, he felt, were
robbing Judaism of warmth, poetry, and psychological
appeal.

A few years before his death, Marshall addressed the
opening session of the 1923 Convention of the Union of
American Hebrew Congregations:

"Let us . . . direct our thoughts to a revival, not a temporary, but a continuous one, in our religious lives. Let the call go forth: 'Back to the Synagogue!' Let it be realized by every one of us that the Synagogue, which is the mother of the Church, is one of our most valuable contributions to civilization. I speak not merely of a house of worship built by human hands, but of the temple of the soul, where we may study and cultivate the virtues preached by the great prophets of old which have gone thundering down through the ages; where we may educate our hearts to understand the true meaning of justice and righteousness and love for our fellow men; where we may absorb and be permeated with the doctrines of our Bible, the ethics of our fathers, the poetry of the great singers of Israel, the simplicity of our saints, and the courage and fearlessness of our martyred hosts."

Lillian Wald

*ANGEL OF THE
EAST SIDE*

Y LIFE, hitherto, has been—I presume—a type of
modern American young womanhood, days devoted
to society, study, and housekeeping duties, such as practical
mothers consider essential to a daughter's education. This
does not satisfy me now. I feel the need of serious, definite
work, a need perhaps more apparent since the desire to become a professional nurse has had birth."

These words, appearing in a letter of application, were
written in 1889 by a young girl (then twenty-two years old,
although her application said she was twenty-five) named
Lillian Wald. As the letter suggests, the writer was a
young lady of spirit, independence, and tough-mindedness.
These were the qualities which were to distinguish Lillian
Wald through a long and extraordinary career which began
with that letter to the New York Hospital and which led
ultimately to the foundation of the Henry Street Settlement and to world-renowned record of social service.

Not the least amazing fact about the almost legendary
career of Lillian Wald was the fact that this girl, with her
sheltered background, should have chosen such a career at

all. Lillian was born in Cincinnati, March 10, 1867, into a
comfortable, loving Jewish family. Her mother's parents
had come to America after the abortive liberal revolution in
Germany in 1848. Lillian was one of four children who
grew up in a lively, cultured, affectionate household. Her
financially successful father, Max, tended to recede into
the background of a bustling family which was dominated
by his strong-willed wife, Minnie, and her vivid father,
known to the children as Grandfather "Favey." The family
circle was large enough to encompass a wide variety of
uncles and aunts and cousins who came to the house in
Cincinnati and, later, in Rochester, New York, for visits
of indeterminate duration.

It would be hard to imagine a happier childhood than
that with which Lillian was favored. The house was big,
full of toys and music and books and the ringing laughter of
a gay Jewish household. The colorful "Favey" saw to it that
the children had a pony, a bowling alley of their own, a
large dream-like playhouse. Joyously, he spoiled them by
satisfying their every whim. The children got along well
with one another, particularly Lillian and her older brother,
Alfred, between whom there grew a tender bond of love
and mutual regard. Lillian nurtured the fondest hope that
her beloved Alfred would go on to college and become a
doctor. Perhaps the deepest tragedy in her life was Alfred's
death by drowning at the age of twenty-five. One may
conjecture that, in some measure, Lillian's subsequent career
as a nurse may have been in some measure an effort to carry
on the dream which died with her brother.

Minnie Wald's ambition for Lillian was simple and obvious: to see her married to a nice Jewish boy of good family
and good prospects. Nor did this ambition seem difficult of
achievement. Lillian was educated at the highly fashionable
Miss Martha Cruttenden's School and grew into a tall, at-

tractive girl, with sparkling dark eyes and a commanding presence. There were interested young men aplenty. The problem was Lillian. For some obscure reason, she was "different" from her sister Julia, who exulted in her debut, her dance parties, her beaux and, finally, as it was meant to be, her marriage and family. Lillian didn't want a debut, she wanted only to go to work. Trying vainly to conceal her disappointment, Minnie Wald, worn down by her daughter's stubborn insistence, allowed Lillian to take a job as a correspondent for the Bradstreet Company. Writing dull business reports was not Lillian's ultimate goal in life; but it was a firm step in the direction of weaning herself from the protective, carefully prearranged life which Mommy had charted for her.

One day, when Lillian was visiting her sister, Julia became ill. The doctor insisted that a nurse be assigned, and he sent Lillian to fetch her. Lillian was delighted with the young nurse who came to tend Julia. Contrary to the prevailing stereotype of a nurse, Lillian found a bright, educated person who had received professional training and who was aglow with pride in her profession. Suddenly, Lillian saw nursing as the perfect outlet for her desire to do important work which would be of service to people. To her conventional family, the idea was meshuga (crazy), if not mildly scandalous, and it took all of the twenty-two-year-old Lillian's iron determination to reduce the adamant opposition to a reluctant, sighing acquiescence. Then, as throughout her life, Lillian had an uncanny knack at twisting people around her finger.

So off went the letter of application, containing the little fib about her age in order to circumvent the minimum age requirement of twenty-five. And Lillian was accepted as a probationer on August 20, 1889. The fledgling nurse had no difficulty adjusting to the hard hours, the bare living conditions, the strenuous work. Her superiors quickly recognized her remarkable aptitude for the profession, noting also the fiery temperament and quick impatience with any rules or regulations she regarded as unjust or stupid.

Lillian Wald always regarded her life as having really begun in 1889, with her admission to the nursing school. The gay, laughing years of her childhood were hardly referred to in her autobiography. It was almost as if, in the light of the serious purposes to which her adult life was devoted, Lillian was later embarrassed by the soft upper middle-class life she had known as a youngster. Upon graduation from the hospital, she took her first assignment with the New York Juvenile Asylum, where, characteristically, she stirred up a first-class row upon noting that, when one of her orphan charges was suffering from a toothache, the dentist didn't even bother to examine the tooth and simply prepared to pull it. Remarkably persuasive when she wanted to be, Lillian, when aroused, was like a tigress. The dentist, it need hardly be added, filled the tooth.

When Lillian was twenty-five, she decided that if she could be a nurse, then why not a doctor? The fact that the few women doctors of the time were treated like lepers by the medical profession, and were widely regarded as not quite respectable, did not deter Lillian from her quixotic scheme. However, she never became a doctor. One day a Jewish Sabbath school asked her to teach a class which was being given for young immigrant women. Lillian had never before heard of Henry Street on the East Side, where the class was held. The neighborhood was a shocking revelation to her. The hoarse shouts of push- cart vendors, the teeming tenements, the cacophony of Yiddish and other immigrant tongues, the stinking garbage hurled out of windows, the children asleep on the fire escape, the hollow stares of hopeless people sitting silently on their stoops, the smells and the sounds and the tragic rhythms of slum life—this was a world Lillian Wald had never known. The class itself, with its impoverished and illiterate students, was equally shocking.

If Miss Wald traced the beginning of her career to her letter to the New York Hospital, one could also say that her career received its real direction one rainy day while she was teaching bed-making to her class at the Jewish Sabbath school. Suddenly, a small girl ran into the room, sobbing brokenly about her mother. Without a word, Lillian took the child's hand and followed her from the room, through the dismal streets, past Hester and Division and on to Ludlow Street, and into a rotting and foul tenement. The child led her into an unheated, dark hovel of a flat, where rough boards lining the walls served as "beds" for boarders. Lying in the shadows on a blood-stained rag was the mother, virtually at death's door. For a moment the young nurse was transfixed by the stark poverty and grinding misery which lay revealed before her. Then she went to work, ministering to the hemorrhaging woman, scrubbing the floors, cleaning the children, preparing a meal, and making the sick woman and her children more comfortable. She stayed through the day and into the evening. It was, as she later described it, her "baptism in fire." She never returned to the college. She was afire with desire to tell the public of the degrading conditions she had seen and to correct them.

Lillian decided that she could do nothing effective in the East Side as an outsider; she had to become a part of the community itself. She persuaded a classmate from the training school, Mary Brewster, to join with her. Together they would live in the neighborhood, participate in its community life, share its travail. Finding quarters represented no minor achievement—it was said at that time with little exaggeration that there were only two bathrooms in the tenement district south of Fourteenth Street. The girls found a flat on Jefferson Street, replete with a prized bath and a small closet for supplies and equipment. Although a far cry from the material comforts both Mary and Lillian had known in their family homes, their apartment was more than adequate by the standards of the East Side.

The two young girls—the tall dark Jewess and the fragile fair-skinned Christian—captured the hearts of their neighbors. The immigrants had come to know and to despise the condescending "charity" bestowed upon them by the "Uptowners." But Mary and Lillian came not only to help and to serve, but to live with them. People poured into the little flat on Jefferson Street. "Workers in philanthropy, clergymen, Orthodox rabbis, the unemployed, anxious parents, girls in distress, troublesome boys," Miss Wald recalled in her autobiography,* "came as individuals to see us, but no formal organization of our work was effected till we moved into the house on Henry Street, in 1895." Mary and Lillian gave themselves to the endless demands of nursing the sick, climbing up and down the endless stairs, cleaning the filthy rooms, bathing children, finding food and clothing for the most desperate, and giving comfort and help to the despairing.

Although the nurses accepted a small fee from those who could afford it, most of the patients could not even afford to pay for medicine and many were in dire need of food and money and clothing. Lillian solicited the interest and financial aid of Jacob Schiff, himself an immigrant who became a wealthy partner in the firm of Kuhn, Loeb and Company and who presided over Jewish philanthropy with

---

* *House on Henry Street*, Lillian Wald, Henry Holt and Co., New York, 1915.

autocratic benevolence from his plush office at 52 William
Street in Wall Street. Some $60.00 a month was extended
for each girl's living expenses, with the understanding that
additional emergency funds could be requested when
needed. They were frequently needed, as the "angels of the
East Side" became known throughout the community, and
the top floor of 27 Jefferson Street served as a combination
employment agency, nursing home, food distribution center, and meeting place.

New York City in the 1890's was the Promised Land.
Manhattan was the beacon of hope—and the fetid grave-
yard of broken dreams. Immigrants poured into the city
in an ever-increasing flood, a half-million a year, past the
beckoning Lady in the Harbor and into the steaming caul-
dron of New York City. Manhattan, in 1893, comprised
one and a half million people, 85 per cent of whom lived
in tenements. The death rate was astounding, especially in
the worst of the tenements. Of every four New Yorkers,
three were foreign-born or the children of foreign-born.
And, like an evil magnet, the lower East Side drew hundreds
of thousands of frightened and ignorant immigrants who
huddled together in search of some warmth and anchor,
vulnerable to the exploitation and disease and untold misery.
Into this human jungle Lillian Wald and Mary Brewster
plunged with an eagerness and sense of mission which endured through all the days of their lives.

On one of her daily rounds, Lillian paused at an open
door to chat with a harried immigrant woman. The woman
poured forth her problem. She reported that her twelve-
year-old son, Louis, was "bad" and pleaded with the nurse
to make him "good." Bad? Louis was "bad," the mother
tried to explain, because he won't "cure his head." And
because of that, the teacher wouldn't let him in the public
school, thus dashing all the hopes of the parents that Louis

would learn to read and to become a "real American." Examining Louis, Lillian saw instantly that he had a bad case of eczema. Her questions elicited the information that Louis had gone to the dispensary, had received the proper medicine, but that the medicine had never been applied correctly because neither Louis nor his parents could read English. Patiently, Lillian applied the medicine herself and later taught the mother how to administer it. That fall, Louis was admitted to school and he raced back all the way to Jefferson Street to rattle off the words he had so proudly learned that day.

From then on, Lillian maintained a list of the youngsters like Louis who were kept out of schools for minor, correctable ailments. At the same time, she kept a second list of children who were allowed to attend school despite the fact that they were suffering from contagious disease. The prize example of the latter was Joey, a boy in the last stage of scarlet fever who regaled his classmates by peeling off his skin before their startled eyes. Lillian marched Joey to the president of the Health Department. Acknowledging that terrible overcrowding in the schools made it impossible for teachers to identify individual problems, Miss Wald warned that Joey might easily have infected his entire class and started a full-scale scarlet fever epidemic. The president was as troubled as the young nurse and he informed her that the Board was considering the possibility of regular inspections of all school children by competent doctors. But, he sighed, there would have to be a substantial appropriation for that and, thus far, the Board didn't have enough facts to dramatize the need for such a program.

Lillian and the other nurses now working with her in the East Side set out to gather the facts. Soon they had accumulated a compelling and persuasive case. But, as Lillian came to know through bitter experience, facts did not automatically lead to reforms; many a needed project failed to make its way through the swamp of Tammany politics. In 1897, Miss Wald and her supporters won a partial victory: 150 school doctors were appointed to spend one hour a day in each New York City school. It was a gain, but it was not nearly adequate to cope with the immensity of the need. By 1902 the crusaders had succeeded in expanding the program so that full medical examinations were given in all grades. But there was still no treatment and home care was practically non-existent. Miss Wald launched a campaign to add nursing service alongside of the doctor's examinations.

By arrangement with school authorities, Miss Wald assigned one of her staff nurses, Miss Rogers, to certain schools as an experiment. The nurse visited four schools, got from the doctor a list of the youngsters sent home, and then went to their homes to treat them. In a month she had administered a whopping 893 treatments, visited 137 homes, and sent back to schools twenty-five children who had been getting no medical attention until she had entered their homes. The Board of Estimate could not ignore the efficacy of the work; $30,000 was authorized for twelve municipal nurses, the first school nurses employed anywhere in the world. The program led to the New York City Bureau of Child Health which served as a model for communities throughout the United States and elsewhere in the world. Thanks to Lillian Wald, aided and abetted by Louis's "bad head" and Joey's removable skin, New York City pioneered in a new movement based on community responsibility for the health of its children.

Within two years, Lillian and Mary had outgrown the Jefferson Street apartment and, with the encouragement of Mr. Schiff, found new and larger quarters elsewhere in the district. They settled in a three-floor house on Henry Street, next door to the very house where Lillian had taught for the Sabbath school. The address was 265 Henry Street. The unemployed men and boys who carefully moved the many belongings and furnishings from Jefferson to Henry Street wouldn't accept a cent for their labors. They and the entire neighborhood rejoiced in the move of their "nurses' settlement" to a real home. From 1895, the year of the move to Henry Street, for forty years, Lillian Wald and the House were inseparable. The group of nurses grew from two to four, to seven, to fifteen. Nurse Brewster, petite Mary, grew ill and died shortly after the shift to Henry Street. Lillian was devastated. But work provided healing and Mary was replaced by other nurses, Jewish and Christian, who shared the hopes of Lillian Wald.

Social work was emerging as a profession in the early years of the twentieth century. While Miss Wald had remarkably good luck with her growing "family" of nurses and lay workers, she sometimes had to apply a gentle corrective against the overly academic and impersonal approach of some young professionals. Once she asked a new college graduate to visit a young unmarried girl who was about to have a baby. The young graduate fidgeted. "I will try, Miss Wald, but, you see, I haven't actually had any background in case work." Miss Wald gently informed the young woman that she hadn't asked her to see a "case" but a "girl." No one was ever a "case" to Lillian Wald. They were human beings—boys and girls, men and women, black and white, immigrant and native-born, ignorant and educated—who needed help and affection. Her mission in life was to supply both.

The House on Henry Street reached its beneficent roots into every segment of life in the Lower East Side. Playgrounds were established for the children. Clubs were organized for all ages and purposes—arts, theater, housekeeping, discussion, cooking, dancing, sewing, mechanics,

English. Children were taken to the zoo, to parks, to the country for an exquisitely rare day out of the city. In 1899 the Henry Street Settlement secured a country house of its own, which was soon followed by several others. Tenement youngsters and their parents came to know the delights of fresh air and the wonders of nature. The sick had a place where they could convalesce away from the dankness of the East Side. The House on Henry Street was providing not only a window to the world but also a ray of warmth, hope, health, and color for thousands and tens of thousands of Americans.

The House was never a retreat from the fever of life. The entire world seemed to pour through it. The immigrants brought with them the hated memories of Czarist Russia, and the news of fresh pogroms in Europe swept through Henry Street like electricity. Political discussion boiled in the house. East Siders yearned for a revolution in Russia which would bring an end to the Czarist tyranny from which they had escaped. Ignoring the raised eyebrows of her uptown friends, to whom all talk about a Russian revolution was anathema, Miss Wald eagerly supported relief measures, helped to sponsor meetings, and entertained speakers for Russian democracy.

The House resounded with joy when the revolution actually took place. Shortly thereafter, the new democratic Kerensky regime dispatched a mission to the United States, whose only unofficial visit was to the House on Henry Street. The leader of the mission told the milling throng that the Russians were there to express their appreciation to "a shrine that had burned for Russian freedom." When the democratic regime was overthrown by the Bolsheviks, the House reverberated with debate, with Lillian Wald, mistress of the House, calmly mediating the fierce intellectual storms. The significant role which the House was

assuming in the life of the nation was revealed in a conference which Miss Wald convened during that period, addressed by the U.S. Secretary of State and an official representative of the new Soviet regime.

With all her political idealism and social crusading, Lillian
Wald's first love was unquestioned: children. "The visitor
who sees our neighborhood for the first time at the hour
when school is dismissed," she wrote, "reacts with joy or
dismay to the sight, not paralleled in any part of the world,
of thousands of little ones on a single city block. Out they
pour, the little hyphenated Americans, more conscious of
their patriotism than perhaps any other large group of
children that could be found in our land; unaware that to
some of us they carry on their shoulders our hopes of a
finer, more democratic America, when the worthy things
they bring to us shall be recognized, and the good in their
old-world traditions and culture shall be mingled with the
best that lies within our new-world ideals. . . . They are
irresistible. They open up wide vistas of the many lands
from which they come. The multitude passes; swinging
walk, lagging step; smiling, serious—just little children, forever appealing, and these, perhaps, more than others, stir
the emotions. . . . As a nation we must rise or fall as we
serve or fail these future citizens."*

One morning in 1905 Lillian Wald and her staff gathered
in the House for the usual 7:30 breakfast and, as always,
chewed over the news of the outside world along with the
morning meal. "Aha," said Mrs. Florence Kelley, beginning
her daily ironic commentary on the newspaper, "the Secretary of Agriculture is going down South to investigate the
boll weevil which is endangering the cotton crop." Miss
Wald, spooning her breakfast distraitly, suddenly pushed
back her dish and exclaimed, "Of course! The government

* *House on Henry Street*, Lillian Wald, Henry Holt and Co., 1915.

ought to be concerned about the cotton crop. But shouldn't
the federal government be at least equally concerned about
the country's crop of children? Why don't we insist upon
a federal investigation of the conditions under which children are growing up in America? If we could get the facts
through such an investigation, then we'd have a basis upon
which to demand the reforms that are needed."

Breakfast ended abruptly. "But," said one nurse, "the
cotton growers have a lobby; children don't."

"Right," rejoined Miss Wald, "then we'll be the children's lobby, and we've got plenty of important friends
who will lobby with us."

"Maybe you've got something," said another, suggesting
that President Teddy Roosevelt might even be sympathetic
to the idea.

The House on Henry Street was not merely a forum for
socially useful ideas; it was an unpretentious but no less
powerful base for effective social and political action. Mrs.
Kelley rushed off to bring the idea to Dr. Edward T.
Devine, a sociologist at Columbia, who promptly contacted
the President of the United States. In less than twenty-four
hours, Lillian Wald and Dr. Devine stood in the White
House, presenting a proposal for new legislation and for a
new national organization dedicated to the welfare of children. The President liked the idea. A bill, providing for a
children's bureau in the federal government, was introduced
in Congress.

For seven years the bill languished, victim of the quiet
sabotage of powerful forces which had a vested interest in
the exploitation of children. Miss Wald spearheaded the
long fight which enlisted the aid of many civic and social
welfare organizations. Passage of the measure during the
Taft administration heralded a new spirit of national concern for the welfare of our children, resulting slowly in

better schools, lower death rates, fewer maternal deaths in childbirth, better protection of youthful offenders, more humane treatment of orphans, growing prohibitions against child labor. In this, as in so many other ways, the warm heart on Henry Street pumped a fresh spirit of social idealism into the arteries of the nation.

Lincoln Steffens, sensitive writer and occasional muckraker, once wrote of the "heart-breaking comedies, of the tragic conflict between the old and the new, the very old and the very new; in many matters, all at once: religion, class, clothes, manners, customs, language, culture. We all know the difference between youth and age, but our experience is between two generations. Among the Russian and other eastern Jewish families in New York it was an abyss of many generations; it was between parents out of the Middle Ages, sometimes out of the Old Testament days, hundreds of years B.C.E., and the children of the streets of New York today. We saw it everywhere all the time."

Lillian Wald watched this tragic drama unfold, too, but she was not one of those who felt that equipping immigrants for American citizenship meant sundering the traditions and values of the old-world culture. She struggled to help them to retain their pride in their past. Always she tried to instil in the youngsters an appreciation of the religious and cultural traditions of their parents; a sense that the richness of America was its varied inheritance of national strands and cultural fabrics. Miss Wald wanted no Jew to offer up his inheritance for a spurious "100 per cent Americanism." Integration, yes. Assimilation, no.

Leadership of an institution frequently tends to deter one from controversial stands which might, possibly, antagonize important supporters. But not Lillian Wald. Fiercely independent, she never shrank from a public stand, however unpopular her position. She helped organize trade unions for women. She was the first to protest against the cruel treatment by the police of the girl strikers in the needle-trade. She was a member of the Mayor's Push-Cart Commission, which was established to safeguard both buyers and sellers on the East Side. Even her benefactor, Jacob Schiff, disapproved of her involvement in labor disputes. Other wealthy supporters muttered darkly that the House was becoming a breeding place for socialistic and radical ideas. But Miss Wald answered only to her own conscience. She had no real interest in movements or abstract political principles; she cared only about people and their needs.

She became involved in the campaign for women's suffrage. She was also a prohibitionist, not out of theory but out of bitter knowledge that much of the misery which she had seen in the East Side was caused by drinking and alcoholism. She was delighted by passage of the Prohibition Amendment and she was saddened and angered by its repeal fourteen years later. Again she faced the disapproval of many of her friends and supporters of the House; but by now they knew, or should have known, that Lillian Wald made up her own mind. Perhaps no previous stand occasioned as much controversy as her declaration of pacifism during World War i. "Ever since I have grown to maturity, I have dedicated my life, all that I am and all that I have, to the preservation of life, the promotion of happiness and the development of good will among people. It would follow as the day the night that I could not be in any sense of the word a militarist." In the hysteria of the war, the blundering Military Intelligence Service issued a list of sixty-two Americans it accused of being "active in movements which did not help the United States when the country was fighting." The list included Lillian Wald, Jane Addams, Norman Thomas, Charles Beard, and many others who shared her commitment to peace and the unity of mankind.

In the post-war years, Miss Wald continued a campaign which she had carried on for years to establish "public health nurses" in communities throughout America. She had been the first president of the National Organization for Public Health Nursing. By 1931, the idea had reached fruition: 10,000 public health nurses were working under various auspices throughout the country.

Meanwhile, the House on Henry Street was expanding. It now consisted of several houses, with branches throughout the city, and a network of summer homes serving as camps and rest homes. The Henry Street Music School was established on Pitt Street. A Playhouse was set up on Grand Street. In 1935 the house next to 265 was taken over for workers' education and craft work; and a house at 305 was converted to a workshop. Other buildings were secured for gyms, meeting rooms, nursery school, consultations. Her deepest prayer—that no child would have to grow up in a slum—was still not answered and, perhaps, will never be. But the House on Henry Street brought a spirit of life which even the squalor of the tenements could not completely dim.

The kids grew up, and many moved away. But all remembered the House and the lady who built it with her faith. Alfred E. Smith and Herbert Lehman knew the East Side, and they came to work side by side with Miss Wald. Eleanor and Franklin D. Roosevelt were friends of the House. The then Prime Minister of England, Ramsay Mac-Donald, came to the House whenever possible as one goes to a shrine, seeking spiritual refreshment. Teddy Roosevelt came, and so did senators and poets, and painters and musicians. George Gershwin and Irving Berlin memorialized the rhythms of the streets in their music, and thousands of other former Henry Street children came back, as adults, to sit with Lillian Wald and recall the bitter-sweet days of

their childhood there. Slowly, under the impetus of the
New Deal and the spreading horizons of social welfare,
changes came to the East Side. Public housing began to
rise where rotting tenements had been. City, state, and government began to assume many of the responsibilities for the
sick, the hungry, the unemployed, which Lillian Wald and
her staff had struggled with meager resources to carry. But
the House on Henry Street continued to be needed, as it
had always been.

Lillian Wald suffered greatly the pain of the Depression
and the deathly tragedy of Nazism. At the age of sixty-five,
she was weary and seriously ill. Yielding to the pressure of
her doctors, she stepped down as head worker of Henry
Street, remaining president of the settlement. Her seventieth
birthday, in 1940, was celebrated joyously and messages
poured in from President Roosevelt, the governor, the
mayor, Ramsay MacDonald, and thousands of friends
throughout the world. She died September 1, 1940. She had
never married but her Henry Street children numbered
thousands and tens of thousands. Her life was a blessing.
Well had she fulfilled her youthful quest for "serious,
definite work!" She had found it in selfless dedication to
people in need.

What made Lillian Wald what she was? Did her Jewish
heritage help shape this unique spirit? Certainly not consciously. Miss Wald had little interest in the externals of
Jewish life or of the Jewish religion; she was not active in
the Jewish community. Yet the imperishable optimism, the
unshakable faith in the goodness of people—qualities she
inherited from her warm-hearted mother—find their echoes
deep in the tradition of Judaism. Similarly, whatever her
personal philosophy, Lillian Wald was acting out the best of
a prophetic tradition which reverences life and commands
kindness to the orphan, the widow, the sick, and the disin-

herited. "Do justly," exhorted the prophets of Israel. In the life of Lillian Wald were mingled the finest impulses of an ancient spiritual heritage and a humane, modern democratic faith.

Albert Einstein

POET OF SCIENCE

THE FOLLOWING letter was sent by Albert Einstein to President Franklin D. Roosevelt on August 2, 1939:

> The results of the research recently pursued by E. Fermi and L. Szilard, submitted to me in manuscript, have revealed that we may in the immediate future expect to find the element uranium capable of being transformed into a new and considerable source of energy. This new phenomenon may also lead to the construction of excessively powerful bombs. A single bomb of this type, transported by ship and allowed to explode in a port, could destroy the whole port and the surrounding territory.

This simple letter triggered the Manhattan Project, the crash program which created the atomic bomb. In a sense, Einstein's message launched the atomic age. Moreover, the splitting of the atom would not have been possible without Einstein's basic discoveries decades earlier. Thus, Einstein's name probably will always be associated with the atomic death rained down upon Hiroshima and Nagasaki. What a bitter irony! Not only did Einstein personally have nothing whatever to do with the bomb, beyond writing this letter; but there is evidence that Einstein was never informed of the Manhattan Project. Moreover, he recoiled from the horror of the bomb and urged its banning and complete control by a world government. But, beyond all this, the atom bomb symbolized forces which negated all the values of a lifetime of abhorrence of violence. Einstein was more than a scientific genius. He was a tender poet of science whose greatest hero was not Galileo or Copernicus or Newton—but Gandhi.

Einstein emphatically rejected the accolade, "father of the atomic bomb." He insisted, with perhaps a trace of defensiveness, that his role was "indirect" and that he had not even believed that atomic energy would be released in his lifetime. But the bomb shadowed his conscience to the end. Would Einstein have written the portentous letter if he could have foreseen the tragedy of Hiroshima, the subsequent dwarfing of the A-bomb of a magnitude to imperil human survival, the balancing of a divided world on the razor's edge of annihilation? If he had known, would he have pressed the button? The grave yields no secrets. The only clues lie wrapped in the record of seventy-six years lived by a brilliant and lonely Jew who unlocked the mysteries of the universe.

Albert Einstein was born on March 17, 1879, in Ulm, Germany. His family moved to Munich the following year, and it was there, in the proud capital of Bavaria in southern Germany, fourth largest city in the mighty new empire, that he spent his childhood. His parents were proudly assimilated into the German milieu; they were freethinkers and, while not hostile to Judaism, were coolly indifferent to their Jewish heritage. People of modest means, they lived in an atmosphere of religious tolerance and pleasant comfort. Albert, as a boy, displayed no promise of genius what-

ever. On the contrary, he seemed almost dull. He was a late
talker and was so slow that he almost drove his parents and
teachers to distraction. The family thought he was lazy.
Actually, he was reserved and withdrawn, characteristics
he was to retain throughout his life.

If young Albert was backward in many ways, he was
precocious in at least one: he was anti-military at the age of
five. His mother took him and his younger sister, Maya, to
see a military parade. They watched the high-stepping
troops, the sleek horses, and the haughty Prussian officers
who were the cream of the Bismarck army which, in only
fifteen years, had brought unity and power to Germany.
Germans, lining the Ludwigstrasse, hoarsely shouted their
martial pride. But little Albert burst into tears. "I don't
want to be a soldier," he cried.*

It was the same in the schools. The teachers prided themselves on their military bearing, and iron discipline seemed
the goal of education. Albert hated the schools. He felt he
was being ordered about like a soldier instead of being encouraged to think for himself. In later years, he expressed
contempt for the kind of rote education which was stuffed
into the student's mind—"educational machine," he called
it. The taciturn lad simply refused to permit his mind to be
regimented. When his parents sent him to a Catholic school,
where he was the only Jew in the class, Albert startled
everybody by asserting his Jewishness and going through a
stage of several years of intense Jewish religious zeal. He
moved out of this phase, but he never ceased affirming his
Jewish identity and he never resigned himself to running
with the pack. All his life he distrusted authority and de-
tested all constraints on the free mind and spirit.

As a student, he was good in mathematics and mediocre in
all other subjects. Rarely did he foreshadow the genius that

---

* *They Fought for Freedom*, Elma Levinger, UAHC, New York, 1953.

was to be. Once he received a compass as a gift from his father and his family was flabbergasted by his eager curiosity about the needle and its magnetic action. Later, upon receiving a book on Euclidian geometry, he was shiny-eyed with fascination. Although undistinguished at Munich and almost anonymous in the classroom, Einstein was cultivating maturity and complete independence. At the age of fifteen, he reached a crucial decision without consulting a single living soul, including his parents: to leave Munich and surrender his German citizenship. With the aid of some relatives, whose help stemmed from a sense of Jewish family responsibility rather than out of any faith in the future of the student, Einstein was enrolled at Swiss Polytechnic in Zurich. He decided to become a teacher.

Even at sixteen, Einstein's mind was crowded with the mysteries of the universe. He was plagued by a question: What would be the result if man could capture a ray of light? It was, unknowingly, the beginning of his life's task. Laboratory experimentation intrigued him. But he suffered indescribable agonies under the pressures of examinations— he likened the experience to a guillotine suspended over his head. He also experienced severe physical privation, because he insisted on making himself independent of family help. Despite his lack of sufficient food and clothing, he used part of his small income to pay for his naturalization as a Swiss subject. He became a Swiss citizen and regarded himself as a citizen of the world. Upon graduation, he sought an assistantship but won only rebuffs. Not one professor wanted him. Not one had discerned the rare and creative mind. Swallowing his hurt and humiliation, the young man resigned himself once more to that recurrent sense of failure which then seemed his forlorn lot.

Unable to find a teaching position, Einstein took a minor job in the Swiss Patent Office. It was dull work. "Examining

the patents sent in and making reports for the files is a
shoemaker's job," he said. But the salary did enable Einstein
to marry Mileva Maric, a Serbian Greek Orthodox woman
he had met at the University. Two sons were born to the
young couple. It didn't take much money to satisfy Einstein's needs. He was then and always contemptuous of
materialism. "Well-being and happiness," he once wrote,
"never appeared to me as absolute aims. I am even inclined
to compare such moral aims to the amibitions of a pig."*
The capacity for wonder and reverence was superior, in
Einstein's view, to the capacity for happiness.

At twenty-three years of age it was still not apparent that
Albert Einstein was destined for a special place in history.
He was married—not happily and divorce followed in a few
years—and had founded a small family. His sons gave him
much pleasure and, like high-spirited children everywhere,
some headaches too. He had a job, dull but well-paying, and
time to indulge his love of good music and literature. But the
real life of Albert Einstein was internal. While working in
the patent office or chatting with friends at his home, or
reading to his boys, Einstein's thoughts often strayed completely away from his surroundings. In later years, his
friends talked of this detachment as his "absences," comparing the experience to a kind of religious ecstasy. One
friend, who also became his biographer, commented upon
the strange "departures" of Einstein: "But one never quite
lost the feeling that his presence among us was only a temporary loan."†

What appeared to be absent-mindedness was, of course,
the working of a creative genius. The mystery of the light
rays continued to nag him. He was haunted by a galaxy of

---

* *The Drama of Albert Einstein*, Antonina Vallentin, Doubleday, New
York, 1954.
† *Ibid.*

questions about current concepts of physics. His rich mind was awhirl with shattering insights and extraordinary discoveries. In 1905, the unknown patent office clerk published five rather disparate articles in the *Year Book of Physics,* a weighty German publication. Each was a major and significant paper. One dealt with photoelectric cells and developed the quantum theory of the atom. Another treated with the movement of molecules. But it was an article entitled, "On the Electrodynamics of Bodies in Movement," that was fated to shake and change the world. It was the theory of relativity. The next issue contained an article by Einstein on the relationship between matter and energy reduced to a formula, $E = MC^2$. Exhausted by the delicious agony of creativity, Einstein was ill for weeks. It was years, however, before an apathetic world became conscious that the writings of an obscure failure and a humble civil servant had revolutionized the universe. At first, only a few scientists even sensed that a new physics had been written across the sky. A Polish professor at the University of Cracow looked up from Einstein's article and declared, "A new Copernicus has been born."

The quiet days at the patent office were over. Soon, the scientific and academic world was clamoring for Einstein. He taught briefly at the University of Bern, then accepted a professorship at the University of Zurich and, in 1910, was offered a Chair at the German University at Prague. A revealing incident occurred when he accepted the latter post. At that time, regulations in Austria required a professor formally to state his religion. It was well known that a genteel anti-Semitism then permeated university circles. For this reason, Einstein was urged by well-meaning advisers to do what many other Jewish instructors had done: to go through the meaningless ritual of nominal "conversion" in order to safeguard his bright career. Why not?

His wife was not Jewish, his own Jewish ties had been
broken off in Munich, and his career had carried him far
from Jewish life. But Einstein despised opportunism and
expediency. He wrote "Religion—Israelite" on the ques-
tionnaire in a firm, bold handwriting. In the years to come,
his affirmation became something more meaningful to him
than a mere refusal to conform or to compromise.

There is no need here to review Einstein's scientific
achievements. No scientist in our time has made a com-
parable impression on the public imagination. Few people
were able to give an intelligent interpretation of relativity.
But the name Albert Einstein became legendary, the white-
maned head was recognized by plain people in every land.
He became not merely a celebrity but a world idol. Two
American students once addressed an envelope simply
"Professor Albert Einstein, Europe." The letter was delivered to him. "How excellent the postal service is!" was the
characteristic comment of the man who never learned to
fathom such fame and was never willing to accommodate
himself to it. But our concern here is not with his scientific
triumphs but with the social ideals which moved him and
the causes for which he fought as a Jew and as a humanitarian. "The concern for man and his destiny must always be
the chief interest of all technical effort," he once warned
his colleagues. "Never forget it among your diagrams and
equations."

Einstein had contempt for scientists who rattled around
in their academic ivory towers. "Only a life lived for others
is a life worth living," he declared. He used his unexpected
fame as a vehicle to transport his ideals. One of these was
pacifism.

Einstein was a passionate pacifist. He saw war as a profanation of all the values that made for humanity. "My
pacifism is instinctive," he declared. When the fever of

World War 1 inflamed Germany with mass hysteria, Einstein refused, as always, to succumb to the mob. He was asked to join with ninety-three German intellectuals in support of the war. He not only refused but signed a counter-manifesto entitled, "Appeal to Europeans," pleading for sanity. His was a calm voice in a churning sea of emotion and his dissent from the national Germany policy called down upon him bitter abuse. Einstein lived a life of solitude, and he had no anxiety about personal attacks upon him. Yet he needed an understanding person near him to mediate between him and the outside world. He found such a mate in Elsa, his lovely cousin who had also been divorced and had two children of her own. His dream of peace in the world lay in the smoking ruins of the war. But Elsa filled his private life with peace.

During the war, Einstein published his General Theory of Relativity, suggesting that light rays could be attracted by the gravitational forces of the sun. Moreover, he wrote, this could be proved during a solar eclipse. When the war ended, two British groups set out—one to northern Brazil, another to the Gulf of Guinea—to photograph the eclipse and thus test Einstein's theory. The pictures proved a definite bending of the light rays. Einstein was right in his hypothesis that light does not always move in a straight line. The president of the British Royal Society exclaimed, "[This] is the greatest discovery in connection with gravitation since first Newton enunciated his principles." It was gratifying to Einstein that the correctness of his theory had been proved by former opponents of Germany, thus demonstrating that science transcends national borders. He knew that his world renown reflected glory upon Germany, and he was eager to strengthen the self-respect of a conquered people struggling to achieve democracy. He went out of his way to identify his fame with Germany by be-

coming a German citizen once more—a supreme gesture of
generosity which was later to be repaid to him in suffering.

Einstein understood the ambivalence with which he and
his scientific discoveries were sometimes received. He could
even be wry about it, "Today, I am considered in Germany
as a German scientist and in England as a Swiss Jew, but if
one day I become persona non grata I would be a Swiss
Jew for the Germans and a German scientist for the English." World events were to show the prescience of this
grim joke. They helped make a Zionist out of him.

He was driven to Zionism by his hatred of anti-Semitism
and his disdain for the German and Austrian Jews who for-
feited their self-respect and denied their identity as Jews in
order to gain the crumbs of acceptance from Jew-hating
Christians. "I saw the shameful pretenses of Jews of high
standing," he recalled, "and my heart bled." Einstein was
shocked by the craven manner in which these "turncoats"
turned their backs on their East European brethren lest they
be identified with alien folk. Einstein concluded that "only a
common enterprise dear to the heart of Jews all over the
world could restore this people to health. It was a great
achievement of Herzl's to have realized and proclaimed
at the top of his voice that, the traditional attitude of the
Jews being what it was, the establishment of a national
home, or more accurately, a center in Palestine, was a suit-
able object on which to concentrate our efforts."

Einstein was delighted to learn of the plans to build a
Hebrew University on Mount Zion in Palestine. Spurred on
also by the knowledge of the barriers against higher education of Jews in most of Europe, he gave his warm and full
support to the project.

Einstein was persuaded to accompany Chaim Weizmann,
also an eminent scientist and a great Zionist leader (later the
first president of Israel), on a fund-raising mission to Amer-

ica. German leaders, especially in the University circles, were aghast at Einstein's enlistment in the Zionist cause, fearful that it might be interpreted as a repudiation of the weak Weimar Republic of Germany. Einstein believed in democracy and in the Weimar Republic. He had expressed his support by becoming once again a German citizen, thus joining his fate to the destiny of Germany. But he refused to cancel the trip to America in behalf of the millions of his brethren who were homeless.

Einstein took America by storm, that spring of 1921. He was showered with honors and attention while he looked on in amused detachment. But some people couldn't figure the strange man out. A New York rabbi cabled him, "Do you believe in God?" Einstein replied, "I believe in Spinoza's God, who reveals Himself in a harmony among all people, not in a God who worries about the destiny and actions of man." But most Americans—Jews and non-Jews —were delighted by the professor. Princeton University gave him an honorary doctorate; President Hibben identifying Einstein as a "new Columbus who sails alone across the uncharted seas of thought." The trip was a sensational success, financial and otherwise, and the dream of a Hebrew University had become a certainty. Einstein felt that the irrepressible passion for knowledge was one of the proud qualities of the Jewish people—one that linked him to them. Love of learning, exaltation of life, a fanatical yearning for justice, the sense of wonder at the grandeur of the world— he considered himself heir to this rich Jewish tradition. "These traditional principles of the Jewish people prove to me that it is my destiny to belong to them."

In the post-war world, Dr. and Mrs. Einstein did a great deal of traveling. He was summoned to address scientists in England, the United States, Belgium, and many other nations. In 1922 he and his wife made a tour of the Far and

Middle East, visiting India, China, Japan, and Palestine. Everywhere, the simple man received royal receptions. Everywhere, the plain people stood in packed throngs to catch a glimpse of the famous face and the warm smile. In 1922 also, Einstein was awarded the Nobel Prize in Physics, the first German since the war to receive such an honor. His fiftieth birthday was celebrated all over the world and the flood of gifts included tobacco from a German laborer, a forest in his honor in Palestine, a statue of Einstein in the new Einstein observatory in Potsdam, and a sailboat. Einstein accepted the adulation with shy bewilderment. He still owned no formal clothes, wore a mended sweater and battered sandals as his uniform of the day, and usually dispensed with socks altogether as an unnecessary encumbrance. He had no sense of triumph. He was troubled about war and injustice and brutality.

While many Germans lionized Einstein, there was evident a deep resentment against him in many German circles. Frequently, attacks on the theory of relativity were only thin disguises for the anti-Semitism which lurked beneath the surface. Einstein was aware of the fragility of the Weimar Republic. But he was hopeful that Jews could contribute to the struggling democracy the benefits of their group values, and particularly that concept of the sanctity of life which he felt was the mark of the Jew. Once, Walter Rathenau, martyr of the Weimar Republic, alluded to this characteristic in a conversation with Einstein, "When a Jew says that he's going hunting to amuse himself, he lies." Einstein cherished this comment as a fitting expression of a sublime Jewish quality.

The fight for peace was as important to Einstein as was his scientific work. "A pacifism that does not actively oppose the rearmament of nations is and will remain impotent," he said. He labored for the War Resister's League.

He simply refused to yield to a "judicious silence." Once he wrote, "This subject brings me to that vilest offspring of the herd mind—the odious militarism. The man who enjoys marching in line and file to the strains of music falls below my contempt; he received his great brain by mistake—the spinal cord would have been sufficient. This heroism at command, this senseless violence, this accursed bombast of patriotism—how intensely I despise them! War is low and despicable, and I had rather be smitten to shreds than participate in such things."

In December, 1930, he said, "If you can get only 2 per cent of the population of the world to assert in time of peace that they will not fight, you will have the solution for international troubles. Even so small a proportion as 2 per cent will accomplish the desired result, for they could not be put in jail. There are not enough jails in the world to accommodate them." American followers conceived a button with "2%" stamped on it, and pacifists all over the world thus attested to their principles.

But world events were overtaking him—events that would strain and ultimately shatter his pacifist faith. In 1929 Einstein and his wife secured a lovely bungalow on a lake in Caputh, near Berlin, and for a few precious years they found a new paradise of joy. Einstein, his shock of hair tossing in the breeze, resplendent in a battered sweater, his eyes squinting into the warm sun, was childishly happy in his small sailboat. But he was aware that Caputh was becoming an island in a storming sea. The outside world, with its darkness, pressed in on all sides. Economic tragedy was striking everywhere—America, Europe, Germany. Political tensions were becoming acute in Germany. The Weimar Republic was being strangled. Nazism seemed to be rolling in, as Einstein once said it would, "on an empty stomach." In 1932 Elsa wrote a friend about Einstein's eagerness to return to the "little house." She added, "But this time I feel uneasy about it. Is it wise to stay here in these troubled times —who can tell? I feel very anxious at heart."

On December 12, 1932, Einstein finally yielded to Elsa's fears and their friends' importuning and they left Germany on a journey to the United States, then to France and Belgium. In his absence from Germany, the Nazis came to power. "The little house" would never again be inhabited by the Einsteins. When the Einsteins took temporary refuge in a hostel in Belgium, King Albert urgently requested them to remain in Belgium. Elsa urged her husband to avoid signing manifestoes, or issuing statements, or calling attention to himself in such troubled times. To which Einstein replied that if he should do what she wanted, Einstein would no longer be Einstein. Instead, he issued a declaration which concluded, ". . . I hope that Germany will soon recover her sanity and that in future men like Kant and Goethe will not only be remembered from time to time, but that the principles they taught will prevail in public life and in the conscience of the people."

Nazi Germany let loose its full-throated fury against him. The newspapers accused him of launching an "atrocity" campaign against Germany. His funds in Germany were confiscated, the house at Caputh was rifled and the garden dug up by the police in search of—incredibly—arms. Nazi brochures were published, listing the "enemies" of the German people, all of whom must be exterminated. A picture of Einstein headed the list. Under his picture were the words: "Not yet hanged." The Nazi pack incited the masses to dreams of assassination. Using the power of his pen, Einstein struck back as best he could against the Nazi jackals. But he was sickened by the fact that he got many violent letters from Jews in Germany blaming him for their troubles. Frightened German Jews, certain that Hitler would not harm them, issued obsequious statements, repudiating Einstein, affirming their fidelity to the Fatherland, insisting that they were well treated and had no fear for the future of Germany. They even burned Einstein's photograph. There is no way of knowing how many of these blind Jews later perished in Hitler's crematoria!

Life in Belgium was seething. Rumors that the Nazis had dispatched henchmen to murder Einstein frightened everybody, with the possible exception of Einstein. Elsa begged Einstein to avoid publicity. He accused her of cowardice. Queen Elizabeth and King Albert had Einstein's house surrounded by the police and assigned plainclothesmen to follow Einstein everywhere. He developed an amused pride in his ability to give them the slip. In the fall of 1933, the scientist and his wife made the important decision. They went to America, where he accepted a post at Princeton with the newly-organized Institute for Advanced Studies. Worn out by the years of anxiety and devastated by the death of her daughter, Elsa became ill and died in 1936.

Einstein loved Princeton and the comfortable quarters he found there. He was free to work as he pleased and he worked effectively. He became an American citizen. But he was tormented by the forces which the Nazis had loosed upon the world. His fundamental life principles were put to a terrible test. How could mankind be saved from the darkest scourge ever unleashed? Sadly, reluctantly, heartbreakingly, he struggled through to the reality which could no longer be avoided. "We must," he said, "face even battle when it becomes necessary to safeguard law and human dignity." The world had crushed a part of his faith. He had become a "hardened pacifist."

The world scene haunted him. It "throws a shadow upon every hour of my present life," he said in 1939, on his sixtieth birthday. The tragedy of the gentle pacifist, faced with the inescapable need for defense of freedom against a new Dark Age, was climaxed by the visit from refugee scientists Fermi and Szilard who urged him to write to the President. One can only imagine the pain of conscience with which Einstein must have contended before he agreed to write the letter to the President. Knowing that the Nazis were racing to complete an atom bomb, he was convinced that the future of mankind required America to win the race.

"The war is won but not the peace," Einstein declared at the close of World War II. "The world was promised freedom from fear; in fact fear has increased enormously since the end of the war. The world was promised freedom from want; but large parts of it are faced with starvation while others live in abundance." Einstein's conscience was heavy. Frequently, he described his part in the development of the bomb as merely being a "mail-box" to transmit a letter. "If I had known that the Germans would not succeed in producing an atom bomb, I would not have lifted a finger," he confessed to his friends. But he didn't know. He couldn't know. He devoted the best energies of his last years to his fight for a world government which he saw as the only way of "eliminating the most terrible danger that man has ever faced."

Pacifism, Zionism, and socialism and humanism were features of Einstein's social and political philosophy. But, in none of these movements was Einstein a party-liner or doctrinaire follower. His pacifism, as we have seen, was strongly affected by the rise of Hitlerism. Einstein's Zionism remained intense to the very end of his days. While he exulted in the achievements of the Yishuv and the emergence of Israel, Einstein was not greatly interested in the "dross" of a new, albeit Jewish, nationalism. He saw Zionism as an instrument for the cultural, social, and psychological healing of the Jewish people. He saw the Jewish home as a center for Jewish culture which "shall help to awaken the Near East to new economic and spiritual life."

A rapprochement between the Arabs and the Jews was one of Einstein's fondest hopes. He was warmly sympathetic to Judah Magnes's concept of a bi-national Palestine. In 1938 he addressed the Third Seder of the National Labor Committee for Palestine, meeting in New York City, ". . . I should much rather see reasonable agreement with the Arabs on the basis of living together in peace than the creation of a Jewish state. Apart from practical consideration, my awareness of the essential nature of Judaism resists the idea of a Jewish state with borders, an army, and a measure of temporal power, no matter how modest. I am afraid of the inner damage Judaism will sustain—especially from the development of a narrow nationalism within our ranks, against which we have already had to fight strongly, even without a Jewish state. . . . If external necessity should after all compel us to assume this burden, let us bear it with tact and patience."

Practical necessity did make a Jewish state inevitable, and Einstein extended the fullest support to the fledgling state. Indeed, so revered in Israel was the great scientist that, upon the death of Chaim Weizmann, he was asked to serve as President of Israel. Einstein was then too old, too deeply involved in his own work at Princeton—he refused the high honor. But his heartfelt concern for the Jewish homeland never waned. At his death on April 18, 1955, he was making plans for a television appeal to Jews and Arabs to work out their joint destiny in brotherhood, understanding, and peace.

Einstein's socialism was also an iconoclastic philosophy, deriving less from Marx than from a tender humanism which was appalled by "the crippling of individuals" which he felt implicit in capitalism. Writing in the *Monthly Review* in 1949, Einstein declared, ". . . Unlimited competition leads to a huge waste of labor, and to that crippling of the social consciousness of individuals. . . . This crippling of individuals I consider the worst evil of capitalism. Our whole educational system suffers from this evil. An exaggerated competitive attitude is inculcated into the student, who is trained to worship acquisitive success as a preparation for his future career."

Arguing for a socialist economy, Einstein was far from being oblivious to the possible pitfalls, ". . . Nevertheless, it is necessary to remember that a planned economy is not yet socialism. A planned economy as such may be accompanied by the complete enslavement of the individual. The achievement of socialism requires the solution of some extremely difficult socio-political problems: how is it possible, in view of the far-reaching centralization of political and economic power, to prevent bureaucracy from becoming all-powerful and overweening? How can the rights of the individual be protected and therewith a democratic counterweight to the power of bureaucracy be assured?"

The dignity and fundamental liberties of the human individual were paramount in Einstein's thinking. In his later years, he witnessed the heavy hand of mccarthyism, smashing civil liberties and academic freedom in America. A Brooklyn school teacher, who had refused to testify before a Congressional committee, wrote Einstein for advice. The aging scholar wrote:

> *Dear Mr. Frauenglass:*
>   . . . The problem with which the intellectuals of this country are confronted is very serious. The reactionary politicians have managed to instil suspicion of all intellectual efforts into the public by dangling before their eyes a danger

from without. Having succeeded so far, they are now proceeding to suppress the freedom of teaching and to deprive of their positions all those who do not prove submissive, i.e., to starve them.

What ought the minority of intellectuals to do against this evil? Frankly, I can only see the revolutionary way of non-cooperation in the sense of Gandhi's. Every intellectual who is called before one of the committees ought to refuse to testify, i.e., he must be prepared for jail and economic ruin, in short, for the sacrifice of his personal welfare in the interest of the cultural welfare of his country.

However, this refusal to testify must not be based on the well-known subterfuge of invoking the Fifth Amendment against possible self-incrimination, but on the assertion that it is shameful for a blameless citizen to submit to such an inquisition, and that this kind of inquisition violates the spirit of the Constitution.

If enough people are ready to take this grave step, they will be successful. If not, then the intellectuals of this country deserve nothing better than the slavery which is intended for them.

P.S. This letter need not be considered "confidential."

In his own way, Einstein was a religious man. He did not believe in a "God who plays at dice." He once said, "For me the essence of religion is to be able to get under the skin of another human being, to rejoice in his joy and suffer his pain." He rejected a personal and vindictive God but he believed in a God of the natural order, whose laws are absolute and immutable. He believed in the indomitable quality of man's free spirit. What is the meaning of life? "To know an answer to this question," he wrote, "means to be religious. You ask, Does it make any sense, then, to pose this question? I answer, The man who regards his own life and that of his fellow creatures as meaningless is not merely unhappy but hardly fit for life." He cherished the yearning for social justice which he found in the Jewish prophets, in Gandhi, and in the saints and sages of all religions.

Einstein was a rare human being, a supreme iconoclast, who traveled light, mostly alone—and never in harness. There was a uniqueness also in his Jewishness. "The pursuit of knowledge for its own sake, an almost fanatical love of justice, and the desire for personal independence—these are the features of the Jewish tradition which make me thank my stars that I belong to it. Those who are raging today against the ideals of reason and individual liberty and are trying to establish a spiritless state-slavery by brute force rightly see in us their irreconcilable foes. History has given us a difficult row to hoe; but so long as we remain devoted servants of truth, justice, and liberty, we shall continue not merely to survive as the oldest of living peoples, but by creative work to bring forth fruits which contribute to the ennoblement of the human race, as heretofore."*

---

* *Mein Weltbild*, Querido Verlag, Amsterdam, 1934.

Stephen Wise

GOD'S ANGRY PROPHET

S TEPHEN S. WISE, like no other Jew in his time, strode across the stage of the twentieth century as the very embodiment of the ancient prophet of Israel. He was, to friend and foe alike, a giant, smashing aside the pygmy minds and Lilliputian spirits who sought to restrain him. He was the modern exemplar of God's angry man, excoriating evil in high places and low, proclaiming justice throughout the land. His was the voice of grandiloquence, rumbling like thunder and flashing the lightning bolts of truth. To Wise fell the privilege of revivifying the ancient prophetic tradition, of making a Judaism grown flaccid in America once again a fiery call to action in the political and civic arena. He taught an entire generation that Judaism need not be a sweet soporific; that Judaism can be a revolutionary doctrine which can strike flint and shoot sparks and challenge society. When he died in 1949, he left a noble inheritance and a vacuum which could never be completely filled.

Born in Budapest in 1874, the son and grandson of rabbis, Stephen Wise was brought to New York at the age of sixteen months. He attended the public schools, later enrolled in City College and Columbia University. Determined from childhood to become a rabbi, he studied with his father and other distinguished rabbis in New York before going abroad to complete his studies at Oxford University and in Vienna where he was ordained.

Returning to New York, he became assistant rabbi of New York's Congregation B'nai Jeshurun. Within a year, the senior rabbi died and, though Wise was only twenty-one years old, he was appointed spiritual leader of the congregation. In 1899, after a difficult period of soul-searching, he made his decision, against the advice of many close friends who warned him of self-exile, to accept the call to become rabbi of Temple Beth Israel in Portland, Oregon. In Portland, with his bride Louise, he began an exciting and fruitful ministry which lasted until 1906. During those wonderful years, which he always recalled as the happiest period of his interesting life, his daughter Justine and his son James were born.

The pioneer period which Wise served in Portland foreshadowed the ministry which was to come. There, in the still wild Northwest, Wise visited many small communities, beginning the arduous lecturing and guest preaching which were to carry him later to cities all over the country. There, he perfected the masterful speaking prowess which could hypnotize and overwhelm an audience. And there, as he was to do throughout his life, he flung himself into the fierce controversies of public life, establishing himself as a leader not only in Jewish life but, equally, in general communal affairs wherever moral issues were at stake. He fought against the alliance of gambling and liquor interests; against the blight of organized prostitution which, in collusion with city officials and the police, corroded the life of the city. Members of his congregation did not always approve of these actions; but they soon learned, as many others were to learn, that to try to restrict Wise from doing or saying what he believed to be right was about as safe and profitable as tinkering with the proverbial buzz-saw.

In 1905 Stephen Wise accepted the invitation of Temple Emanu-El of New York City, "the Cathedral Synagogue of the Country," to preach a series of trial sermons. This invitation represented a singular tribute to the young rabbi, then only thirty-one, and to his rapidly growing reputation. After a trial sermon, Wise was approached by a committee headed by Louis Marshall to discuss conditions under which he might be invited to serve as rabbi. Wise quickly announced that, whatever the arrangements would be, one thing would have to be understood clearly from the outset: the pulpit, like his pulpit at Temple Beth Israel in Portland, would have to be free.

Marshall retorted immediately that such a condition was out of the question inasmuch as "the pulpit of Emanu-El has always been, and is, subject to and under the control of the Board of Trustees."

Wise replied instantly, "If that be true, Mr. Marshall, there is nothing more to say."

In the course of the next week, the rabbi had three visits from various members of the Board, pleading with him to reconsider and insisting that Marshall's arbitrary decisions should not be taken too seriously. But the die was cast. Wise returned to Portland. When he received a letter from Marshall restating his position on the status of the Emanu-El pulpit, Wise replied, on January 5, 1906, declaring that he felt constrained to "address this Open Letter to you on the question of the freedom of the Jewish pulpit" because the "steadily waning influence of the church and the synagogue is due in no small part, I hold, to the wide-spread belief that the pulpit is not free." The oft-quoted letter to Marshall, which stirred wide-spread debate in the Jewish and in the general press (even the *New York Times* published an editorial opposing Wise's view), stated:

"The chief office of the minister, I take it, is not to represent the views of the congregation, but to proclaim the truth as he sees it. How can he serve a congregation as a teacher save as he quickens the minds of his hearers by the vitality and independence of his utterances? How can a man be vital and independent and helpful, if he be tethered and muzzled? A free pulpit, worthily filled, must command respect and influence; a pulpit that is not free, howsoever filled, is sure to be without potency and honor. A free pulpit will sometimes stumble into error; a pulpit that is not free can never powerfully plead for truth and righteousness."

The following year Wise returned to New York to put the flesh of reality on a dream he had nurtured for many years: the founding of the Free Synagogue. Services were held in the Hudson Theatre near Times Square and later in mammoth Carnegie Hall.

"The task proved more difficult than I had foreseen," Wise recalled in his autobiography. "I soon found myself facing a rather wide, if not deep-seated hostility, on the part of temple and synagogue groups within the community. The hostility sometimes verged upon the vulgarity of abuse, as in the case of one of the so-called leading rabbis of New York, who described the Free Synagogue in its earliest days as 'a hall, with an orator, an audience, and a pitcher of ice water.' "

Wise then, and later, was not one to back away from a fight, particularly where his own convictions and his own highly-developed ego were at stake. "An unexpectedly hospitable response greeted my first addresses or lectures," he wrote years later. "Some supporters, I do not doubt after all these years, were attracted by the mere novelty of the undertaking. . . . Among these supporters were such as were appealed to by the vitality and freshness of the venture, seeing that there had been nothing new and vital in American synagogue life for a generation. I made clear beyond all doubt that the Free Synagogue would never become a retreat or asylum for faint-hearted and pusillanimous Jews, that it was to be wholly, unequivocally a Jewish adventure, that it would be deeply, unreservedly, and even rejoicingly Jewish."

In his first "address," Wise set out to answer the question: What is a Free Synagogue? "The Free Synagogue," he explained, "is not to be an indirect or circuitous avenue of approach to Unitarianism; it is not to be a society for the gradual conversion of Jewish men or women to any form of Christianity. We mean to be vitally, intensely, unequivocally Jewish. Jews who would not be Jews will find no place in the Free Synagogue, for we, its founders, wish to be not less Jewish but more Jewish in the highest and noblest sense of the term."

On what principles would the Free Synagogue be based? Wise and his small group of co-workers set down the guiding principles as follows:

1. Absolute freedom of the pulpit.

2. Abolition of distinction between rich and poor as to pews and membership privileges.

3. Direct and full participation of the synagogue in all social services required by the community.

4. Complete identification not only with the Jewish faith, but with Israel's fate and future.

Wise and his Free Synagogue were ridiculed from pulpit and press, but the new institution began immediately to fill a pressing need. Within a year, the Free Synagogue had received many requests to found a branch on the East Side. Wise responded by establishing a branch at Clinton Hall for the masses of immigrants "who had not forsaken their Orthodox Jewish moorings and yet were eager . . . to hear the word and the message of an intensely loyal Jewish

liberal." Beginning with Friday evening services, the branch
soon added a religious school to provide an education and
a friendly meeting place for Jewish young people. Like the
main Free Synagogue uptown (which began in a church
building on West 81st Street before moving to its present
building on 68th Street in uptown Manhattan), the Clinton
Branch embarked upon a host of social service projects
throughout the teeming neighborhood.

Within a few years, the much-maligned Free Synagogue
had grown into a large congregation. Even more, it became a bright new symbol in American Jewish life and,
particularly, in the Liberal Jewish movement throughout
America. In the Free Synagogue, the ethical principles of
Judaism were boldly applied to the social issues confronting
society. Wise proclaimed the cause of civic purity, of social
justice, and the Free Synagogue consecrated itself to the
highest values of the Jewish heritage.

Wise appointed Rabbi Sidney Goldstein to head the
Social Service Division of the Free Synagogue. An idealistic
young rabbi who, like Wise, identified Judaism with concrete efforts to improve the lot of all people, Goldstein
began an association with the Free Synagogue which was to
continue until his retirement in 1950 and his death in 1955.
Goldstein organized the social service program which he
later termed the "noble experiment" and which made the
Free Synagogue a unique institution in Jewish life. Volunteer synagogue members provided organized social service
for the Jewish patients of Bellevue and Montefiore Hospitals. A factory was set up for tuberculosis patients, affording an opportunity for part-time employment under medical
supervision. Later, Louise Wise was to spearhead the famous
Child Adoption Center of the Free Synagogue, a Center
which now bears her name. In virtually all areas of community life—psychological, recreational, medical, and economic—the Free Synagogue, as an institution, played an

impressive role. In 1913, 45 per cent of the synagogue budget was spent for social service activities.

Even before the Free Synagogue was established on a firm footing, the young David who was its leader had his sling-shot cocked and ready to take dead aim on the powerful Goliaths in New York civic and political life. "I felt very early in my ministry," he said in his autobiography, "the necessity and advantages of the minister going into politics. To me neither religion nor politics was remote or seques-tered from life. Religion is a vision or ideal of life. Politics is a method, or modus vivendi. To say that the minister should not go into politics is to imply that ideal and reality are twain and alien. Politics is what it is because religion keeps out of it.

"I am persuaded," Wise continued, "that the minister can go into politics without partisanship, without compro-mise, and most important, he must seek nothing for himself or his church, and accept nothing. Convinced that the ideals of religion, separated from their day-to-day application, were meaningless, I early entered into one area of contro-versy after another that many might call political, and which I recognized as part of the socio-political life of America. . . . For me the supreme declaration of our Hebrew Bible was and remains: 'Justice, Justice shalt thou pursue.' "

New York City soon came to regard Wise as a formidable Jewish spokesman and a factor to be reckoned with in political affairs. In 1907 the notorious former Tammany boss "King Richard" Croker, was tendered a public wel-coming dinner upon his return from virtual exile in Ireland. Many New York Supreme Court judges, as well as the district attorney, attended this dinner which was devised to serve as a vehicle for the public rehabilitation of Croker, preparatory to his return to leadership of Tammany Hall. But Rabbi Wise threw a monkey-wrench into this political scheme.

The night after the dinner, Wise had the opportunity to address the Ethical Social League. He let loose a blistering indictment of political degradation, in which he characterized the Croker smoker as "New York's Night of Shame." Wise showed no mercy in raking the judges and other New York officials for uniting to do honor to a dishonorable politician. New York papers and *Life* magazine picked up the "Night of Shame" theme, political cartoonists had a heyday with it. Thanks to Wise's rousing of public opinion, the Croker reincarnation plan died aborning.

Within a few years, the fame of the aggressive young rabbi had spread from coast to coast. A San Francisco newspaper, learning that Wise had made parenthetical reference to San Francisco graft cases in the course of an address on civic problems in New York City, wired New York to request that the entire speech be telegraphed to it in San Francisco.

Wise's social zeal catapulted the Free Synagogue into renown, but inevitably it also created controversy within the congregation. True to the original statement of purposes, Wise had democratized the new synagogue by establishing its financial support in voluntary contributions instead of the conventional dues system. In addition, he initiated the unassigned pew system in place of the prevailing practice of the sale of fixed pews. Thus divesting control from the hands of the wealthy, Wise was free to preach his prophetic message without serious let or hindrance. These democratic innovations were emulated in many synagogues, thus bringing an increasing measure of democratic life to the American synagogue.

But Wise's penchant for plunging into the thorniest of public controversies angered and pained some of his congregants. His stands on these issues led to continuing loss of members. The liberal company he chose to keep caused strain also. For example, when Wise participated in a series of union meetings with two neighboring churches, some of his largest contributors left him.

Wise subjected New York City government to sharp scrutiny and weighed the conduct of public affairs against the highest standards of morality. Anybody who took liberties with the public trust could expect to face the implacable moral indignation of Stephen Wise. In 1912 the rabbi preached a sermon entitled, "A New Year's Vision of a New City," in which he labeled Police Commissioner Waldo as "a menacingly incompetent and incorrigibly stupid creature whom his chief maintains in office lest he be thrown to the wolves, though in the meantime the life of the city is thrown to the dogs." What had provoked the fearful Wise ire was the fact that a gangster by the name of Rosenthal had been murdered and that the police officer whom the mayor chose to investigate the affair was himself suspected of the crime. Upon Wise's demand, a civic committee was appointed not only to bring the murderers to task but also to make sure that "the blackmail and plunder organized to a fine science . . . under which the Police Department of New York collected revenue for Tammany and even employed murderers to enforce its thievery, should be revealed to the citizens of New York and thus ended." The civic committee helped curb some of the worst of the abuses spotlighted by Wise.

Like the prophet Nathan who pointed the accusing finger at the king of Israel himself, Wise did not shrink from combat with the breezy and popular mayor, Jimmy Walker. When a magistrate of Walker's appointment behaved in an improper manner, Wise fired a telegram to Franklin Delano Roosevelt, then governor of New York, demanding action. Simultaneously, he released the wire to the press, thus forcing reluctant action from the governor. Soon thereafter, the City Affairs Committee, of which Wise was the vice-chairman, petitioned the governor to give Walker a full and fair trial to determine whether he should be removed from office for corruption and irresponsibility. In reply, a piqued Roosevelt suggested that Rev. John Haynes Holmes, chairman of the committee, and Rabbi Stephen Wise devote more attention to religion and less to politics. Years later, when President Roosevelt and Stephen Wise were close and loyal friends, the rabbi teased the smiling President about this remark.

In 1932, when the nation was in the throes of the depression, members of the city government, including Mayor Walker, planned a salary grab. When Wise confronted Walker about the proposal to raise his own salary from $25,000 to $40,000, Walker sought to absolve himself by saying that others, not he, had proposed the increase. "What could I say to them?" the Mayor complained. Wise told him, "Your answer, Mr. Mayor, should have been, 'Is thy servant a dog that he should do this thing?'" The proposal was quickly shelved.

Wise's pressure on the ineffable Walker was unrelenting and, at one point, helped persuade the mayor to take a sudden boat trip. Mayor Fiorello LaGuardia once said, referring to Walker's hurried trip to England, "When Rabbi Wise talks about mayors, there is usually a run on Atlantic steamship accommodations."

At a time when sympathy with labor was regarded as radical and/or queer, Rabbi Stephen Wise took his stand as one of labor's staunchest friends. Wise's concern for the rights of labor harked back to 1895, when he held his first pulpit in New York. Some street car workers were killed during a Brooklyn strike over wages and hours. In his sermon the following Sabbath, Wise excoriated the conditions which led to death for persons who sought only the right to live decently. Although severely criticized by officers of the congregation, he affirmed, "I shall continue to speak for the workers whenever I come to feel that they have a real grievance and a just cause."

In his Oregon pulpit, Wise had been "one of a small group . . . which knowing of child-labor conditions in the fish canneries, brought about the introduction and ultimately the legislative adoption of a child-labor law. This created a State Child Labor Commission of which I became a member by gubernatorial appointment, serving on it until 1906 when I returned to New York."

Feeling against organized labor ran high in 1911-1912 when the Los Angeles *Times-Herald*, long a "hot spot" in the field of industrial relations, was wrecked by dynamite. Wise raised his voice in an address at Carnegie Hall, "As long as labor organizations are denied a hearing save just before election seasons; as long as they are treated with scorn and contumely; as long as they are cast out and denied, it is not to be wondered at that the leaders, finding themselves and their organizations outlawed, should in turn be guilty of outlawry; that being cast out, they should resort to the weapon of the outcast; that being denied a hearing after the manner of destructive and unreasoning foes, they should make themselves heard after the manner of destructive and unreasoning foes."

John Haynes Holmes, Wise's perennial partner in social struggles, also delivered an address in which he said, "I would rather be in the McNamara cell than in the office of the president of the Steel Trust. . . . I say that there is more peril to America in the criminal corporation than in the criminal laborer, and I say this also, that if I had to make my choice between being leader of the corporations or being sent to the dungeons of San Quentin, I would choose the latter." For these and similar sentiments, Wise and Holmes were dubbed by *American Industries* as "the McNamaras of the pulpit," and they were depicted in cartoons as the Jekyll and Hyde of organized labor.

Criticism seemed only to whet Wise's delight in the good fight. In 1911, for some inexplicable reason, he was invited to speak at the annual banquet of the New York Chamber of Commerce. The banquet was ornamented by America's greatest captains of industry. Wise laced into everyone in the room, challenging them with their God-given duty to protect—not deny—the rights of workers, appealing to their Christian conscience to improve—not undermine—the security and welfare of their laborers. Wise was never invited to address this august body again.

A climactic moment in Wise's support of the rights of labor came in 1919. Having become convinced through his experience in industrial conflicts that no real improvement in working conditions was possible without collective bargaining, Wise felt deeply involved when employees of the United States Steel Corporation went on strike to gain the right to organize. Wise was outraged by the knowledge that half the employees of United States Steel worked an average of twelve hours a day. Their efforts to organize had been impaired by the company's use of the black list and the labor spy as anti-union weapons. In June, 1919, Wise wrote to Samuel Gompers, the leader of the strikers, expressing his pleasure that the American Federation of Labor was proceeding to organize the steel workers. Wise offered his assistance in any way the labor leader could use it.

Wise resolved to speak his mind on this ethical issue from his Free Synagogue pulpit. He was not unaware of the possible consequences. Just before he delivered that celebrated sermon, he commented sardonically to his wife, "My sermon this morning will light a million-dollar blaze." The address was entitled, "Who Are the Bolsheviks at Home and Abroad—How Shall We Know Them?" His sermon sought to expose the charge of Judge Elbert H. Gary, who represented the steel companies, that the demands of the workers were Communist-inspired. Wise fired his volley in these words:

"The men in the iron and steel industry are striving for a fundamental right of industry . . . the right to organize and to deal organizedly with their employers. . . .

"I charge Mr. Gary with having made it impossible for me as an American citizen to know what the thought and what the will of the workers in the steel industry is. They have never been free to utter themselves. They are not free today.

"I charge the United States Steel Corporation with resorting to every manner of coercion and even of violence . . . in order to avoid the organization of the workers." Wise termed Gary "the most prolific breeder of bolshevism in America" because of his union-busting.

Wise's allusion to a "million-dollar blaze" had reflected his premonition that many substantial pledges for a new synagogue structure would be canceled as a result of his address. The rabbi was correct. Condemnation poured in from many quarters. Many large pledges were withdrawn. So many members of the congregation resigned that Wise felt duty-bound to submit his resignation to the synagogue board. The board refused his resignation, defended his right to speak, and explained that the rabbi spoke to, and not for, the congregation. The Free Synagogue and its rabbi survived a testing challenge. But the synagogue building was set back so far that the new structure was not completed in Rabbi Wise's lifetime.

During the Depression, Wise was bitterly critical of the economic system that permitted large-scale unemployment and human suffering. He urged a swift program of relief, unemployment insurance, and other ameliorative measures.

Wise supported Roosevelt and the New Deal and hailed the
improved status of organized labor.

Against all forms of religious or racial intolerance Wise
was indomitable. Throughout his life he fought for Negro
rights. He was, with several other distinguished white persons, a founder of the National Association for the Advance-
ment of Colored People which was destined to play an
historic role in striking down the barriers of segregation
which separated man from man. In 1915 Wise poured out
his wrath on the film, "Birth of a Nation," an anti-Negro
film which Wise felt reinforced negative stereotypes about
the Negro people. Until his death, Wise was a fervent advocate of such civil rights legislation as the Fair Employment
Practices Law.

While many of Wise's social ideals were realized in his
lifetime, he was doomed to heart-breaking disillusionment
in some others. Especially was this true of Wise's passionate
yearning for a world in which the ancient Peace Vision of
Isaiah would be fulfilled upon earth. Like many of his colleagues in the Central Conference of American Rabbis,
Wise was a pacifist at the time World War 1 burst upon
mankind. Viewing the war as an incalculable calamity,
Wise nonetheless associated himself with President Wilson
in the belief that the Allied cause was just. He draped his
pulpit with an American flag and announced that it would
remain there "until the morning of the dawn of peace for
humanity." He posed the issue in these words: "The question is not whether we shall successfully wage war . . . but
whether we will be equal to the infinitely difficult task of
gaining a victory over the German government without
losing our own souls. The question is whether we shall be
great enough to suffer no malice nor uncharitableness to
invade our souls."

The post-war world turned his idealistic hopes to ashes.

Having poured out his prodigious energies in behalf of U.S. support for the League of Nations and of guarantees of minority rights in the peace treaties, Wise was filled with gloom by the disenchantment of the '20's. He publicly apologized for the endorsement he had given to the war (his friend John Haynes Holmes had persisted in his pacifism) and promised "without reservation or equivocation never to bless or support any war whatsoever again." Again, the hurricane of events was to force Wise to retreat from what he had hoped was a fixed moral position. The emergence of Hitlerism led him to abandon all vestiges of pacifism, and Wise threw himself unsparingly into the struggle against fascism.

His profound reverence for democracy moved Wise to challenge the lack of democracy in the management of Jewish affairs in the United States. Until World War 1, a small number of wealthy and influential philanthropists constituted themselves the self-appointed spokesmen and representatives of the Jewish community. The masses of Jews, whose numbers were constantly swelling as a result of the stream of Eastern European migration, had virtually no choice in determining the issues by which they were vitally affected. These masses were increasingly and articulately discontented with the "shtadlanim" who presumed to speak for them. They liked the taste of democracy which America had afforded, and they wanted the same democracy extended to the internal processes of Jewish life.

Wise became a powerful advocate of democratization of Jewish life. With the outbreak of World War 1, the time seemed ripe for American Jewry to take the management of their affairs into their own hands. Three major problems faced the Jewish people: (1) the desperate need of Jews in war-torn countries; (2) the grave necessity of protecting the minority rights of the populous Jewish belt in

Eastern and Central Europe; (3) the hope that Palestine would be legally secured as a Jewish national homeland. These tasks required the full mobilization of the resources of American Jews. Under the impetus of these exigencies, the idea of an American Jewish Congress, uniting all Jewish groups within a democratic framework for common action, appealed to the imagination of large segments of American Jewry. The warm tide of enthusiasm and the sense of urgency which coursed through the Jewish community overwhelmed those powerful and wealthy who instinctively shrank from mass action and who frowned upon Jewish nationalist aspirations.

And so the American Jewish Congress was born. Louis Brandeis gave the new movement its clearest expression. The Congress was organized initially to represent American Jewry at the Paris Peace Conference. It was to be strictly a temporary machinery, to be dissolved as soon as its functions with respect to the Peace Conference had been discharged. Wise and Louis Marshall, his perennial opponent who earned Wise's grudging admiration by submerging his private and organizational prejudices into the policies hammered out by the Congress, carried much of the onerous burden of the Congress delegation to the Peace Conference. The delegation did its work well, persuading the Allies to include formal guarantees of minority rights, and also setting the stage for the Balfour Declaration of 1917 in which England pledged its aid in the establishment of a Jewish national homeland in Palestine.

When the Peace Treaty was signed, the Congress adjourned as agreed. But a large body of delegates immediately reconvened in a conference for the formalization of a permanent American Jewish Congress "determined that the gains made in bringing democracy into Jewish life should not be lost." Rabbi Wise sounded the keynote, warning that it was too late to return to "the undemocratic, un-American, un-Jewish method of dictation from above however well-meaning in intent, however soft-spoken in manner." Louis Marshall and the leaders of the American Jewish Committee cried "double-cross" and blasted the American Jewish Congress. But the new body was established and would continue as a rival and thorn in the side of the more austere and aristocratic American Jewish Committee.

Under the leadership of Stephen Wise, the American Jewish Congress made a substantial contribution to the Jewish people and to American life. It helped to develop a World Jewish Congress to protect the rights of Jews throughout the world. It pioneered in a comprehensive, dynamic and effective program of civil rights for all Americans, based on the philosophy that Jewish security in America is dependent on the extension of democratic rights to all Americans regardless of race, creed, or national ancestry. This was a radical departure from the so-called Jewish defense attitude, characterized largely by anti-defamation and behind-the-scenes influence-peddling. The American Jewish Congress spurned the timid defensive policies it condemned as "sha-sha" and, through law and mass action, unhesitatingly expressed its views on such public issues as Negro rights, employment discrimination, Zionism, and church-state relations.

To Stephen Wise fell the task of rallying Jews and non-Jews to an understanding of the rising menace of Hitler and fascism. Repeatedly, Wise conferred with President Roosevelt and with leaders of both political parties to warn them of the ominous cloud on the world horizon. He mobilized the American Jewish Congress to an unremitting struggle against Hitlerism. In 1933 he organized a gigantic mass meeting at Madison Square Garden to throw the klieglight of world opinion on Nazi atrocities against the Jews. At the

World Jewish Congress, Wise secured the unanimous adoption of a resolution calling for a world Jewish boycott of
Germany. While many Jewish organizations in the United
States joined in the boycott, there was from some quarters
violent, almost hysterical, opposition to the whole idea of
strong public anti-Nazi actions by American Jews.

Some Jewish leaders in Germany tried to silence Wise.
In October, 1932, Wise sent a representative to Germany
to interview thirty leading Jews to ask what, if anything,
could American Jews do to avert the dreaded rise of the
power of Hitler? All except one declared that "Hitler
would never come to power." Several of them sent a sarcas-
tic message to Wise, "Say to Rabbi Wise that he need not
concern himself with Jewish affairs in Germany."

Wise was astonished by the lack of foresight of Jewish
leaders, not only in Germany, but in the U.S. as well. Ten
days before Hitler's ascent to power, Wise met with representative leaders of the American Jewish Committee and
the B'nai B'rith. Reciting this episode in his autobiography,*
Wise wrote, "We pressed home again and again the question, 'What shall we do if Hitler comes to power?' The
chairman of the American Jewish Committee, Dr. Cyrus
Adler, made the reply destined to become classic as an
exhibit of unwisdom and lack of prescience on the eve of
tragic events, 'We will cross that bridge when we come to
it, not before.' The penalty of foresight is always inflicted
upon the foreseeing by the blind, whom foresight reproaches
and exacerbates but never teaches."

This fundamental difference in strategy between the
American Jewish Congress, on the one side, and the American Jewish Committee, on the other, persisted throughout
the tragic period. The latter contended that mass meetings

---

* The Challenging Years: The Autobiography of Stephen Wise, Put-
nam, New York, 1949.

and boycotts by American Jews would only worsen the plight of German Jews, that the wiser strategy would be to seek somehow to ameliorate the delicate situation of Jews in Germany. Proposals were advanced for deals with Nazi Germany that would have enabled some Jews to preserve some of their property and possessions. Lashing such suggestions, Wise exclaimed in 1936:

"We are resolved to make possible the transfer of the largest number of Jewish exiles from Germany into Palestine. But one thing we will never do. We will never take any step or adopt any measure or resort to any device or stoop to any subterfuge which shall bring financial help or any reinforcement of strength to the Nazi Reich. To do that were to betray the hopes of mankind, so far as these be in our Jewish keeping. . . . We will not become 'Hitler's drummers.' We refuse to act as Hitler's agents or commercial travelers. Not only do we reject out of hand with scorn and contempt any and every proposal which would ensure the security of some Jews through the shame of all Jews, but we declare that if any attempt be made in America or in England, or in any land, to facilitate the exodus of Germans through strengthening and reinforcing the financial status of Nazi Germany, we will do what men can do in order to wreck and destroy such proposals. The honor of Israel, the values of civilization, the ideals of mankind are even more precious than life itself."

Wise spent himself in the titanic struggle against Nazism. He hounded and harried U.S. Government leaders who sought to sit on reports of anti-Jewish atrocities for fear of provoking public opinion in America. He importuned President Roosevelt to extend every possible aid on American shores to Jewish refugees from Hitler. He traveled frequently to Europe to confer with representatives of Jewish groups and to lead the World Jewish Congress. He labored, with only partial success, to stir the Christian conscience in America to speak out with vigor against anti-Jewish atrocities. The destruction of 6,000,000 Jews was the supreme sorrow of his life. It must have been through God's mercy that this weary warrior lived to see the total defeat of the Nazi Empire and, rising out of the blood and agony of the holocaust, the fulfilment of a shining dream he had cherished for fifty years and his people for twenty centuries—the creation of the State of Israel.

This is a partial picture of Stephen Wise, a modern prophet of Israel. It is a picture of a picaresque and gallant fighter—eloquent, sometimes arrogant, somewhat vain, frequently mercurial, and even opportunistic, but a man who faced the challenging years with courage and dignity and without fear. But, even so, this is not the whole picture of Stephen Wise. For, beyond the renowned public figure was Stephen Wise, the man—the husband, the father, the gentle grandparent, the friend, the Rabbi in Israel. One has only to read, *The Personal Letters of Stephen Wise*,* lovingly edited by his children—Judge Justine Wise Polier and James Waterman Wise—to sense the deep currents of feeling which sustained him, the unexpected softness which suffused his relations with those near to him, and the pulsating zest for life which animated this vital man. His letters to his wife—he sometimes wrote her three times a day while away on a lecture trip—reveal a lyrical and tender love story which continued to the day of her death in 1947. With her death, something of the inner spirit of Stephen Wise began to dim.

Stephen Wise died in New York City at the age of seventy-three. He left the following letter for his children:

---

* *The Personal Letters of Stephen Wise*, edited by Justine Wise Polier and James Waterman Wise, Beacon Press, Boston, 1956.

I am not tearful or maudlin as I write this, but I am so wretched that I would be insensitive and stupid not to write as I do. When something happens to me, Ed knows about the things I prefer for the Service. [Edward Klein was then associate rabbi of the Free Synagogue and became Rabbi Wise's successor.]

Ed, of course, is to have charge of the Service, whether at the Synagogue House or in Carnegie Hall, where I preached for thirty years and with which I became associated during the stronger years of my life—or, best of all, in the new building.

In view of the large part which the [American Jewish] Congress and Zionism have had in my life, I think that, just as in the case of Mummie, I would like Dave [Petegorsky, the brilliant young director of the American Jewish Congress who died in 1956] to speak the word of farewell if he were equal to it. Dave has grown very dear to me. He knows what it is that I most deeply care for: The State of Israel and freedom and justice for Jews everywhere. . . .

I would like a prayer or the reading of a poem by my beloved friend, Holmes.

You won't see this while I am alive. When you do see it, I beg you to understand that my release, whenever it comes, is a great mercy. I am far from well and comfortable. As you know, I hate to leave you both and Shad and Helen and my precious grandchildren, but I feel the time is drawing very near for me to go Home. If God will, it will mean the reunion of my spirit with that of Mummie's, and you know that I want my dust to be placed in the niche wherein she lies.

All love forever to you who have taken such

wonderful care of me and will do so, I know, to my end, whenever it is to be. You will love and care for each other always.

Into the Hand of God I commend my spirit. May He continue to vouchsafe me His grace and mercy.

Henry Monsky

GAMBLER IN FUTURES

HENRY MONSKY was an abstemious man. His strongest drink was hot chocolate. To the dismay of his loving wife, he seldom noticed what food was placed before him. But Henry Monsky was also a gambler in futures—in Jewish futures. He staked his energy and his strength—indeed his life—to make the Jewish future better than the present. He pledged himself and all his resources to the conviction that American Jewry could unite all its factions and fractions and help shape its own future together.

Anyone who knows Jewish life knows that, when you bring three Jews together, you will probably get four committees. Monsky knew that too. But he also knew, and believed with all the conviction of a vibrant Jewish soul, that behind the clamoring differences and disputes there was one people, under one God, bound together by an irrevocable history, joined by the bonds of shared ideals, sharing a common fate and destiny. To Monsky, this spelled the need for Jewish unity and to this ideal he consecrated his tremendous talents and his tireless energies.

But Henry Monsky was a man of many parts. When he

died, Walter Winchell caught some of these parts in his
column:*

> New York Novelette: An item of Americana
> muffed completely by the Big Burg's obit writers
> was this story. . . . Remember the little Jewish
> tailor in MGM's film "Boys Town"? His role
> tugged at the heart with his earnest efforts to
> help Father Flanagan found the famed colony
> for homeless boys. . . . He was never really an
> immigrant tailor as shown on the screen. He was
> a prominent American lawyer, without whose
> aid (the good Padre always said) they might not
> have succeeded. . . . He not only helped conceive
> and raise funds for Boys Town, but he also served
> on its Board of Trustees and handled all legal
> details. . . . He refused to have himself glorified
> in the movie. . . . So the scripters changed the
> lawyer to a tailor. . . . This man (always in the
> background) became a confidant of presidents
> and statesmen—a two-fisted fighter for human
> rights. . . . Catholics made him a member of their
> National Catholic Welfare Conference, Protes-
> tants turned to him for guidance, Jews honored
> him with the presidency of their oldest and
> largest organization, B'nai B'rith. . . . He died
> Friday at 57 . . . Henry Monsky, Human Being.

Monsky grew up in Omaha, Nebraska, and was a friend and
adviser to Father Flanagan from the inception of Boys
Town. Separated by religious creed, the two men were
nonetheless remarkably alike in many ways. In each, the
flame of social justice burned strongly. Each had a deep
sympathy for underprivileged and rebellious youngsters
whom society dubbed "bad kids" or "juvenile delinquents."

---

* *Henry Monsky: The Man and His Work*, Mrs. Henry Monsky and
Maurice Bisgyer, Crown Publishers, New York, 1947.

Boys Town was testimony to what love and understanding can do for a troubled boy. To this cause, Monsky, like the famous priest, brought a faith in kids which sometimes bordered on the quixotic.

Father Flanagan once concerned himself with a boy in Iowa who had been charged with murder. The facts indicated that the youngster had been driven to violence by a sadistically cruel relative. Because of the seriousness of the crime, bail was set at $25,000. Father Flanagan was determined to get the lad out on bond and take him to Boys Town for the months before the beginning of the trial. The banks, fearful of lending money for a person held on a murder charge, had reluctantly refused the priest. Monsky was in New York where he received the following letter from Father Flanagan:

Henry dear:
The bank would not lend me the money for ———'s bond. I consulted Billy (Henry Monsky's partner) who says I may not legally advance it from funds of the Home. But, Henry, this home is for saving boys, and we cannot let that boy stay in jail over there. He is a good boy, so I borrowed the money from a cooperative Board member, who is understanding and paid the bond. The Home should reimburse the Board member, so I hope you will present the matter properly at the next meeting of the Board, and explain what has been done.

As was so frequently the case, Monsky matched the Father's blind faith. He presented the case "properly," and then persuaded the Board. The boy became a model member of Boys Town who discovered, for the first time, that somebody trusted and wanted him. But what if he had jumped bail? Wouldn't he have made Father Flanagan and Monsky look not only impractical but irresponsible? Perhaps. But they would jump off that bridge when they got to it. And rarely was their faith abused.

Henry Monsky came to leadership in the Jewish community through the B'nai B'rith, the largest Jewish civic organization in America. The son of East European immigrants, Henry, in his youth, was devoutly Orthodox in his observances. Even at conventions of the B'nai B'rith, Monsky would have felt guilty if he had forgotten his *t'filin*, phylacteries which an Orthodox Jew puts on daily. Once his mother mailed them to him at a convention in Lake Harbor, Michigan. From his parents, young Monsky also learned the ethical traditions of the Jewish heritage and gained a warm and positive identification with all aspects of Jewish life.

In Omaha, Monsky contributed his talents to the general and Jewish community. Leader of numerous Community Chest campaigns, president of the Jewish Welfare Federation of Omaha, president of the Mid-Western District of B'nai B'rith, and member of the Executive Committee of the national Order, Monsky early displayed the great attributes of personality and leadership which were to propel him into the national scene.

In 1938, at the age of 47, Henry Monsky became the president of the largest Jewish organization in America. At a time of supreme gravity for the Jewish people, B'nai B'rith plucked from the Midwest heartland a leader unlike most of his predecessors. A man without wealth or social station, Orthodox, the son of Russian immigrants, a staunch Zionist, Monsky was elected unanimously to the high office. When he was installed, he received the following telegram in Yiddish from his mother, then ninety years old:

"Mazel tov glick und gesundt und langi yoren stop azloche fun Gott as ich hob derlebt zu zen dem kovod fun mine zun stop love to you and Daisy. Mother" ("Congratulations, luck and health and long life. Thank God that I have lived to see this honor bestowed on my son"). Deeply moved by the telegram, Monsky read it in Yiddish to the delegates, some of whom had probably never heard the language before.

Monsky led B'nai B'rith decisively onto an emergency footing. Lodges and chapters stepped forward with contributions to European war relief. When disaster struck the United States at Pearl Harbor, B'nai B'rith placed all its resources and manpower behind the war effort. A complex war service program was initiated, with thousands of volunteers furnishing day rooms and canteens; providing recreation for the armed forces; visiting the sick; giving blood; and helping out in every possible way which the imaginative president and his staff could conceive.

Throughout the war years, Monsky was obsessed by the fate of Jews abroad. He had no patience with any "business as usual" attitude by Jewish organizations seeking to go it alone. Jewish unity, to him, was an ideal constantly to be pursued; but, in a time of such crisis, it was an absolute imperative. In December, 1942, Monsky asked the heads of all major Jewish organizations to join with him in a single delegation to the White House. The delegation urged President Roosevelt to warn the Nazis as forcefully as possible "that they will be held to strict accountability for their crimes." In addition, they urged that "an American Commission be appointed at once to receive and examine all evidence of Nazi barbarities against civilian populations, and to submit that evidence to the bar of public opinion and to the conscience of the world."

This was the beginning of the inquiry into German war crimes which would culminate later in the Nuremberg war trials. But the pronouncement did not slow the savage massacre of European Jewry by Hitler. Monsky was a driven

man. He could not rest. He organized protest meetings,
joined in working out emergency rescue and aid programs
for European Jews, labored with the Adopt-a-family plan
of B'nai B'rith. Membership swelled under his vigorous
leadership from 60,000 to 300,000 men and women. But
Monsky's goals transcended the successes of B'nai B'rith or
any organization; the desperation of the Jewish communities
abroad had fired him with the necessity of a united American Jewry, and he could not be content until that vision
could be made real in his time.

On January 6, 1943, at the height of the war, Monsky
issued the following invitation to the leaders of all Jewish
organizations to meet with him in Pittsburgh on January 23,
1943:

"American Jewry, which will be required in large measure
to assume the responsibility of representing the interests of
our people at the Victory Peace Conference, must be ready
to voice the judgment of American Jews along with that of
other Jewish communities of the free countries with respect
to the post-war status of Jews and the upbuilding of a
Jewish Palestine. . . . The purpose of the Conference is to
bring together the representatives of major national Jewish
membership organizations, in order that they may consider
what steps should be taken to bring about some agreement
on the part of the American Jewish community."

Thirty-two national organizations were represented. Two
—the American Jewish Committee and the Jewish Labor
Committee—did not participate. The thirty-two cooperating groups represented a variety of ideologies, covering
virtually the entire spectrum of Jewish life. Zionist and non-
Zionist, Reform and Orthodox, working man and businessman—all came, but it took a Henry Monsky to keep them
away from each other's throats and concentrating on the
"crucial need for the restoration of that lost position (of the

Jew in Europe) and for its fortification upon enduring foundations of equality and justice," and for securing a Jewish Palestine.

Monsky worked ceaselessly on the back-breaking preparations for the convening in New York City of the American Jewish Assembly. With patient diplomacy, he negotiated with the American Jewish Committee, finally persuading it to join the united body on the understanding that the over-all body would be called the American Jewish Conference instead of Assembly ("Assembly implies a separate political enclave," the American Jewish Committee charged), and that any participating organization had the right of dissent from decisions of the Conference. The Jewish Labor Committee came in with the American Jewish Committee.

In an atmosphere heavy with history and the gravity of world events, the American Jewish Conference was called to order by Monsky at the Waldorf-Astoria Hotel, New York City, on August 29, 1943. Present were 500 delegates representing 64 national organizations and 375 communities. Monsky opened the meeting, precisely as Nathan Straus had opened the American Jewish Congress in 1918, by reciting the Hebrew, saying, *Hineh mah tov u-mah na-im shevet ahim gam yahad!* "Behold, how good and how pleasant it is for brethren to dwell together in unity." Monsky continued, "One of the essential virtues of the conference is that it comprises leadership democratically chosen from the ranks of American Israel. It is the antithesis of the prevalent practice of representation by 'shtadlanim.' The spirit of democracy and the development and appreciation of democratic processes have changed the whole concept of Jewish leadership. Leaders must be responsible to the yearnings, the aspirations, and the hopes of those for whom they presume to speak."

But unity was not an easy thing to draw out of the conference. There were sharp voting blocs. There were volatile and ambitious leaders. There was an electricity of tension in the air which made progress even harder. There were unavoidable conflicts of philosophy, attitude, and personality. All of these factors made themselves felt as the delegates strove to harmonize their differences and to hammer out basic agreements. It was quickly evident that, while there would be no insoluble disagreement on what should be done to protect the post-war status of the Jewish survivors of Nazism, the Palestine resolution touched a painful nerve of division and discord: "We call for the fulfilment of the Balfour Declaration, and of the Mandate for Palestine whose intent and underlying purpose, based on the 'historical connection of the Jewish people with Palestine,' was to reconstitute Palestine as the Jewish Commonwealth. . . ."

The storm broke. The National Council of Jewish Women and the Union of American Hebrew Congregations made statements indicating reservations on this resolution. Despite the most painstaking precautions and the masterful direction of the sessions by Monsky, the American Jewish Committee and the Jewish Labor Committee withdrew from the conference. The rupture broke the solid unity which Monsky felt was indispensable to meeting the momentous world crisis of the times. But the American Jewish Conference persevered, despite noisy internecine controversies about the role and scope of the conference, and Monsky continued to tax his immense skills of leadership.

In 1945 Henry Monsky was elected by the conference as its official consultant to the United Nations. He went to San Francisco full of hope that the nations of the world would, at last, give concrete reality to the ancient peace vision of the Jewish prophets. But he was quickly jolted back to reality. He listened to the statesmen of the world, representing no less than fifty-one nations. He heard their eloquent words. Vainly he searched through the generalizations and the tinseled platitudes, seeking some recognition of the fate of the Jews during the war. Stettinius, Eden, Smuts—the great leaders—had not a word to say of this. It remained for the Minister of Haiti to remind the world of the destruction of six million Jews.

Monsky, together with the growing corps of Jewish leaders pouring into San Francisco, sought to amplify the small voice into an urgent demand that the first victim of Hitlerism not be overlooked in the fashioning of a peaceful world. Said Monsky, "The right to self-determination cannot, by definition, be exercised vicariously; liberty is not enjoyed by proxy. In the peaceful and orderly reconstruction of the world, all peoples must have a voice in the determination of their future. We ask that this right be granted to the Jewish people."

San Francisco was alive with excitement. Henry Monsky was never far from the eye of the hurricane. Almost daily he met with the American delegation to the U.N., or their advisers. Each day, Monsky reported, as consultant of the American Jewish Conference, to the many representatives of Jewish organizations. Common approaches and strategies were evolved. In May, 1945, a joint memorandum was submitted to the UNCIO (United Nations Conference of International Organizations) by the Jewish groups, urging a commission on human rights and pledges by member organizations to observe basic human rights. Indeed, partly as a result of the insistent appeals for protective clauses, the drafters amended the language of the United Nations Charter so that the U.N. clearly committed itself to "promote universal respect for and observance of human rights and fundamental freedoms for all without distinction as to race, language, religion or sex."

What did the conference achieve? Dr. Israel Goldstein, one of Monsky's staunch fellow workers in the conference, described its accomplishments in the following words, "If at San Francisco the trusteeship chapter was so phrased as to protect the existing rights of the Jewish people with regard to Palestine; if before our government and before American and world opinion, and recently before the Palestine Inquiry Committee, there was a voice which could speak for the overwhelming majority of American Jewry in protest against the British White Paper and in espousal of the aim of the establishment of Palestine as a Jewish Commonwealth; if conditions in the German camps have been improved in no inconsiderable measure as a result of our persistence with the War Department in Washington, with UNRRA, and with other bodies; if the entry of Jews from Poland into the American zone has not been stopped as had been often threatened; if the Jews in the camps have been able to meet a representative team of American Jews who did not make them feel as others did—that they came to make things easier for Bevin—but who made them feel that they and we are one people with one destiny; if 20,000 Jews in Shanghai have been saved from deportation as enemy aliens; if a coordinated representation, consisting of the American Jewish Conference, the World Jewish Congress, and the Board of Deputies of British Jews, has been formed to present a united front on behalf of the great majority of the Jews of the world; it is due to the fact that the American Jewish Conference has existed and has functioned."

Dr. Goldstein could have added that it was, in large part, due to the sagacious leadership of Henry Monsky, whose statesmanship bridged the divergencies and rivalries of Jewish life and fashioned a cooperative unity, that the conference was able to function at all. The conference was a fragile body. Internal pressures made the very atmosphere combustible. At least three Jewish organizations, not in the conference, had their own headquarters in San Francisco. There were, within the conference, organizations which were determined to broaden its scope and to make it a permanent organization. Others, including Monsky himself, were equally determined that the conference must not go beyond the specific areas in which it was authorized by its Charter to function, and that it had no right to become a permanent organization.

Indeed, on May 2, 1947, the day of his death, Monsky was presiding over a meeting of the Conference's Interim Committee, to which the Committee on Future Organization, under the chairmanship of Rabbi Maurice N. Eisendrath, president of the Union of American Hebrew Congregations, reported. The majority report was adopted, but not without sharp wrangling and dissent, which evoked from Monsky a fervent statement on the urgent need to accept the majority report and to reconstitute the American Jewish Conference without infringing the autonomy of any organization then within or outside the conference. It was Monsky's last speech. A few minutes later, he was stricken with a heart attack and died.

No one can say for certain, but it is not without significance, that the American Jewish Conference also died shortly thereafter. Henry Monsky's premature death, at the age of 57, was a grievous loss to the Jewish community and to the structure of unity which he had built as the work of his hands.

It is similarly impossible to estimate the full effect of Monsky's death upon another agency of Jewish unity which he helped build: the National Community Relations Advisory Council. At the time of Monsky's accession to the presidency of B'nai B'rith, a bitter debate was raging in the

American Jewish community about duplication and over-
lapping in the field of "defense" or "civic-protective" work.
It was common knowledge, and scandalous, that the American Jewish Committee, the American Jewish Congress, and
the Anti-Defamation League of B'nai B'rith, along with
some less powerful organizations, were competing fever-
ishly for funds and credit, were duplicating one another's
activities, and were creating confusion and dismay in Jewish communities throughout America. In revulsion against
this spectacle, the Jewish community was aroused and the
mounting demand was to knock heads together and create
a single or "unitary" agency for Jewish community relations and defense work.

Monsky and others fought against such a centralized control as being undemocratic; instead, they suggested a
cooperative machinery for common planning, for joint
policy-making, and for joint action by all the defense
agencies and local community councils. It was to be a "fish
bowl so that all can see what is going on." The fish bowl
was created. It was the National Community Relations
Advisory Council (NCRAC). Charter national organizations were the American Jewish Committee, the Anti-
Defamation League, the American Jewish Congress, and
the Jewish Labor Committee. Later, the Jewish War Veterans and the Union of American Hebrew Congregations
joined. In recent years, the United Synagogue (Conservative) and the Union of Orthodox Jewish Congregations also
became members. The roster of local Jewish community
councils has risen from fourteen in 1944 to more than fifty
in 1960.

The NCRAC was conceived as a "fish bowl." It served
that function. For the first time, the national defense
agencies shared their programs and plans with other
agencies and with the Jewish community at large. For the

first time, efforts were made to hammer out united policies on such matters as civil rights, religion and public education, American immigration policy, combating post-war anti-Semitism. But, if it was a fish bowl, it was also a cockpit in which long-standing organizational and personality conflicts simmered and occasionally exploded. While it was usually possible to work out agreement on broad policy, the scramble for supremacy for credit and for funds continued unabated. The Jewish welfare funds, which raised the considerable funds utilized by Jewish defense agencies, began to express dissatisfaction anew that the NCRAC had not been given sufficient power to solve the stubborn problems which continued to afflict the field.

What would have happened if Monsky, the apostle of unity, had lived? Would his own organization, the B'nai B'rith, have resorted to attacks upon the integrity of Professor Robert M. MacIver because that gentleman, in an evaluative report on the NCRAC, recommended thoroughgoing changes in the field and even in the functioning of the Anti-Defamation League? Would Monsky have risen, as his successor did, to denounce the MacIver Report as a "fraud and a tyranny"? Is it conceivable that Monsky, after the overwhelming majority of the delegates endorsed the MacIver Report, would have withdrawn B'nai B'rith from the cooperative process of the NCRAC, as did his successor? Is it possible to imagine that Henry Monsky, whose life was devoted to the building of a Jewish unity, could have joined hands with the American Jewish Committee to turn his back in isolation upon the bulk of the American Jewish community? Many who knew Monsky intimately are convinced that the shape of the Jewish community today would be altogether different had Monsky and his immense influence endured a few years more.

Henry Monsky marked the emergence of a new kind of

leader in American Jewry. Zionist, Orthodox, a son of East
European immigrants, Monsky was representative of those
Jews whom the then-accustomed rulers of the Jewish community viewed with ill-concealed distaste. Indeed, Henry
Monsky and Daisy Hirsch, who first met in 1912 and who
were devoted to each other from the start, acted out a
modern Romeo-Juliet tragedy of Jewish significance. Her
parents were austere Reform German Jews; they "shared a
popular dislike and distrust of East European Jews."
Henry's parents looked upon Reform Jews as traitors to
Judaism, and thus something worse than "goyim." The
young couple knew, as Daisy wrote years later in a tender
recollection, that "any suggestion of our marriage would
have created unhappiness for all of our parents, and stirred
up a hornets' nest of opposition. So we wrote finis—or
thought we did—to a devotion that was based on so many
shared ideals that it seems incredible we did not know how
to rise above a barrier that we both realized was stupid and
unwarranted." The mistake of their youth was rectified
twenty-five years later. Daisy, who had been married to
Albert Rothschild, was widowed. Henry, who had been
unhappily married, was divorced. Henry had had three
children by his first wife; Daisy had one child by her first
marriage. On November 3, 1937, in the fulness of maturity,
they were married.

It was a richly fulfilling and happy marriage, despite the
frenetic pace of Henry's organizational life.* Indeed, the
marriage was launched in the hectic atmosphere which was
to mark their relationship until Monsky was stricken ten
years later. Henry showed up late for his wedding. Immediately after the ceremony, the bride, the groom, and one of

---

* Mrs. Monsky became an important Jewish leader in her own right,
rising to the presidency of the National Federation of Temple Sisterhoods
in 1957.

Monsky's importunate clients boarded a train for Chicago. The three of them enjoyed a wedding dinner in the drawing room, and the next morning at 7:30 A.M., two of them— Monsky and his client—left for Springfield, Illinois, for two days. It was not an auspicious, only a characteristic, beginning to a marriage which was nonetheless blessed with sweetness and rare companionship to the very end.

Monsky was a new kind of Jewish leader in a deeper sense. He felt an obligation beyond his own particular organization. He regarded himself not merely as a servant of B'nai B'rith, but as a servant of his people. Democracy, to Monsky, was no mere shibboleth, to which to pay homage in Fourth of July addresses. Democracy was a supreme value to be cherished and defended in American life and, equally, in Jewish life. He burned himself out upon the altar of Jewish survival and unity. When a heart specialist reported sadly that Monsky had suffered a rupture of the heart, his wise wife said, movingly and simply, "His heart broke for his people."

Henry Cohen

THE HEART OF TEXAS

WHAT IS a rabbi? What makes a great rabbi or a great minister? Some, like Stephen Wise, were great because of the grand qualities—the flaming social passion, the thundering eloquence, the majestic vision, which burned their mark upon an entire nation. But there are other clergymen whose greatness lies, not in the grandiloquent sweep of drama, but in the small deeds done lovingly and well; not in the blare and color of vista-vision but in the simple black-and-white close-up of ordinary community life.

Henry Cohen, the rabbi of Galveston, was such a man. His influence did not spread far across the land, but it sank deep, deep into the rugged soil and zesty spirit of a Texas town. For more than fifty years, Henry Cohen was the rabbi of Galveston—with a love as broad and as non-discriminating as Galveston Bay, stretching out to the gulf.

Everybody knew Rabbi Cohen. He was a permanent part of the city landscape—as bustling as the Strand, paralleling the raucus wharf-front, and as indestructible as St. Mary's Cathedral. On almost any day of the week, the little, bespectacled man could be seen hurrying through the streets of the city on his daily rounds of social service. As you watched, he paused for a moment, peered down at his white shirt cuff, scratched another name off the list scrawled on the cuff, and darted off to the hospital, the prison, or somebody's home for another good will visit. His spirit warmed the community and, while he was the rabbi of Congregation B'nai Israel he was, in truth, a spiritual leader of the entire city.

There was hardly a Galvestonian—Jew, Protestant, Catholic, or heathen—who didn't turn to Rabbi Henry Cohen, at one time or another, for help or comfort or advice. He was at once an employment agency, marriage counselor, parole board, male nurse, immigration service, social reformer, and lobbyist for the public weal. He was Henry Cohen, the rabbi of Galveston, and that was all he was or ever wanted to be. Never did he regard Galveston as a stepping-stone to national prominence and fame. Galveston was his community, his life's work. Henry Cohen, "the man who stayed in Texas," was a great rabbi.

He was born in London, England, in 1863. Son of poor parents, he was boarded out at the age of nine to Jews' Hospital. He decided in early boyhood that he wanted to be a rabbi. Working by day and studying at Jews' College by night, the intense young man quickly revealed a quick wit and plucky determination. He interrupted his rabbinic studies at an early age, and with his brother Marc, spent a year in Africa, where he mastered several African languages, was caught up in a Zulu war, soaked up the smells and sounds of a strange and mysterious continent which was to intrigue him throughout his lifetime, got his head bashed and retained a scar as a permanent souvenir of his youthful adventures. Returning to England, he settled down to the grind of earning his *semicha* (rabbinical ordination). In the year 1884, Henry Cohen became a rabbi.

The young rabbi's first pulpit was in Kingston, Jamaica. It was a memorable interlude, a kind of spiritual civil war more akin to the Zulu battles he experienced in Africa than to anything he learned about synagogues at Jews' College. The S'fardic Jews, who had lived in Jamaica since the fifteenth century when they fled from Spain and Portugal, were the aristocrats of the island; the Ashk'nazim, who emanated from Central Europe and had different religious customs and traditions, were regarded as Johnnies-come-lately. The rabbi had been informed that the two groups were now united into one peaceful congregation. But he quickly learned, to his dismay, that this was a vain illusion. Factional bickering was the favorite sport of the congregation. A small intramural "pogrom" almost erupted when, in the midst of the Sabbath service, a S'fardic member interrupted the rabbi's reading of the Torah and loudly accused him of pronouncing Hebrew Ashk'nazi fashion. Rabbi Cohen stayed in the West Indies for an unquiet year.

Sick of the factional warfare he had suffered through in Kingston, Henry arrived in New York to book passage for home. He was depressed about the sterile controversies over ritual he had just left, and he was also reluctant to go back to England where he would have to submit to the authority of the Chief Rabbi in such matters. While he waited, he chanced to meet a Reverend Henry Jacobs of New York who told him of a position that might be available in Woodville, Mississippi. Rabbi Cohen braced himself and took off for the cotton belt of the New World.

New World indeed! Instead of the liquid Spanish accents he had grown used to in the Island, his ear now had to become attuned to the soft and lazy Mississippi drawl. Having turned his back on the cacophonous quarreling among divergent Orthodox factions, Rabbi Cohen now found himself ministering to an ultra-Reform congregation, most of whom even kept their places of business open on Saturday. Shocked, Rabbi Cohen handed down a virtual ultimatum: respect the Sabbath or find yourself a new rabbi. Impressed by his sincerity, the congregants stifled their first impulse to dispatch the brash youngster who, in addition to his excessive zeal, had a clipped British accent which was aggravated by a slight but unhelpful stammer. They compromised, kept their stores closed on Saturday morning, and went to the temple for Sabbath services. And their respect for their religious leader grew into genuine affection, fully requited.

Among the many speaking engagements which began to pour in upon Rabbi Cohen was one from the synagogue in Galveston, Texas. Galveston, in 1888, was the boom town of Texas—lusty, flourishing, cosmopolitan. Henry fell in love with the city, and it was a love affair which was to last the rest of his life. When the Galveston congregation offered him its pulpit, he left Woodville with sadness. But his closest friends in Woodville insisted that he could not refuse the invitation to lead one of the largest and most distinguished synagogues in the South.

How did it happen that a small, young Jewish clergyman, with an alien-sounding British accent and a stammer, could become a legendary figure in so unlikely a place as Galveston, Texas? Nobody knows what a strange spiritual chemistry joined the man and the wondrous island city which stuck like a tropical sliver into the southern flank of Texas. Nor did it happen overnight. Indeed, during the young rabbi's trial sermon (on "Africa," no less), two pretty young ladies giggled impertinently every time the preacher stuttered. Other members of the congregation objected to a stuttering rabbi, while still others didn't relish the idea of an Englishman rabbi, with or without stuttering.

However, Rabbi Cohen took to Galveston like a Texan

to oil. He went down to the shore, and, like Demosthenes, filled his mouth with pebbles, and practiced speaking until the stammer was gradually overcome. He strengthened his congregation and developed an efficient congregational routine. Then, realizing that the state of Texas had 12,000 Jews dispersed throughout its 260,000 square miles, most of them without services of a rabbi, he took up the burden of serving Jewish communities throughout the state. Each week he would go out to a few different towns, "from Nacogdoches on the east to Brownsville on the border, teaching, marrying, burying, preaching the words of the fiery Old Testament prophets."[*]

But it was in Galveston, itself, that Henry Cohen fulfilled himself. First off, he courted and married brown-eyed Millie Levy, one of the two impertinent and giggling young ladies, and they set up their home (quaintly referred to as the "rabbinage") at 1920 Broadway, on the corner of Twenty-fourth and Avenue I. During the next half-century and more, many of the people of Galveston—and incidentally, a good share of the waters of Galveston Bay which ran wild in the storm of 1900—were destined to pass through that house.

At least one of the qualities of Rabbi Cohen which appealed to bluff, outspoken Galvestonians was his open-handed honesty. He refused to kow-tow or to tailor his principles for anybody. Not long after his arrival in Galveston, he was struck by the fact that the *Galveston News*, in reporting a fire in a store, identified the merchant as a "Hebrew." The rabbi fumed but waited until, one day, there was a similar item about a fire in another store, except that in this story the religion of the owner was not referred

---

[*] *The Man Who Stayed in Texas*, Anne Nathan and Harry I. Cohen, Whittlesey House, London, McGraw-Hill Book Co. Inc., New York, 1941.

to. Storming downtown, Rabbi Cohen slammed the paper on the desk of the editor and demanded to know why the story didn't indicate the religion of this Christian merchant, just as it had indicated the religion of the "Hebrew" merchant a few weeks earlier. Red-faced, the editor apologized to the rabbi and solemnly promised that it would never happen again. It never did.

When it came to defense work—defending the rights and reputation of the Jewish people—the little rabbi from Galveston was a one-man anti-defamation agency. He didn't carry a gun but he was remarkably quick on the verbal draw and he could cut down a big-mouthed bigot before you could say, "Remember the Alamo."

Rabbi Cohen worked and fought side by side with his best friend, the Catholic priest, Father Kirwin. Together, they maintained the tolerant and civilized atmosphere which characterized Galveston. In the early years of the twentieth century, the Ku Klux Klan made a dramatic comeback, stirring discord and hatred throughout the state. But it couldn't get off the ground in Galveston. When the local sheriff hedged on a Klan issue, the people threw him out of office. A scheduled Klan parade down Market Street was hastily canceled when Father Kirwin announced that he was all set to shower the paraders with a dose of lachrymal gas from St. Mary's Infirmary.

Reader's Digest sent a writer, Webb Waldron, into Galveston to find out why "at a time when the world is full of racial hatred, Galveston, Texas spreads a shining light of good will and tolerance." Waldron wrote:

> . . . In the recent mayoralty election, the two chief candidates were a Catholic and a Jew. The Catholic came to his padre seeking his support. "No, my son," said the padre, "I'm going to vote for Adrian Levy. Levy has been a good mayor

and I think we ought to keep him on the job."
The priest told me that hundreds of parishioners
voted as he did. Levy was elected, though the
Jews form less than 2 per cent of the population
of Galveston. The priest said to me, "Why is it
we judge a man in this town not for his race or his
creed, but for *what he is himself?* The answer
is—Rabbi Cohen."

The rabbi's religion was rooted in social justice and social
service, and in its application it was universal. Everybody
had a claim upon his energies and upon his help. Once, while
Rabbi Cohen was heavily engaged in the burdens of the
Galveston movement (described below) he heard that a
man was being detained at the immigration detention center, slated for deportation to Russia for illegal entry. The
man, who had been a boiler maker in Russia, had escaped
as a stowaway. If returned, he would probably be executed
by the Czar. Local immigration officers had wired Washington but had been informed that they must put the
Russian on the next ship, regardless of the personal consequences. Rabbi Cohen packed a bag, rushed to the station,
borrowed $100 from a congregant, and sped to Washington.
Every official he talked to expressed regret but insisted there
was nothing that could be done. So the rabbi wangled an
appointment with President Taft.

The President was sympathetic and affable but regretted
that his hands were tied, since this was clearly a case of
illegal entry and the Department had already decided upon
deportation. As the rabbi wearily rose to leave, the President
expressed his admiration for "the way you Jews help each
other out—traveling all the way up here from Galveston,
Texas, when a member of your faith is in trouble."

"Member of my faith!" exclaimed Rabbi Cohen. "He's
not a Jew, he's a Greek Catholic."

The President gulped in surprise. "You mean to say, you traveled all the way up here at your own expense to help out a Greek Catholic?"

"He's in trouble; they're going to deport him on the next ship, and he'll face a firing squad when he gets back to Russia. He's a human being, Mr. President; a human life is at stake. That's the way I see it."

"Wait a minute," said the President. He rang for a secretary, who hurried in. "Take a telegram. It goes to the Chief Inspector of Immigration at Galveston. Say, 'Hold Lemchuk in Galveston and release in the custody of Rabbi Cohen on his return.' Say they'll hear direct from the Department," said the President of the United States.

Immigration was the momentous adventure of America in the first quarter of the twentieth century. The Golden Door was thrown open, and the Statue of Liberty beckoned to the poor, the unwanted, and bedraggled of the Old World. Jews, fleeing from Russian pogroms, were among the grateful beneficiaries of American humanity. Between 1870 and 1910, some 2,000,000 Jews, mostly from Eastern Europe, poured into America. So vast a transplantation of Jewish communities could not be achieved without some dislocation and misery. The Jewish community of the United States, striving mightily to receive and integrate the hundreds of thousands of immigrant Jews, found itself virtually overwhelmed by the immensity of the task. One of the most serious complications was that the immigrants, pouring into Castle Garden and later Ellis Island, confused and bewildered by a strange tongue and culture, tended to huddle sheep-like for mutual security on New York's East Side. Jewish leaders tried to evolve ways to divert the tide away from the squalid ghettos of New York City and into the broad heartland of America. The Galveston movement was the most ambitious of such projects.

In the autumn of 1906, a young social worker named Morris Waldman knocked on the door at 1920 Broadway, Galveston. He came to outline a plan developed by Jacob Schiff, prominent Jewish philanthropist of New York City. Briefly, the plan was to divert immigration of Jews to ports of entry from which the immigrants would have ready access to the less-populated and open sections of the Midwest, South, and Far West where they could more easily come to terms with a new, free society. Waldman proposed that Galveston be used as a major port of entry. The city had ship connections with European ports, was a terminus for important railroads spanning the Far West. Moreover, it was likely that the immigrants would pass on to other sections of the nation, instead of sinking into the first refuge of America, as they were doing in New York City. Waldman looked over the city and the rabbi and rushed a telegram back to Schiff: this was it.

The Galveston movement was the personal pinnacle of Rabbi Cohen's career. What a blessed opportunity for a man who gloried in human service and whose mission in life was to ease the burden of people in trouble! On a blistering summer day in June, 1907, months of meticulous planning reached a climax. The rabbi raced his bicycle down to the wharf and waited, impatiently, for the docking of the "Cassel," arriving from Hamburg. He studied, for perhaps the fiftieth time, a dog-eared sheet of paper, bearing the names of the sixty passengers who would shortly become the first group of Jewish immigrants to debark at the port of Galveston. The immigrants would be received, lodged in headquarters of the Jewish Immigrants Information Bureau, fed, taught English, and ultimately sent off to another city in the Midwest where jobs in their trades would be waiting for them and where teachers and religious leaders were alerted to guide them in the process of adjustment.

It was a dream come true for Rabbi Cohen. And, if for the rabbi, then for Galveston, too. They straggled off the ship, the refugees, clumsy and sweating in their foul-smelling smocks and heavy boots, huddling together in their despair and fear, behind them the hell of Kishinef and ahead of them—what? The rabbi was all over the place, dropping a Yiddish word of encouragement here, carrying a bawling infant there, patting their backs in encouragement, allaying their anxiety. He had arranged this ceremony up to the hilt. Mayor Landes, speaking in his broad southern drawl, welcomed the immigrants to Galveston and shook hands with every one of them. Rabbi Cohen translated into Yiddish. Most of the immigrants held back, still frozen with fear. But one Russian suddenly walked forward, and, with great difficulty and deep emotion, told the mayor that where they had come from this kind of scene could never take place. He pulled up his sleeve and showed an arm red and angry with scars. "The knout," he said, "was our greeting. You have clasped our hands. A time may come when your country will need us; we will not hesitate to serve you with our blood."

And so they came—twenty-six on July 14; seventy on August 6; eighty-nine on August 24; eighty on September 14; and on through the years—to Galveston. It was a pittance compared to the waves which continued to deposit their human cargoes on New York City. Considered as a solution to the problem of the East Side ghettos, the Galveston movement was a failure, and an expensive one at that. But Henry Cohen had not the stomach for statistics and no interest in people as a mass. He cared about the person, the individual who needed help. He worked like a horse, with no thought of compensation or recognition. His reputation became legendary in gloom-ridden cities of the Russian steppes, where despairing Jews whispered the name Rabbi

Cohen to each other as a modern-day Moses who would lead them out of the wilderness.

By the time the Jewish Immigrants' Information Bureau closed down at the start of World War 1, more than 10,000 Jews had been welcomed in Galveston. A small but efficient staff of social workers had carried on the technical tasks of caring for the refugees. But everybody knew that while the financial sinews were provided by Jacob Schiff, the inspiration and spirit of the Galveston movement issued from the heart of Rabbi Henry Cohen.

The motif of his life was the Jewish injunction to seek justice. When he first came to Texas, the age of consent for a woman was ten years. The rabbi was infuriated when he heard that a man who had raped a twelve-year-old girl was set free. Enjoining his wife, Molly, not to lay hands on the shirt he was wearing (for fear of "washing out" his next day's appointments), he went up to the state capital in Austin and demanded that the State Legislature correct that evil law. Year after year, he badgered the legislators. Finally, perhaps in self-defense, they amended the law; by 1918 the age of consent was a more respectable eighteen.

Rehabilitation of prisoners was another of Rabbi Cohen's intense concerns. The sheriff of Galveston used to say, "There's nobody whose judgment I'd trust the way I do the rabbi's. If he says there's good in a man, I'll take his word for it. He's never guessed wrong." Local judges developed the habit of paroling men to Rabbi Cohen, knowing that he would straighten them out, give them a few dollars to keep them going and find them jobs.

The rabbi believed that society had a responsibility to rehabilitate prisoners and not merely to lock them up in vengeance. And, if circumstances required it, he was not above knocking some heads together to see that such an enlightened approach was followed. Once a boy was flogged in a state institution. Upon investigation, the rabbi concluded that the boy would undoubtedly be ruined if he were kept under the medieval conditions then existing. He went to the judge, who had the power to parole, and asked that the boy be released in his custody. The judge flatly refused. Whereupon, the rabbi went to the door, locked it, put the key in his pocket, and announced that he wouldn't unlock the door until the judge released the boy. "You are a fine one to refuse to give him a chance," the rabbi exclaimed. "We picked you out of the gutter dozens of times, a confirmed drunkard. Yet, you reformed. Here you are, in a position of responsibility in the state. How can you—of all people—refuse this boy a chance to become a decent, self-respecting citizen?" The young man was paroled in custody of Rabbi Cohen.

Along with other public-spirited citizens of Texas, Cohen worked furiously to ignite the public conscience to the dire need for prison reform. The rabbi was a moving force in the Texas Committee on Prisons and Prison Labor. A searching report, published in 1924, focused attention on the basic evils in the Texas prison system. When legislation was finally adopted in 1925, Governor Moody appointed Rabbi Cohen as one of the eight non-salaried members of the new prison board. But the rabbi was still not content and he fought hard and successfully for stronger legislation. Finally, he felt constrained to resign from the prison board. He was getting tired. He didn't like to acknowledge that he was getting old. Each day was still back-breakingly full, and the cuff still carried a long list of daily appointments. But the rabbi no longer wheeled around on his bicycle. He now sat in the back of a chauffeur-driven automobile and he found he didn't have the strength to "assist" at so many operations as before. In three years he would be 70 years old.

In 1938 Rabbi Cohen celebrated his fiftieth anniversary of service in Texas. The public celebration, lasting all day and half the night, was a rare outpouring of pride and love. Five thousand Texans filled the city auditorium to honor their rabbi. People of all faiths came from every city in Texas to pay their respects to the little man who, they knew, had refused tempting offers from large synagogues and organizations in the East—the man who preferred to stay in Texas. The Episcopal minister spoke, "In my church it is high honor when a minister becomes a bishop, with the title Right Reverend and Father in God. To me, Rabbi Cohen always is Right Reverend and, in all sincerity, my Father in God." Said a young man, son of the former president of the congregation, speaking for three generations of Galvestonians, ". . . Some of us you have clothed, some of us you have fed, but to all of us you have taught the ideals of charity, mercy, and justice—that there is one God who has created us all, and that, regardless of race or creed, we have the same Father. . . ."

Henry Cohen lived to the age of 87, beloved in the ripeness of his years as was the stammering young rabbi fresh off the stage-coach from Woodville. The Biblical mandate reads: "Separate not thyself from thy community." It took death itself to separate Henry Cohen, a small person who became a big man in a big state, from the community he served with all his heart, all his soul, and all his might.

Henrietta Szold

MOTHER OF A PEOPLE

H ENRIETTA SZOLD'S first memories were of Abraham Lincoln and the Civil War; her last memories were of the nightmare of Hitler and World War II. Her life spanned eighty-four years—kaleidoscopic years, saturated with history. It was not, however, the length of her days which stamped Henrietta Szold as the greatest Jewess of the age. She was to the Jewish people what Eleanor Roosevelt has been to America—a plain woman of such love and sensitivity as to rise almost to saintliness. Miss Szold's life was long and incredibly full. But her gift of self to her people necessitated the sacrifice of a profound need of her own: to marry and bear children, "many children." She died a spinster. Yet she is hallowed in memory as mother of Hadassah, the largest Zionist organization in the world; mother of 8,000 children, snatched from Hitlerism and brought to Palestine by Miss Szold's Youth Aliyah; and, in some measure, mother of the vision which gave birth to modern Israel only three years after her death.

Few children have received so rich a heritage as was vouchsafed to Henrietta Szold. Born December 21, 1860, in the city of Baltimore, the first of eight girls (three died in infancy), she was raised in the image of a remarkable father and mother. Her father was Rabbi Benjamin Szold, who had been ordained in Vienna at the age of fourteen and had come to America after fighting in the unsuccessful liberal revolution of 1848. Brilliant, humanitarian, and intensely Jewish, Rabbi Szold had come to Baltimore with his bride in 1859 to assume the pulpit of Congregation Oheb Shalom. Rabbi Szold was a cultured man to whom Judaism was not a creed but a moral way of life. He quickly shocked the slave state of Maryland, during the hysteria of the Civil War, by boldly preaching abolition and the need to preserve the Union. Principle was more precious to him than peace, even in his congregation.

On Henrietta was lavished the kind of tender care and education which, in those days, were usually reserved for the first-born son. Her mother, Sophie, filled the house with flowers, music, books—and love. Her father enriched it with culture and Jewish thought. At the age of eight, Henrietta was happily familiar with both Jewish and general classics. Reverence for learning, faithfulness to the highest standards of conduct, commitment to Jewish religious tradition—these values were part and parcel of the Szold household. They were spiritual values which helped to shape Henrietta Szold and which impelled her throughout her life. Rabbi Szold was a Conservative rabbi, unable to go along with the sweeping changes then being instituted by the early "Reformers"; but he was modern and flexible and accepted the necessity of altering ceremonies and rituals which he regarded as out of harmony with the modern world.

When Henrietta was fourteen, the family moved from Eutaw Street to a new house on Lombard Street in Baltimore. Everything was packed. The van was loaded. Hen-

rietta had shepherded her younger sisters into the carriage.
But where was father? He was nowhere to be found. Mrs.
Szold began to sob. "We followed the vans up to Lombard
Street," Henrietta recalled, "everybody carrying something. We found my father in the garden back of the
house, planting a vine and a fig tree."* Judaism sweetened
every event of daily life in the Szold household, and Henrietta always recalled the house on Lombard Street as a
sanctuary "that makes for sympathy and understanding."

Henrietta was graduated from the Western Female High
School on June 28, 1877. She was the only Jewish girl in
the class of forty-eight. Most Jewish families in Baltimore
did not send their daughters to high school. First in the class,
Henrietta delivered the major speech. Sending a girl to college at that time was all but unthinkable, so Henrietta ended
her formal education and returned to school as a teacher.
She taught German, algebra, French, and an assortment of
other subjects, serving also as a private tutor of individual
children in Hebrew and German.

The mild-looking school teacher, not yet seventeen,
doubled in brass as a columnist for various English-Jewish
publications under the pen name of Sulamith. In words that
still retain the sting of accuracy, she poured forth her scorn
for the commercialism and vulgarity which, she felt, were
corrupting Jewish life: ". . . Jewish life seems to consist
entirely of Jewish betrothals, Jewish entertainments, Jewish balls, and Jewish boasting, interlarded with a dose of
caustic disputation and rabbinical sarcasm and, as the one
good ingredient, Jewish charity." The sprightly columnist
didn't hesitate to cross editorial swords with such weighty
opponents as Isaac Mayer Wise and his *American Israelite*,
which jeered at her as a "dear pot-and-pan scourer."

---

* *Henrietta Szold: Life and Letters*, Marvin Lowenthal, Viking Press,
New York, 1942.

Actually, Miss Szold had little sympathy with the cool, austere, increasingly prosperous German Jews, most of whom had emigrated to America between 1840 and 1880. Her heart went out to the Russian Jews, who began to come to the United States around 1880 and whose numbers mounted into a human torrent in the early part of the twentieth century. It was not merely the sympathy she felt for these victims of Czarist cruelty and pogroms. It was their warm Jewishness, their "Jewish heart," which captured her. "There is something ideal about them," she wrote. "Or has the suffering through which they have passed idealized them in my eyes? At all events, I have no greater wish than to be able to give my whole strength, time, and ability to them."

Jewish refugees from Russia began to make their way to Baltimore after the bloody pogroms of 1881. Alien in dress and tongue, the immigrants evoked a frigid response from most of Baltimore Jewry. In the home of Rabbi Szold, however, the newcomers found warm friendship and unqualified acceptance. The immigrants called the Szold house their "Wailing Wall." Out of this relationship grew Miss Szold's idea of a night school for the Russian immigrants—one of the first adult education programs in America. Henrietta Szold became the principal. Classes were held in a loft. In the first semester alone, 650 men and women were enrolled, learning the rudiments of English as well as many other practical subjects. Years later, Mayor LaGuardia, in giving Miss Szold the key to New York City, referred to her pioneer night school and said, "If it weren't for you, I wouldn't be here."

Miss Szold was already demonstrating the stamina which always dazed her friends and associates. The following, taken from a letter she wrote in 1891, outlines one typical day's activity in the life of Henrietta Szold:

Monday—up at 5:30 A.M.

6:30: Correspondence with teachers of the Russian school and others; telephone calls for substitute teachers (made from the corner drug store as there was no telephone in the Szold house); breakfast;

9:00-3:00: Teaching at the private school kept by the Misses Adams;

After 3:00: Shopping for books, pencils, etc., for two new classes organized because of the unexpectedly large registration; meeting of Botany Club until 6:00; supper at home;

7:00: Russian school;

11:30: Home (no dinner).

Her sympathy for the Russians and her quickening admiration for their fervent Jewish spirit helped to make a Zionist out of Henrietta Szold. She regarded them as symbolic of 1900 years of Jewish homelessness and persecution. To her, it seemed clear that the Jewish people needed a home, not merely as a haven for the persecuted, not only as a spiritual and cultural center, but to give dignity and psychological health to Jews all over the world.

Henrietta Szold continued to make her livelihood as a teacher until 1893. In that year she was asked by the Jewish Publication Society to become a full-time editor. For several years prior, Henrietta had contributed her services, on a voluntary basis, to this important educational project. Indeed, it was a report she had done on Graetz's *History of the Jews* which so impressed the editors that they decided to appoint her Secretary to the Publication Committee. Miss Szold, then twenty-three, moved to Philadelphia, site of the J.P.S., and eagerly embarked on the heavy chores of proofreading, translating, and rewriting. In 1903, a year after the death of her beloved father, Henrietta moved her mother and herself to New York City, where they settled in an apartment on West 123rd Street, just across from the Jewish Theological Seminary, the school for Conservative rabbis. Her apartment became an informal center for professors and students from the Seminary, including Dr. Solomon Schechter, its president, who called Miss Szold his "Minerva."

She served as secretary for twenty-three years. Her letters during that period described "the crazy orgy of work." As Louis Lipsky described her work, "she gathered into her motherly care the accepted manuscripts, the work of translation, the proofreading, the compiling of indexes and appendices, and the preparation of advance notices." When she left the Society, the J.P.S. had published almost 100 volumes and had begun to pierce at least the outer walls of illiteracy and ignorance of Jewish literature.

Even during the arduous years of work with the J.P.S., Miss Szold had freely contributed her extra hours—which she somehow found after a sixteen-hour daily schedule of work—to Zionist affairs. She was a member of the Executive Committee of the Federation of American Zionists (later known as the Zionist Organization of America) and served as its honorary secretary and honorary vice-president. Her unusual capacity for service was, by now, apparent to leaders of the Jewish community. In 1915 Judge Julian W. Mack, distinguished Zionist spokesman, and a few other men of vision took a far-seeing step. They relieved Miss Szold of any further need to make a livelihood. Through their generosity, they made it possible for her, from that moment on, to make a gift of herself to the welfare of the Jewish community. Many years later, Miss Szold acknowledged that this stipend had given her the opportunity to make her latter years both active and productive.

Hectic as her life had been, and eminently useful, her first fifty years were, nonetheless, a prelude to the main theme. From 1907, Miss Szold had been associated with the Hadassah Study Circle, a rather academic group of New York women who met to hear papers on Pinsker, Herzl, Judaism, and related topics. (Miss Szold confessed that the Zionist Organization "looked upon us as organizers of a strawberry festival.") Then, in 1909, Miss Szold and her mother visited Europe and Palestine. Henrietta was moved by the Holy Land, but she and her mother were oppressed by the wide-spread poverty and disease they saw there.

One day they visited the Jewish Girl's School in Jaffa and they wondered at the clear, healthy eyes of the pupils in contrast with the emaciated children outside the building, their eyes sick and covered with deadly flies. How come? The doctor explained: The school was fortunate in that it had doctors and a nurse who came regularly. Most of the children of Palestine never saw a doctor. This, concluded Henrietta's mother, is the kind of thing that you and your Study girls back in the United States ought to be doing something about, practical work in Palestine, instead of reading papers and drinking tea.

Upon her return to America, Henrietta set out to convert the Hadassah Study Circle into a national organization of Jewish women to undertake practical work in Palestine. The first meeting of the new organization was held February 24, 1912, at Temple Emanu-El, New York City. Miss Szold was elected president. By the end of the first year, 157 members and thirty-seven associates had been enrolled. In 1914 the first national convention was held in Rochester, New York, and representatives of seven chapters—ranging as far west as St. Paul, Minnesota—attended. Miss Szold applied her creative genius to fashioning out of the tiny organization a mighty instrument for study and service. She succeeded. Many years later, when she was in Palestine, she was importuned to "appeal" to Hadassah for emergency funds. "No," she said, "to Hadassah we send no 'appeal.' To Hadassah we send only information. . . . To Hadassah we tell only what the need is."

Miss Szold wasted no time in directing Hadassah toward practical work in Palestine. "By the end of 1912," as she recalled many years later, "we had in our treasury about $283. Then Mr. and Mrs. Nathan Straus appeared on the scene and asked me to visit them. They told me they had heard our purpose was to introduce visiting nurses in Jerusalem; they wanted to know why we didn't do it. I said we had only $283 in the treasury. They said, that doesn't matter! Start! I said there was no money; and Mr. Straus repeated, that has nothing to do with it. Mrs. Straus kept nodding her head behind his back as if to say, 'The Lord will provide.' "*

Nathan Straus contributed the cost of passage for two nurses. Others contributed funds to cover the nurses' expenses for the first year in Palestine. Miss Szold scoured the countryside, building the organization, founding new chapters, recruiting new leaders, raising funds. By 1917, the infant organization was reaching respectable proportions. With forty-seven chapters and 4,000 members, Hadassah was ready and willing to confront larger challenges. The war had made medical conditions in Palestine, poor to begin with, virtually intolerable; the shortage of doctors and medicine was acute. Hadassah rose to the occasion by accepting the obligation of setting up and financing an entire medical unit and dispatching it to Palestine. Forty-four persons formed the medical staff and more than $50,-000 worth of equipment and drugs arrived in Palestine in

---

* *Ibid.*

1918. A budget of $250,000 was set up. While the American
Joint Distribution Committee raised part of the sum,
Hadassah, under the leadership of Miss Szold, gladly as-
sumed the lion's share of the responsibility.

It is difficult to imagine the desperate health problems
which the Yishuv (the Jewish community of Palestine)
faced at the time Hadassah entered the scene. An average of
five to ten persons lived in one room, with little air, light,
water. Most Jewish women bore their children without the
benefit of a doctor. Mortality rates were frightening.
Malaria and trachoma were epidemic. There was not a
maternity ward in any Jewish hospital, and the few Christian hospitals were notorious in mixing missionary activities
with medical assistance. In the entire city of Jerusalem, there
were three doctors serving 50,000 Jews. Hadassah's first
objective was the development of a district nursing service,
along the lines of the Henry Street Settlement created by
Lillian Wald in New York City.

In 1919 Miss Szold herself was sent to Palestine. Despite
disturbing evidences of a bad heart, she seized the opportunity to go to Erets Yisroel—for a two-year stint, as she
believed—to help smooth out the workings of the Medical
Unit. She could not have imagined that the two years would
stretch to twenty-four and that, with only a few interludes,
the rest of her life would be spent in Palestine. She was
60 years old when she arrived in May, 1920. Many Jews,
not much older than she and with hearts no stronger, came
to the Holy Land to die on the sacred soil. Henrietta Szold
came to live, as full of ideas and energy as a bouncing
pioneer. At 60, she began the great adventure of her life.

Gradually, the Hadassah medical units began to raise the
health standards of both Jews and Arabs in Palestine.
Malaria was conquered. Trachoma was obliterated. The
mortality rate declined sharply. The sneers, which at first

dismissed the Unit as mere American-style charity, quickly turned to heartfelt appreciation and respect as the work of Hadassah brought healing and balm to the Promised Land. And the guiding spirit of the enterprise was a gray-haired little woman who worked sixteen to twenty hours a day, whose labors carried her into the most primitive sections of the country, sometimes by donkey, and whose name became a household word through every city and kibbutz in Palestine.

Miss Szold drew the inner strength to absorb the stresses of such an adjustment at the age of 60 from her wondrous exhilaration at seeing the Zionist promise reaching toward fulfilment. The idealism of the chalutsim thrilled her. She exulted in the mounting stream of refugees and immigrants returning to their ancestral home. But harsh difficulties were legion, and even Henrietta Szold was frequently torn by despair. Great Britain had pledged, in the Balfour Declaration of November, 1917, to create a Jewish national homeland in Palestine. But between the word and the reality stretched years of conflict, deception, and bloodshed.

Arab riots, culminating in the bloody massacre of 1921, left her sick in spirit. But, unlike most Zionists, she saw the outbreaks as a solemn warning and as an indictment of the Jews as well as the Arabs. "If our cause is just, wholly just and righteous," she wrote, "we are bound to find just and righteous and peaceful means of conciliation. We shall ally ourselves with the best of our Arab fellows, to cure what is diseased in us and in them. *Arukat bat ammi* and also *arukat ha-goyim*—the healing of the daughter of our people and the healing of the nations!" Miss Szold always insisted that the moral test of the success or failure of Zionism would be reconciliation between the Jews and Arabs. Together with Dr. Judah Magnes, president of the Hebrew University, she maintained this position even in the face of harsh propaganda and political attacks upon her by her fellow Zionists in Palestine and in America. Henrietta Szold was a Zionist; but she was a respecter of no party line. Her conscience and her deepest Jewish values determined her positions.

Miss Szold never ceased regarding herself as an American. She yearned to return to her own country. In September, 1921, she wrote to a friend in America, . . . "If I am needed here, I'd rather stay my self-assigned term out, and then go home for good; but home I must go, if not now, then in the not too distant future." But, except for brief returns to America, and those mostly for fund-raising missions for Palestine, Miss Szold was destined to live out her days in Palestine. The spry little lady, then in her 60's, somehow kept growing. "I find that, old as I am, in a certain sense I have not stopped growing. While I don't understand, while my intellect is an organ of narrow limitations, my inner world—perhaps it is my world of feeling, of instinct —expands." And so did the world of responsibility which was loaded on her shoulders. When she completed her medical work, she was pressed into straightening out the educational system, then on into social welfare, then youth work, always a new task and an urgent one, always the insistence that only Henrietta Szold could bring it to a successful completion, always the capitulation to duty.

In the spring of 1933, Henrietta Szold toured her beloved Palestine for what she was certain would be the last time. Tenderly, she bade silent farewell to the colonies, the cities, the mountains, the lakes she had come to know and love. She had definitely decided to return to her own America. But, again, it was not to be. Hitler came to power in Germany, and his lengthening shadow was a dark portent of things to come. Henrietta Szold felt in her bones that a new dark age was about to descend, and she knew that her people would need her in Palestine. Reluctantly, she ac-

ceded to her own merciless sense of duty. She was driven by
the need to rescue the children of European Jewry. The
vehicle she fashioned to achieve this purpose was called
Youth Aliyah.

Youth Aliyah was a gigantic program through which
youngsters fourteen to seventeen were trained, in Europe,
for life in Palestine and, with infinite care, settled in the
Holy Land. Central to the plan was not merely the physical
rescue of Jewish children; it was their spiritual and social
regeneration, "the building and the being built." The children, trained for life in a kibbutz, were received by Pales-
tinian Jewry with rejoicing and understanding—"a religious
poem," was the way Miss Szold described their induction
into the kvutza. In 1935 a colony was established in her
name. Kfar Szold (Szold Village) was set up in the Negev
and, later, was moved to its present location in the north,
near Mount Hermon.

Miss Szold's schedule was geared not to her age but to the
necessities of her people. She was a woman in a whirlwind,
lining up teachers, writing to parents in Europe, sweating
out the financial problems, trudging through the mud to
look after the children's needs, receiving reports on every
child, arranging transportation, looking after the occasional emotional problems of her charges, standing at the
dock to meet newly arriving boys and girls. Twice she
traveled to Berlin, where she met with the heartbroken
parents who smiled through bitter tears as they said good-
bye, for the last time, to their children. Her first trip to
Germany came on the very day the infamous Nuremberg
laws were promulgated. To the parents, who sensed their
own doom, Henrietta Szold seemed an emissary from God,
a life-giving angel, who would safeguard their seed. They
clutched at her dress, they showered her with pathetic
kisses, they begged her to give messages to loved ones. Some

came merely to draw comfort from the sight of an old woman, who, somehow, symbolized a better future and a better world.

Henrietta Szold became a legend during her own lifetime. Tales of her stamina raced across Palestine. One morning, when an enervating *chamsin*—desert storm—had kept most of the staff from their offices, Miss Szold was found at her desk, as always, at 8:00 A.M. What was she doing there? "What do you mean?" she replied. "I feel like a young girl of 70." Only on the Sabbath, a day she cherished for physical and spiritual refreshment, did she relax. She was never absent from her customary pew in the synagogue. To her sunlit home in Jerusalem, Palestinians and visitors came as to a sanctuary. One day two youngsters knocked at her door and explained, "Please excuse us; we have come to Jerusalem to see the Wailing Wall and Miss Szold."

Wendell Willkie was one of those who came to visit. It was 1943, World War II was reaching its agonizing climax, and Henrietta Szold was 82. They talked of persecution against the Jews. "I cannot live comfortably in America while it is unsolved," she told him. "The Jews must have a national homeland. I am an ardent Zionist but I do not believe that there is a necessary antagonism between the hopes of the Jews and the rights of the Arabs. I am urging my fellow Jews here to do those simple things that break down the prejudices, the differences between people." Mr. Willkie had been subjected that day to a withering barrage of political propaganda from both Arab and Jewish spokesmen. He was puzzled by the gentle words which fell like rain on parched sand. "But as I sat there that late afternoon," he reported, "with the sun shining through the windows, lighting up that intelligent, sensitive face, I, at least for the moment, wondered if she in her mature, selfless wisdom might know more than all the ambitious politicians."

The war blazed toward its inevitable end. The awesome destruction was beyond calculation. Out of the blackness came soul-sickening reports of the murder of six million Jews. Almost as frightful was the callousness of the Christian world, their doors slammed tight against the ragged Jews who survived the disaster and begged for sanctuary. Only Palestine offered a gleam of hope. By war's end, Youth Aliyah alone had saved 8,000 children. Wrote Miss Szold: ". . . I have never been concerned with anything in the way of public work which as impressively as Youth Aliyah made me feel that I am an instrument in the hands of a Higher Power; hence, no self-esteem. As for its value in all respects, one has but to look at the brawny young men and the spirited young women the movement develops to be impressed with the human and citizenship material shaping itself to the uses of a New Palestine."

Honors poured in upon her. Honorary degrees were given by the Jewish Institute of Religion, Dropsie College, Boston University. The work of her hands was now being carried on by many others. Her Hadassah had grown into a vast organization of 300,000 women, and its hospital in Palestine (Rothschild-Hadassah University Hospital) had become the largest in the entire Middle East. Her "children" grew to maturity, equipped in body and spirit to assume the sudden burden of nationhood. But the work-wracked years took their toll; the bottomless vitality was no more. There was pain now, and sickness, and then lapses of consciousness. On February 13, 1945, in the cool of the Palestine evening, Henrietta Szold died. Although she lived many years beyond the Biblical three-score and ten, she died too soon—too soon to see the miracle of our time, the rebirth of the Jewish homeland.

Although, like Moses, she was not destined to see the ultimate fruit of her labor, Henrietta Szold left a standard toward which modern Israel can aspire: ". . . The future is full of the gravest responsibilities. We are promised a place in the sun—not to ravage and dominate, but to serve our people, ourselves, the world. Standing in the sun we shall be seen clearly as never before. Our abilities will be on trial before a world full of nations, who will judge us in the light of a glorious past of ideal service to mankind. For Israel, election has never meant anything but obligation. Clearly, rehabilitating a nation is not a pastime. It is a task, a heavy task, a holy task."*

---

* *Henrietta Szold, Record of a Life,* Rose Zeitlin, Dial Press, New York, 1952.

Edward Israel

YOUNG RELIGIOUS NEW-DEALER

T HE HANDSOME and rugged young man bulked large as he rose to speak. As always, his eloquence and commanding presence seized the attention of every person in the room. He spoke rapidly, vigorously—then, suddenly, he hesitated, raised his hand to his chest and slumped forward. He died almost instantly.

Thus Rabbi Edward L. Israel, age 45, died on Sunday, October 19, 1941, while attending a meeting of the Executive Board of the Union of American Hebrew Congregations in his native Cincinnati. Called to serve as executive director of the Union, the national association of Reform synagogues, Rabbi Israel was being formally installed in that distinguished position that very day.

Earlier in the day, in an address which many present regarded as the most brilliant Rabbi Israel had ever delivered, he had outlined his conception of Jewish life and his plans for the future of the Union. He said in part:

"This is a critical generation, and I feel it depends upon the strength, courage, and forthrightness of religious organizations as to where we are going to end up. The sole reason for the existence of the Jew in the world is his spiritual heritage, and whatever aspect of Jewish life there may be, whatever direction it may take, in any form at all, be it philanthropy, social welfare, or anything else, it has to be rooted in the firm foundation of religious motivation, or else it is meaningless.

"Despite the infinitely dark situation in which we live, we can have sound reason for encouragement. I think we are swinging away from that materialism which has engulfed us, and I think that we are going to embark upon an era in which the religious interpretation of Judaism and Jewish life is going to play a role in our American environment, which for us is practically the entire Jewish world, as never before. With the collapse of Jewish centers throughout the world, what the Jew and Judaism do in America now is going to determine the course of Jewish history for the rest of all time. What we do is not going to affect just another community, it is going to affect the whole course of Jewish history."

Edward Israel was ill at the time he accepted the heavy challenge of leading Reform Judaism in America. His heart had already been seriously strained by a many-sided career to which he had committed his boundless energy, magnificent vitality of spirit, and great idealism. As a rabbinic colleague said of him, "He used his energy to the utmost and, rather than rust away slowly in carefully guarded invalidism, he preferred to burn up his life in the flame of human service."

The career of this devotee of the future was snuffed out before all of its limitless promise could be realized, but not before Edward Israel gave testimony, by his own life, that prophetic Judaism can work with revolutionary power in the life of society. Edward Israel was a social justice rabbi par excellence. His entire life was a demonstration that

Judaism and its majestic social ideals can and must function
to make a better society for all men in the here and now.
"Religion must not be an anodyne but a stimulant," he once
said. Israel was a stimulant himself—and the positive impulses which he set into motion are the legacy he left behind. President Franklin Delano Roosevelt called him "one
of the great liberal leaders of our time."

Born in Cincinnati in 1896, Israel was raised in that city
in the shadow of the Hebrew Union College. Cincinnati
was then the unquestioned Mecca of Reform Judaism in
America: both the Hebrew Union College, the seminary,
and the Union of American Hebrew Congregations were
located in that midwestern city. In his early childhood, Israel
caught frequent glimpses of the then-ancient patriarch, Isaac
Mayer Wise, who had been the builder of the institutions
of Reform Judaism in this country. As a boy, Edward
dreamed of entering the magical, ivy-covered campus of
Hebrew Union College on Clifton Avenue. After studying
at Harvard and Cincinnati Universities, he enrolled at the
Hebrew Union College.

Big and rugged, even at seventeen, Ed Israel quickly established himself as a natural leader. He was beloved by his
fellow students and teachers alike. His scholarship was
superior; he averaged ninety-four or better every year. But
Israel was not a bookworm, and he always had time for the
harmless revels which enlivened the grind of rabbinical
training. A classmate, reminiscing after Israel's death, recalled his friend at HUC, "How clearly I can hear Ed's
peals of laughter as he hit upon some outrageous pun. How
his eyes shone as he threw back his great head in a roar.
Then he would set his lower jaw just a little off center to
stem the avalanche, while his shoulders heaved and his black
curls danced. . . ."

Israel had been at the College only a year when a minor

crisis developed. Rabbi David Mendoza of Norfolk, Virginia, took ill just before Rosh Ha-shono and the harried congregation sent an urgent wire to Dr. Kaufmann Kohler, then president of the College, pleading for a substitute. To his great consternation, Dr. Kohler found there was not a rabbi or upper class rabbinical student who had not already been placed. What to do? He picked the best youngster in the Preparatory Department, snatched some sermons from a file for him, and dispatched Edward Israel, with a few hours' notice, to be a rabbi—at eighteen! The poised youngster made a deep and favorable impression on the congregation.

The sure signs of greatness were on him. When he was ordained in 1919, at the age of 23, he was one of the youngest graduates in the history of the College. The powerful young man, with the crackling humor, the burning idealism and the gentle modesty, was also one of the most popular men produced by the College.

It was in the city of Baltimore that Rabbi Israel became one of the luminous figures in the American rabbinate. After brief tenures in synagogues in Springfield, Illinois, and Evansville, Indiana, the rabbi was summoned in 1923 to assume the pulpit of Temple Har Sinai in Baltimore. How paradoxical that Israel should have flowered as a prophet of social justice in this particular congregation! For it was Har Sinai, which, in 1865, had dismissed and virtually expelled from the town their spiritual leader, Rabbi David Einhorn, for the heinous crime of preaching against slavery.

Rabbi Israel served Har Sinai for eighteen years, until he left to accept the leadership of the Union of American Hebrew Congregations and to meet his premature death. During this period, he worked a virtual revolution in his congregation and his community. His pulpit became a shofor call to action against the evils of society. Far from skirting controversy, Rabbi Israel insisted that religion, and especially Judaism, had to face up to moral issues and stand for principle. *The American Jewish Archives*, in an article by Rabbi Leonard Mervis in the June, 1955, issue, lists the following topics which were among the sermon subjects preached by Israel between 1928 and 1935:

"Political Parsons" (a sermon preached in protest against the bigotry of the Hoover-Smith presidential campaign and in defense of the right of ministers to speak on political themes); "Penitentiary Riots and Kindred Subjects" (a denunciation of conditions in the prisons in Maryland); "Let Freedom of Education Ring"; "Essence of Social Service"; "Social Responsibilities"; "Unemployment"; "Birth Control"; "Mayor Walker and the Mooney Case"; "The Negro Problem"; "Rugged Individualism—Is It Our Answer"; "How the Other Two-Thirds Lives"; "This Man Huey Long."

Rabbi Israel regarded the industrial age as a sharp challenge to religion. He felt that the mechanization of life had to be balanced by spiritual strength and by the translation of religious principles into practice on the economic scene. The rabbi attributed the emptiness of churches and synagogues to the failure of clergymen to confront the stuff of life. He directed an acidulous ridicule upon those clergymen who "were almost bored with social problems."

Hurling himself into social causes in Baltimore and beyond, Rabbi Israel became identified with that "social religion" which came to grips with unemployment, labor, civil rights, crime, and politics. He was impartial arbitrator for the men's clothing industry of Baltimore, chairman of the Municipal Commission on Employment Stabilization of Baltimore. Quickly, his reputation spread. He served as chairman of the Religious Board and member of the Report Committee of the White House Conference on Children in

Democracy (1939-1940); member of the Board of the National Public Housing Conference.

He gave unstintingly of his time and energy to Jewish as well as non-Jewish causes. The Zionist Organization of America, the American Jewish Congress, and the Synagogue Council of America were among the many organizations through which he channeled his tireless energy. But it was as a member and, later as chairman, of the Social Justice Commission of the Central Conference of American Rabbis, that Israel should, perhaps, best be remembered. Together with such passionate fighters for justice as Rabbi Ephraim Frisch, whom he succeeded as chairman in 1927, Rabbi Israel transformed the Social Justice Commission into a powerful instrument of social action on the American scene. To the delight of the rabbis, and to the consternation of many Reform laymen, the CCAR's Social Justice Commission not only spoke out in a spirit of radical liberalism, it sparked important and far-ranging action on controversial issues. Never before, or since, has the Conference joined hands with Protestant and Catholic leaders so effectively in bread-and-butter, practical social action. This period was the "shining hour" for the CCAR as a vital examplar of prophetic Judaism.

The year was 1926. A bitter labor dispute swirled about the Western Maryland Railroad. The railroad called it a strike. Many, including Rabbi Israel, saw it as "in reality a lockout of several hundred employees by a hard-fisted management which determined to make a heavily over-capitalized railroad pay dividends by resorting to a breaking of the labor union and a drastic cut in wages." Strike or lockout, the union dispute festered and threatened to explode into severe violence. Deeply troubled, local clergymen of Hagerstown and Cumberland, Maryland, urged the national religious bodies—Protestant, Catholic, and Jewish—to investigate the conflict. The Federal Council of Churches, the National Catholic Welfare Conference, and the Commission on Social Justice of the CCAR agreed. Each designated representatives to conduct an on-the-spot investigation.

Rabbi Israel and his Catholic and Protestant colleagues studied the records, interviewed the parties, analyzed the issues. The religious leaders worked together in complete harmony. In the course of their inquiry, they discovered that aged pensioners of the railroad had been ordered back on the engines as strike-breakers under threat of having their pensions cut off. The religious leaders put it to the company: revoke the order or face the glare of national publicity about the contemplated injustice. The order was canceled. In 1927, after months of study, the three organizations published their report. This was not an airy sermon, mounted on platitudes. It was a detailed, factual, hard-hitting study and was widely acclaimed as a pioneering document in the field of industrial relations.

Such activities imposed a heavy drain upon the young rabbi, and this was aggravated by the inevitable resistance to his "meddling," as some disgruntled congregants put it. During the Western Maryland investigation, for example, an attorney of the railroad company was sent to the secretary of the board of the temple, demanding that the rabbi be silenced. The board refused to take action.

Taking note of the undercurrent of disquiet among some of his congregants, Rabbi Israel felt constrained to make the following explanation in a sermon:

". . . You may sincerely feel that because of my official position, I have not the right to interest myself in public controversies where I feel that a moral issue is at stake. If this is your point of view, I am sorry that I cannot follow you in it. As I interpret religion, it is the application of the individual conscience to the problems of life. . . . For one to keep silent merely because he may be expressing an adverse opinion is a type of moral cowardice to which I cannot submit. . . ."

In 1928 Rabbi Israel was again catapulted into the storm of controversy. The religious bodies were once more requested to investigate a labor dispute. Although the Catholic group was engaged in other activities and could not cooperate, the Protestant Council and Social Justice Commission agreed to go in. The Real Silk Hosiery Company of Indianapolis and its employees were locked in combat. The investigators found that "the employers were paying wages in many instances far below a decent living standard and working their employees, especially the girls, far beyond the recognized eight-hour limit of our Social Creed." The final outburst came when the workers were forced to sign "yellow dog" contracts or lose their jobs; and to join, instead of a legitimate union, an "Employees' Mutual Benefit Association." The investigators branded the Association a company union, with no semblance of real industrial democracy. The report helped to awaken public opinion against a flagrant abuse of social justice.

Rabbi Israel was not merely respected; he was beloved. Both the Jewish and the general community of Baltimore were enchanted by his warmth, his humor, and his charm. Once, in 1930, the popular Baltimore rabbi was invited to match wits with Clarence Darrow, the well-nigh invincible lawyer and agnostic, along with a Protestant and a Catholic speaker. The subject of the debate was religion and agnosticism. The place: the Lyric Theater. The audience: everyone who could fight his way into the packed theater.

Here is how the *Baltimore Post*, the following day, described the event:

"A callow youth, quite unsophisticated in the dangers of the world, stood on the stage of the Lyric Theater last night and made Clarence Darrow, eminent Chicago lawyer, look like a new member of the bar pleading his first case.

"Not that the defender of Leopold and Loeb—the man who talked rings around the golden-tongued William Jennings Bryan in the famous Tennessee 'monkey-trial'—did not prove himself an eloquent and convincing orator. Darrow was all of that.

"But Rabbi Edward L. Israel, of Har Sinai Congregation, who explained 'Why I Remain a Jew' was even more. His very first sentence—in which he confessed his lack of sophistication and consequent unwillingness to stick his 'head in a lion's mouth' by debating with Darrow—brought a volume of applause which almost amounted to an ovation.

"And from then until the moment, some thirty minutes later, when he brought his speech to a close, his remarks were punctuated by bursts of applause."

The depression, with its agonies of unemployment and misery, shook Rabbi Israel deeply. He was stirred by the need to establish curbs upon a free enterprise economy which seemed to be out of control.

The election of Franklin Delano Roosevelt, and his aggressive and imaginative New Deal, heartened the young rabbi immensely. Roosevelt, for his part, had been aware of the zealous religious leader. Rabbi Israel had caught his eye while Roosevelt was still governor of New York. Indeed, Roosevelt had publicly quoted Rabbi Israel, saying, "We must have a revamping of the entire method of approach to these problems of the economic order. We need a new type of social conscience that would give us courage to act. We are here to serve notice that the economic order is the invention of man and that it cannot dominate certain eternal principles of justice and God."

In 1934 he was appointed by President Roosevelt a member of the regional Labor Board and a member of the consultative group of the advisory commission on Social Security. Later, he served as chairman of a citizen's committee in the men's clothing industry and in the ladies' cotton garment manufacturing. He was successful in hammering out an agreement with the union, although the entire field had been non-union.

He was proud, as he had every right to be, of the cooperative actions undertaken by the three major religious groups. Rabbi Israel and such liberal spirits as Monsignor John Ryan, director of the Social Action Department of the National Catholic Welfare Conference, and Dr. James Myers, industrial secretary of the Federal Council, were able to bring to bear upon the thorny issues of the day the meaningful impact of the religious conscience. A typical example was the "Interfaith Conference on Unemployment" which was held in Washington in June, 1940, and which focused the spotlight of public opinion on the "ethical issues and moral consequences of unemployment and its influence on American life."

Edward Israel lived life with a fierce zest, as if the times were too momentous to permit a normal pace. This was particularly true in the way he approached his appointment to the directorship of the Union of American Hebrew Congregations in 1941. A good friend and colleague, Rabbi James Heller, later recalled this period. "It was a sacred call to him. All of his love for his own faith was revealed in the words he spoke, to individuals and at the few meetings he was able to attend. He looked forward eagerly to the privilege of giving himself utterly. That privilege, not as he envisaged it, came to him too soon. . . . Not often can a life come to so fitting an end, one veritable *Bin'shikoh*, 'ending with the kiss of God.' "

There are so many men—and some rabbis among them—who go through life with one eye on posterity, acutely aware of their own role in history. Such men usually have their autobiographies and neatly-assembled notes bulging in a bottom drawer, confident that history will sustain their own judgment of themselves. Edward Israel was not such a man. His life was too full, too demanding, and raced too swiftly to permit of such narcissism. He was too busy fighting today's battles to pause to record yesterday's victories. There is nowhere a complete account of Israel's work and activities. His loyal widow, Amelia, and his son, Charles, treasured his "papers"—cardboard boxes, overflowing with scraps of letters, notes for sermons, skits spoofing his classmates and teachers at Hebrew Union College, handwritten manuscripts, a heated exchange of correspondence with the *Brooklyn Tablet,* sudden bursts of poetry, book reviews scrawled in Edward Israel's personal hieroglyphics, long and lyrical notes about a trip to Palestine, yellowing newsclips. Among the sea of papers is a yellow card containing the following, scrawled in pencil, titled simply "E.L.I." undated and uncompleted:

"I am filled with nostalgia. Unashamed, unembarrassed, and with the sound conviction that none of my middle-aged generation will dispute us, I 'long for the good old days of our youth.'

"I have no regrets. I am glad that my life is approximately two-thirds lived [ed. note: this was probably written only a year or two before his death]—or even less. I wouldn't change places for a moment with those who are twenty years younger than I. For I have at least known that which they in all probability will never know—a world of beauty and of hope.

"I lived my youth amid those early decades of the twentieth century when life was gay and buoyant. . . . Yet lived in a world of hope and the golden glow of kingdom of the spirit to be conquered. . . ."

Edward Israel lived his youth to the brim—and died, while still youthful. His dreams were captive to a greater tomorrow. In the outpouring of his spirit, he symbolized, at its purest, the prophetic vision: "Behold, there shall come a day...."

David Dubinsky

JEWISH WORKER

THE AMERICA of mid-twentieth century is a world removed from the America of 1850, or 1900, or even
1930. Breath-taking changes have taken place. What is true
of America is true of American Jewry—perhaps more so.
Today, there are more than five million Jews in America.
(There were 700,000 in 1880.) Half of the Jewish population resides in the New York City area and almost all the
rest are clustered in and around a handful of large northern
industrial cities. With Jewish immigration to the U.S. slowed
to a trickle, American Jewry has lost its immigrant status;
80 per cent of American Jewry is native born. The Jew
is an urban animal. Where 12 per cent of the American
population is engaged in agriculture, only 2 per cent of
the Jews work on farms. The Jew is an educated citizen.
Comprising only 3 per cent of the population, he con-
tributes more than 8 per cent of the total enrolment in the
nation's colleges. In a nation on the move, the Jew is unusually mobile: The Jewish population of Los Angeles increased by more than 150 per cent in one decade, Miami by
500 per cent, and a Jewish exodus from the city to the sub-

urbs characterizes every large city. Politically, the Jewish voter tends to be liberal, internationalist, democratic.

But one of the most striking changes in the character of American Jewry has been its sharp economic shift. While about 20 per cent of the American people are now engaged in commerce and the professions, half of the Jews earn their livelihood in these fields of work. The Jew has moved in a generation from the laboring classes to the middle class. The son of the immigrant worker has become a doctor, lawyer, engineer, white collar worker. The garment unions, the so-called "Jewish labor unions," once overwhelmingly Jewish both in membership and in leadership, have grown steadily less so and are now about 25 per cent Jewish. The American Jewish community is prosperous.

The American Jewish businessman or professional, catching the 8:12 morning special which will speed him from his glistening suburb to his air-conditioned office in the city, is hardly conscious of how far and how fast he has gone from the ghettos of his immigrant parents or grandparents.

Jews contributed much to the development of the American labor movement. The American Federation of Labor was founded in 1886 by Samuel Gompers, a Jewish immigrant from London, who led the organization until his death in 1924. Although Gompers was Jewish, he had little rapport with the intense and radical East European Jews who poured into America after 1880. Indeed, the Jewish labor movement came to represent a sharp challenge to the conservative philosophy of Gompers and the A.F. of L. which was based on the simple maxims of "reward our friends and punish our enemies" and "more, more." The A.F. of L.'s emphasis on immediate economic objectives, together with its aversion to involvement in politics, stood in direct contrast to the tendencies of the Jewish labor movement which was, at its inception and for several decades, expressive of a yeasty socialist philosophy which conceived of unionism as an instrument for the waging of the class war and for the elimination of capitalism. The zealous Jewish workers wanted more than higher wages and shorter hours. They were fighting for nothing less than a new world, a messianic age, the true brotherhood of man.

That conditions in the garment industry toward the end of the nineteenth century cried out for unionism was obvious to any fair-minded observer. Working conditions in the industry were wretched beyond description. With the invention of the sewing machine in 1846 and the gradual rise in production of ready-made garments, the industry expanded quickly and, in the 1880's, there developed a shortage of skilled tailors and cheap labor. Russian Jews, 580,000 of whom fled to America between 1880 and the turn of the century, filled the need. Unfamiliar with the language, dazed by the new ways, unprepared by their lives in the Russian Pale for physical labor, desperate for work, penniless, eager to cling to the seeming security of the Lower East Side—these pathetic souls were "ready-made" for the garment trade.

And how they were exploited! The notorious sweat-shop system kept men, women, and children at back-breaking labor eighty-five hours a week in dingy tenement rooms, at an average pay of $6.00 a week. Said the official report of an inspector in 1886, "They usually eat and sleep in the same room where the work is carried on, and the dinginess, squalor, and filth surrounding them is abominable."* Despite mounting protests of social workers and some alarmed public officials, neither the government nor the employers felt called upon to do anything about the jungle conditions of the garment industry. In an age of "survival of the fit-

---

* *American Labor Leaders*, Charles A. Madison, Harpers, New York, 1950.

test," and "dog eat dog," the immigrants were fair game. But some of the Jewish intellectuals were determined that exploitation was not to be tolerated in the land of freedom. Socialists and anarchists mounted soap boxes and filled the air with radical views. But the first and immediate need, they knew, was a labor union. Year after year, the effort to organize was made. The task seemed hopeless. A newspaper reported in 1886: "Almost every year the cloakmakers have been organized and every year the union went to pieces."* The Jewish workers seemed incapable of maintaining the discipline needed for a trade union. Rancorous political arguments—between the anarchists and the socialists, the left-wing and the right-wing and within each clique —repeatedly tore the fragile seams of unionism. The United Hebrew Trades was formed in 1888 and it made some gains but Jewish labor did not emerge as a significant force until after the turn of the century.

The major creations of the Jewish labor movement were the two powerful unions in the apparel industry: the Amalgamated Clothing Workers of America, representing men's clothing, and the International Ladies Garment Workers Union, "born of despair, with poverty as the midwife." The Amalgamated was organized in 1914 and the ILG in 1900. These were the unions which put an end to the evil sweatshop system in the garment industry and made possible decent wages and working conditions. Their growing economic power conquered the disease-breeding conditions; the endless hours of toil; the starvation wages; the human slave-market on Essex near Hester Street which was a "labor exchange" but which was properly called the "Pig Market"; the infamous "contract system" which was built upon human exploitation. The apparel unions were not content merely to curb these practices. They charted new

---

* *Ibid.*

trails for the entire American labor movement in industrial unionism, cooperative employer-employee relations, and social welfare.

Jewish leadership created these unions which, at their inception, were made up almost completely of Jewish laborers. Sidney Hillman served as president of the Amalgamated from 1915 until his death in 1946. This restless Jewish immigrant from Russia who, as a boy had studied in a Russian yeshivah to become a rabbi, became in America an influential preacher of the gospel of progressive unionism. He launched most of the great social projects of the Amalgamated and he rose to national prominence as a leader of the CIO and as one of Franklin D. Roosevelt's key advisers. ("Clear it with Sidney.") Hillman was a labor leader of stature. Indeed, few in his time wielded so much power and influence, and few achieved so much for their followers.

Another, of similar stature, and also an immigrant Jew, is David Dubinsky who was usually linked with Hillman in common cause but, occasionally, stood as a rival in political and labor affairs. Dubinsky is the leader of the International Ladies Garment Workers Union. Both Hillman and Dubinsky were giants of labor. But Hillman, the ex-yeshivah bocher, seemed to sunder most of his Jewish roots upon coming to America. Dubinsky, no less busy, has maintained his warm contact with the Jewish labor movement and the Jewish people.

Dubinsky was born in Brest-Litovsk in Russia in 1892, the eighth of nine children. His family moved shortly thereafter and he was raised in Lodz, a large and ugly Polish industrial city. David's father, Bezalel, had a bakery, but his mind dwelled on the glories of the Talmud rather than money-making. David went to a modern Hebrew school until he was eleven; then he quit to work in his father's bakery. Soon the lad was a "master baker." But, like all bakers in the city, young Dubinsky had to toil some eighty hours a week to eke out even the barest living.

Then the bakers' union came to the city. It was formed by the General Jewish Workers Union—known as the Bund. The Bund was composed of Jewish radicals who caught the imagination of both the masses and the intellectuals with a vision of socialism, revolution, and free trade unions. Unlike the Zionists, who preached redemption of the Jewish people in Palestine, the Bundists advocated cultural autonomy for the Jews within the Russian Empire.

Young Dubinsky became a passionate Bundist, and thanks to his familiarity with both Polish and Yiddish, was named assistant secretary of the bakers' union before he reached the age of Bar Mitzvah. When the bakers struck, they won their wage increase; but the leaders were quickly arrested, David, aged 15, among them. Upon his release, David returned to the union only to be arrested again and exiled to Siberia as a political prisoner. For two years the youngster was shipped from city to city, from jail to jail, across the width of Russia and into the wastes of western Siberia. There, he managed to slip away from his guards and make his escape. Fully aware that Siberia, or worse, awaited him if he were caught again, Dubinsky welcomed the opportunity represented by the steamship ticket to America which his brother had sent from New York. Thus, on New Year's Day, 1911, when a vessel called the "Lapland" carried 700 steerage passengers into New York harbor, one of the wide-eyed passengers was David Dubinsky. He was not yet nineteen. He had $20.00 in his pocket.

David felt at home in New York's East Side and its boiling dynamism, and he delighted in the new horizons of opportunity which were immediately open to all. He learned to be a cloak cutter, a highly-prized and well-paying craft in the garment industry. Only seven months after landing at

Ellis Island, David Dubinsky was admitted to the Cutters' Union, Local 10, of the International Ladies Garment Workers Union.

The ILG was in the midst of a rocky period when Dubinsky appeared on the scene. It had made little progress in the decade since it was organized, with high hopes, by eleven workers who owned $30.00 among them. But in 1910, the ILG amazed and electrified New York City by winning two great strikes involving the shirt-waist and cloakmakers. Nobody believed that the "Uprising" could succeed—except the strikers. At a mass meeting at Cooper Union on November 22, 1909, one of the girls leaped to her feet to interrupt a speaker who was counseling caution and exclaimed in fiery Yiddish, "I am a working girl, one of those who are on strike against intolerable conditions. I am tired of listening to speakers who talk in general terms. What we are here for is to decide whether we shall or shall not strike. I offer a resolution that a general strike be declared—now."* With deep emotion, 2,000 workers rose, voted for the strike, and solemnly repeated this Jewish oath, "If I turn traitor to the cause I now pledge, may this hand wither from the arm I now raise."

America's largest strike started by women took place the next morning, and it raged through twelve cold, miserable, and incredible weeks, during which the picketing girls were pushed around by hired guerrillas and harried by hostile police and courts. One judge sentenced a girl picket with these imperishable words, "You are on strike against God and Nature, whose firm law is that man should earn his bread by the sweat of his brow." The strike was won in a compromise settlement which was made possible by the skilful mediation of Louis Brandeis and Louis Marshall who fashioned the famous Protocol of Peace. The Protocol was subjected to heavy stress in the following years but it established

---

* *Tailor's Progress*, Benjamin Stolberg, Doubleday, New York, 1944.

a stable pattern of labor relations and stability which was far ahead of the rest of the country.

The Great Revolt stirred public opinion. It demonstrated that the ILG was a permanent force to be reckoned with. The first mass strike in the needle trade showed that women too could be organized and could accept hardship and discipline to achieve economic justice. Only a year after the strike, however, another event occurred which further outraged the public conscience and set the stage for additional thorough reforms in the garment industry. It was the Triangle Waist Company fire. One hundred forty-six workers, mostly girls, were consumed by flames in this disaster. The only fire exit on the floor had been sealed, reportedly to keep out union organizers. The disaster stirred public indignation and, as a result, strengthened the ILG.

Dubinsky played practically no role in these historic developments. Within weeks after coming to the U.S., he joined the Socialist Party. Evenings, he would mount a soap box and talk himself hoarse in alternating Yiddish and English, denouncing capitalism, and exhorting his listeners to join the class struggle. He was much more concerned with socialism and the cooperative movement during these years than in the work of the ILG. In 1912 the Socialists seemed to be getting somewhere, with Debs rolling up 900,672 votes for President, the highest vote ever turned out by the Socialist Party. But President Wilson took much of the wind out of the socialist sail by enacting some of their legislative proposals. World War 1 tore the party to shreds, with bitter divisions between the pacifists, led by Debs who went to jail, and supporters of the war. Dubinsky helped sell Liberty Bonds and strongly supported the war effort. When the Russian Revolution erupted, and the Bolsheviks smashed the democratic forces, the ardor of American socialists cooled even more. Dubinsky turned his attention increasingly to the ILG.

Once started, Dubinsky rose like a rocket in the ILG. By 1918, he was a member of Local 10's Executive Board. By 1920, he was vice-president and, in 1921, president of the local. The next year he became a member of the ILG's General Executive Board. In 1929 he was unanimously elected ILG secretary-treasurer. When the incumbent president died in 1932, Dubinsky agreed, reluctantly, to accept the presidency. He was 40 years old. He assumed the burden of leadership at one of the grimmest hours in the history of the union and the nation, amidst the gathering darkness of the Depression and a swiftly deteriorating international situation.

Many of Dubinsky's friends shook their heads and said that "D.D." had accepted to serve as "undertaker" for the union.* The ILG was in bad shape. The industry was sick. Half the workers were wholly or partly unemployed. ILG membership sank to 33,000 members, only a third of the total which the union had reached in 1918. There was no money for the union payroll; officials received $20.00 "on account." To make matters worse, morale had been seriously shaken by the internecine warfare which had raged within the ILG throughout the 1920's. Dubinsky had been a leading figure in a deadly double struggle—against anti-union manufacturers on the one hand, and against a militant communist drive to take over the union on the other hand. The internal struggle had virtually bled the union white. Dubinsky's strong, ruthless fight against the Communists and their rule-or-destroy tactics eliminated the internal threat to the union; but it left deep wounds which festered for years.

Dubinsky dedicated himself to revitalizing the International. He had an unexpected ally in Franklin D. Roosevelt, who was elected President the same year and whose program promised a "new deal" for labor. Section 7a of the Recovery

---

* *David Dubinsky: A Pictorial Biography*, text by John Dewey.

Act, prohibiting the company union and making it illegal for employers to prevent the organization of labor, was a kind of Magna Carta of labor's rights. The International drafted a model code for the industry which was presented by President Dubinsky and ailing Morris Hillquit, who had to be brought to Washington in an ambulance plane. The governmental code for the industry was drawn largely from the recommendations of the ILG. Aggressive organizing campaigns and strikes were launched, and the union's strength multiplied. By 1934, the membership had zoomed to 200,000; the heavy debts of 1932 were paid off and assets reached $850,000. Dubinsky has kept the union rolling in high gear ever since.

Nobody has ever run a union with quite the éclat with which Dubinsky runs the ILGWU. His control is personal and firm. At conventions, he wields the gavel like a sword and frets about every minor detail personally. He speaks extemporaneously, sometimes interminably, with an undisguised Yiddish accent, as well as a streak of sentimentality which frequently moves his audience and, just as frequently, fills his own eyes with tears. But, when a principle is involved, Dubinsky is all business. For example, during the second day of the 1934 ILG Convention at the Medinah Club Auditorium in Chicago, Dubinsky learned that the auditorium officials were mistreating Negro delegates. Next morning Dubinsky moved the entire convention, bag, baggage, and 750 delegates out of the auditorium and installed them at the Morrison Hotel where non-discrimination was pledged. With characteristic gusto, Dubinsky led a gigantic horn-blasting motorcade through the heart of Chicago with banners proclaiming their mission. Dubinsky greeted the roaring delegates at the Morrison with the promise that the "ILG practices what it preaches concerning civic equality of all people and will continue to help in that fight against race discrimination outside and inside the labor movement, until it is won."

Another of Dubinsky's articles of faith is his conviction that Communists are the "eternal enemies of the American labor movement." Today, when the Communists have long been expelled from the labor movement, this statement has a hollow ring. But in the 1920's and 1930's, there was powerful sentiment, in the labor movement and elsewhere, for a "united front" between the liberals and the Communists against the "common enemy." Dubinsky had learned his lesson the hard way through bruising personal experience in the ILG, during which he bitterly fought off the repeated efforts of the Communists to infiltrate and take over the ILG. Dubinsky preserved the integrity of the ILG and distinguished himself as one of the labor movement's most astute students and opponents of Communist tactics.

It was "D.D." who gradually broke the socialist mold of the ILG and brought it into the mainstream of the liberal-labor coalition which became known as the New Deal. His philosophy was spelled out clearly: "Labor should be a social pressure group, pushing its views on great social questions, lobbying for progressive legislation, keeping our society in balance. Labor must be in social politics, not party politics." In this spirit, Dubinsky "de-politicized" the ILG and broke the socialist traditions which the garment unions had maintained from their beginnings. In 1936 Dubinsky resigned from the Socialist Party. This action, which withdrew the ILG from the old radical movements, immediately reduced the factionalism which had hampered the ILG. Dubinsky made the break clean by becoming a presidential elector in the Democratic Party that year. Later, he became a founder of the ALP—and, when that became Communist-dominated, he helped to found the Liberal Party and also the Americans for Democratic Action—to provide the ILG with a political base which combined all-out New Deal support and political independence. No other union plays a more vigorous role in the political arena than the ILG.

Under Dubinsky's buoyant leadership, the ILG has grown into a mighty and far-flung labor union, which extends myriad benefits to its 450,000 members. The union owns no less than seventeen health centers throughout the country, the immense New York Center operating out of a twenty-seven-story skyscraper office. There are $246 million in the treasury, of which $150 million are reserved for health and welfare benefits. Among the many fringe benefits secured for its members is a retirement pension which, like all other welfare benefits, is secured from employer contributions. The apple of his eye is Unity House, an immense and modern non-profit resort in the Pocono Mountains of Pennsylvania which the ILG maintains as a vacation paradise for every ILG card holder. Unity House can handle some 1,200 guests.

The ILG was a pioneering union. Its list of innovations is dizzying and includes: the forty-hour and, now the thirty-five-hour week; market-wide pooled retirement funds; employer-contributed vacation funds; union health centers; an unemployment insurance plan conducted by the union; an educational program for the workers; its own Broadway labor shows; publication of full annual financial reports for the union; a political action department in the union, etc.

The ILG is a most generous union. It has contributed upward of $25 million for foreign relief. It has always been quick to express its warm sympathy for progressive causes and needy institutions. Through voluntary contributions, the ILG has raised substantial sums for such purposes as the following: Histadrut (Israel Labor Federation); Father Flanagan's Boys Town in Omaha, Nebraska; Roosevelt Marine Trades Institute for orphans in Mondello, Sicily;

United Jewish Appeal; March of Dimes; flood relief. These sums have been vast. More than $1,000,000 went to the Histadrut alone and $7,000,000 went into Israeli housing bonds, and a gigantic hospital is now being built in Israel with ILG funds. ILG also helped to launch a housing project in Puerto Rico, a boys' town in Italy, a school in France.

In addition, the union has gone into the business of co-operative housing in New York City. The ILG Co-Opera-tive Village embraces four twenty-two-floor buildings in twelve acres along the East River, containing 1,668 modern apartments renting at an average of $18 a room. The union put $15 million into this investment for democracy which Dubinsky, at the dedication, described as ". . . social divi-dends of our faith in unionism. They are the 'profit' of our great strikes. . . . In our time, slums and poor housing are as out of date as the anti-union sweat-shop."*

Dubinsky and his union have come a long way. The road is marked with paradoxes. The flaming Socialist, who preached class warfare, has become America's finest exem-plar of class collaboration and free enterprise. Dubinsky taught the manufacturers that they and the union had a common stake in a healthy industry. To the dismay of many old-time labor men, Dubinsky's ILG made loans to manage-ment when the industry became shaky; once even built a plant and leased it to a manufacturer; had his staff draw up proposals to help employers increase the efficiency of their plants. Among the many guests at Unity House, there is, usually, a sprinkling of employers.

Once, in a hot wage dispute in the garment industry, management agreed to have Dubinsky, the head of the union, serve as "impartial" arbitrator. Management returns the compliment, frequently inviting Dubinsky to address

---

* *The World of David Dubinsky*, Max D. Danish, World Publishing Co., Cleveland, 1957.

them and to socialize with them. All this helps to explain an unparalleled record of labor-management peace, stretching from 1933 to 1960 with only one flurry of a strike, which lasted six days. The employers swear by his honesty. Dubinsky's rigorous standard of ethics had a great deal to do with the recent expulsion of corrupt unions by the united labor movement.

The ILG is a social laboratory. It is also a melting-pot in action. Jews, Puerto Ricans, Negroes, Italians, Poles— many of the locals are like United Nations in miniature and they represent democracy in action. Shrewd, pragmatic, explosive Dubinsky has carried his union to a pinnacle of unquestioned dominance of New York City's largest business, which produces $6 billion worth of women's garments a year. Dubinsky's sense of rectitude is almost painful. Only recently did he permit his own salary to be raised from $15,000 to $26,000, and his union officials grumble that his frugality holds down the level of their salaries. "If we took more we would not give a damn about the workers," he says.* He is almost fanatical in his principles, and his critics charge that labor has had to pay too heavy a price for the ruthlessness of his crusades to extirpate corruption and Communism from the labor movement.

Dubinsky has always maintained his link with Jewish life. "I am not a professional Jew," Dubinsky has said. "I am a Jewish worker, and I am proud of it. The labor movement has given me an inspiration and a key to world problems, and I am grateful for this as well. Many people ask why Jews are so responsive to all appeals for aid, not only coming from Jews. The answer to that is quite simple; the Jews have suffered for centuries from all kinds of persecution and injustice and they know what it means to suffer. . . .

"But we, Jewish workers," he went on, "feel that as labor

---

* *Life* magazine, "Great Americans," August 18, 1958.

people we should help other workers irrespective of nationality—whether they be Italians, French, Chinese, yes, even
Germans, once we conclude that they are being persecuted.
To us Jewish workers, help for workers everywhere means
a great deal because we realize that if there is a prospect of
solving the Jewish problem, that prospect lies with the
working masses of the world."

Dubinsky is proud of his Jewishness. He has contempt for
those Jews who seek to deny or efface their Jewish background. Dubinsky recalls a conversation he once had with
President Franklin D. Roosevelt who surprised him with
the question, "What is the matter with you Jews? Why are
you so alarmed?" The President went on to explain that
he had come to expect a committee of scared Jews to call
upon him every time he was known to be considering the
appointment of a prominent Jew to an important post. The
same thing had happened when the President was planning
to name Felix Frankfurter to the Supreme Court. When the
usual committee of timid Jews descended, the President
sternly lectured them about the meaning of America where
all people are free and equal under the law, and he told
them that Frankfurter was being named not because he was
a Jew but because he was the best man for the job. And then
the President told Dubinsky something which the labor
leader has remembered vividly, ". . . I have never yet seen
any Irish leaders coming here to complain when Irishmen
are appointed to important offices. Jews need not be so ap-
prehensive, for this is their country no less than that of any
other citizens. Frankfurter will surely be a credit to Jews
and non-Jews alike."*

Dubinsky's Jewish interests and loyalties have been expressed, in large measure, through the Jewish Labor Committee. The JLC was founded in 1933 to rescue liberals and

_____
* *Op. cit.*, Danish.

Jews from Hitlerism. Its membership was drawn from the Jewish trade union movement. During the 1930's, the JLC was prominent among the Jewish organizations which spearheaded a world-wide boycott of Nazi goods. Hundreds of labor leaders and intellectuals and socialists were saved from liquidation in these activities in which Dubinsky played an active role as a member of the Executive Board of the JLC. But neither Dubinsky nor the JLC could be satisfied as they witnessed the enveloping tragedy. "Please, in the name of humanity, give us a loan of 100,000 visas at this trying hour . . . ," Dubinsky appealed to Washington during the war. "Lend-lease us an advance quota of sunshine, of free air, of free humanity, a loan that will afford these escapees from hell a chance to regain human dignity among their fellow men. . . ."

Dubinsky is strong-willed and stubborn when his conscience is outraged. An example of this came during the height of World War II, at a moment when the American people were thrilling to the heroism of the Russians, our warm allies. A report came to Dubinsky that two great Polish labor leaders, Jewish socialists, had been executed by the Soviet Union as "Nazi agents." Henryk Ehrlich and Victor Alter had been well known to Dubinsky and other American labor leaders. They, and liberal leaders like them, represented a glimmer of hope for a democratic post-war Poland. It had been known that the Soviets were keeping them prisoners. News that they had been murdered by the Russians, and on so grotesque a charge, infuriated the labor movement. Dubinsky called a mass meeting of protest in New York City. A clamorous controversy erupted. How could he embarrass an ally, fighting valiantly against the common enemy? Wasn't he endangering the war effort? Dubinsky went through with the meeting, and his own address set the keynote:

"As free American citizens, as workers and as democrats, in registering our fiery protests against these executions we shall assert and reassert to the end of time our unshakable belief in their innocence and their stainless idealism. Ehrlich and Alter died as martyrs. They died because even at the price of life itself they would not renounce their convictions, the principles of a free democratic world."

The Communist press, after striving desperately to prevent the meeting, set out to destroy Dubinsky and his reputation in a campaign of unmatched vituperation. They accused him of causing the fall of Kharkov. They denounced him as a betrayer of the war effort, as leader of the anti-Semitic forces, spokesman of American fascism, etc., etc. Whether Dubinsky was wise or not in staging the protest meeting in the midst of the war, his object was to pierce the misty veil of illusion through which an emotional public opinion viewed the Russians. In the immediate post-war years, the American public experienced the disillusionment of seeing the veil fall off, exposing the aggressive and brutal face of Stalinist Russia. The cold war was a vindication of Dubinsky's cold assessment.

Although philosophically an anti-Zionist, Dubinsky was stirred by the remarkable achievements of Jewish pioneers in Palestine. The Histadrut, Jewish labor movement of Palestine, won his whole-hearted admiration. Dubinsky was profoundly moved by the establishment of Israel which he saw largely as a haven of refuge for homeless Jews and by the Israeli victory over invading Arab nations. In the difficult years of Arab boycott and blockade, Dubinsky's ILG extended the firm hand of friendship and assistance to the new State.

Once, during World War II, when the destruction of European Jewry was reaching its climax, Dubinsky received a letter from a Jewish boy, soon to reach his Bar Mitzvah, asking for advice as to whether it would be wise for the

youngster to maintain his Jewish identity. Dubinsky sent
the following reply:

> *My dear boy:*
> At this time when the Jewish people in other
> lands are enduring the most terrible trials, some
> think "perhaps if the Jews lost their identity as a
> people, the prejudice against them would dis-
> appear and they and future generations of Jews
> would be spared suffering the persecution." Al-
> ways there have been a few weak in mind and
> spirit who would seek such an easy way out.
> Study and reflection, however, supported by a
> knowledge of Jewish history, shows that those
> who seek to hide or who prefer to forget their
> origin are not spared when the tide of anti-
> Semitism rises. In some parts of the world today,
> some who had almost forgotten their Jewish
> origin have become victims of the worst intoler-
> ance. Perhaps their lot was even harder than
> others. . . .
> In all of this there is a great moral lesson. Jews
> must retain their identity. They must carry on a
> knowledge of their history and preserve their
> culture, but they must at the same time work
> hand in hand with enlightened people of all faiths
> and creeds all over the world to liberate human-
> ity, end age-old injustice, and establish a new
> order of freedom and righteousness for all.
> The salvation of the Jews, therefore, lies in the
> salvation of humanity. . . . The best wish I can
> voice for you and your parents is that you will
> be a good American, an upright Jew, and a lover
> of humanity.*

That is also the cloth from which Dubinsky himself is
cut.

---

* *Ibid.*

Samuel Mayerberg

CRUSADER FOR CIVIC DECENCY

THE OFFICE of Reed McKinley, city manager of Kansas City, was jam-packed on November 9, 1959. Some 100 happy politicians, hangers-on, and assorted lackeys were on hand to see Dr. George V. Feist sworn in as city director of health. One man, however, was there to see that Dr. Feist was *not* sworn in. He was Rabbi Samuel S. Mayerberg, for thirty-one years spiritual leader of Temple B'nai Jehudah—and, for all that time, extraordinary crusader for civic decency and goad to the conscience of Kansas City.

As the city clerk prepared to administer the oath of office to the new director of health, Rabbi Mayerberg rose:

"Just a moment!" he exclaimed. "Before the oath is read . . ." The mood of light-hearted gaiety fled. Suddenly, the air was electric with tension as the familiar figure demanded permission to read a prepared statement before the new health director was sworn in. Obviously fearing what he would say, the crowd drowned out his words with a chorus of catcalls, boos, and hoarse shouts of, "He's out of order!"

Banging on his desk for silence was the city manager, his face ashen and eyes carefully averted from the rabbi. The clerk will now proceed with the oath, he ruled, and the rabbi can make his statement afterward. Dr. Feist was sworn in amid sighs of relief from the audience. As the rabbi left the room, the crowd jeered, savoring a sweet, if temporary, victory.

In 67-year-old Rabbi Samuel Mayerberg, however, they knew they had a most formidable foe who had learned, through years of bruising battles, that wars for clean government are never decided in the initial skirmish. Some twenty-seven years earlier, Rabbi Mayerberg had led the successful drive to smash the Pendergast machine in Kansas City.

His brand of Judaism impelled him to challenge every kind of social evil. In recognition, he had been widely plaqued, scrolled, cited, and feted by Christian, Jewish, and interreligious organizations, even including the Daughters of the American Revolution.

But perhaps the most appropriate honor was his selection by the governor of Missouri in 1956 to serve as one of four police commissioners of Kansas City to direct, along with the mayor, a large police department with a budget of $7,000,000 and an enviable record of performance. In appointing him to a four-year term, Governor Blair had said, "Rabbi Mayerberg will put the fear of God into the hearts of the underworld."

Having served the people of Kansas City for so long and so well, approaching the ripeness of a beloved emeritus status in his congregation, what induced Rabbi Mayerberg to expose himself once again to still another thorny Kansas City struggle?

The background was simple. A new administration took office in Kansas City in the spring of 1959. Before long, it became clear that a spoils system was being reinstituted which was wrecking the City Charter and its provision for a merit system of appointment. Dissatisfaction came to a boil when a group in the city council forced the resignation of the experienced director of the health department and announced, through the city manager, the appointment of Dr. Feist. Feist was a general practitioner, innocent of any experience or background which could qualify him for this vital public post.

Infuriated, the doctors of Kansas City filled the air with protests. They appealed to Rabbi Mayerberg to gather religious leaders of all faiths in a campaign to block the appointment. Rabbi Mayerberg, who had never been accused of running from a good fight, helped organize an Interfaith Committee for Civic Action. He became co-chairman, along with Dr. Stanley I. Stuber, executive secretary of the (Protestant) Council of Churches of Greater Kansas City. The committee, including clergymen and lay leaders of all faiths, strongly challenged Feist's fitness for the job. What had been sporadic sniping now broke into a major, all-out conflict, and Kansas City reverberated with explosive charges and counter-charges.

The city counselor (a member of Rabbi Mayerberg's temple) rendered a legal opinion, advising that the charter did not require any special training in public health or hospital administration for the director of the health department. A general practitioner, he insisted, was amply qualified under the law.

The counselor's ruling was raked by community leaders. Desperate, the Feist forces announced, straight-faced, that their man was indeed qualified, that he had received a "special course" in hospital administration during the past summer.

This gas-filled balloon was quickly shot down by the newspapers who revealed that the good doctor had not taken any "course" and that all he had done during the summer was to have some chats with the dean of a medical school and with miscellaneous officials of a few hospitals in California. The Jackson County Medical Association announced that it would join with the Interfaith Committee in a court test to challenge Feist's qualification under the charter.

Rabbi Mayerberg and his committee jolted the citizens of Kansas City from their somnolence, stung their civic pride, and forced them to turn their bleary eyes away from the private-eye thriller on television to the whodonit in their own city council. Membership in the Interfaith Committee increased and, to the consternation of perspiring politicos, the committee began to expose the firing of other experienced public employees by City Hall and their replacement with unqualified hacks.

Confirming the suspicions of the Interfaith Committee, a member of the city council admitted that the former Director of Hospitals, Dr. Gelperin, had been discharged because some of the councilmen had wanted to close down General Hospital, the city institution providing services to many of the city's indigent. Dr. Gelperin's heresy was that, far from yielding to this plan, he had insisted upon expanding services to the needy.

Mayerberg and his co-workers were now convinced that the city manager was acting as a tool for certain members of the city council. Armed with facts and with a daring which startled the people of Kansas City, the rabbi and three other clergymen descended on City Hall to ask for nothing less than the resignation of City Manager McKinley.

The stage was set for one of Kansas City's sensational political Donnybrooks. While the clergymen read their statement, some of the councilmen made an elaborate show of boredom. One slouched, head in hand, staring out the window. Another clipped his finger-nails.

One of the councilmen, who had been a principal target of the committee's criticism, took the floor as soon as the clergymen's statement was completed. Flushing angrily, a trembling finger stabbing the air, he glared at Rabbi Mayerberg and demanded that, if the rabbi was so interested in politics, why didn't he run for office himself? "Is it fair to assume," he stormed, "that he is shirking his duties at his temple while his handsome salary continues to roll in?" The councilman spilled out the full litany of political vituperation, denouncing Rabbi Mayerberg as, among other things, a "stooge" and "dictator."

Dr. Mayerberg replied, "I've entered all the fights of Kansas City with the full right of a man of religion to fight for right and truth."

The rabbi then developed his charge that the city manager was a prisoner of certain members of the council. With heated righteousness, each of the named councilmen denied the charges. So did the city manager. Recalling conversations he had had on this subject with McKinley in the past, Mayerberg fixed him with a cold stare and said, "Reed, I hope your conscience will let you rest. My conscience is clear."

The struggle was far from over, but the tide of battle had begun to turn. Shortly thereafter, Mayor Bartle blasted the city council and declared it had flouted the City Charter. He repudiated the handling of the city hospital situation and reported that a small group of councilmen had acted without clearing with him and contrary to the best interests of the city.

That afternoon the city manager made a dramatic announcement: Dr. Feist had resigned. The medical fraternity was jubilant, but the Interfaith Committee had made a more probing diagnosis of the illness of Kansas City. They continued to press for major political surgery.

A few days later, the city manager held a press con- ference. Grimly, he acknowledged that for months he had been under severe pressure from members of the council and from political faction leaders and that he had not been free to do what was best for the city. It was a complete vindication of everything the rabbi and the com- mittee had contended.

In its last stages, the struggle became even more acute. Fighting for their political lives, some politicians reverted to the tactics of the alley-fight. The deadly weapon of character-assassination was dusted off and aimed at the respected Dr. Stuber. Ugly whispering campaigns were started. Statements were made over the radio, insinuating that Stuber was a Communist or, at the very best, a fellow traveler. The National Council of Churches immediately came to Stuber's defense and sharply branded the attack as slanderous and reprehensible.

Councilmen also approached congregational leaders in an effort to silence the clergymen who were leading the campaign. A politician buttonholed the president of Rabbi Mayerberg's temple and suggested that a councilman be allowed to meet with the board of the temple. The presi- dent rejected any such suggestion. Instead, the board adopted a resolution commending Rabbi Mayerberg for "his courageous efforts to safeguard the health services to the needy and indigent patients at General Hospital and to assure compliance with the requirements of the city charter." For good measure, the board authorized the Social Action Committee to join the struggle for clean govern- ment in Kansas City.

As the New Year of 1960 began to unfold, a bright day dawned in Kansas City. The city manager was dismissed. An immediate investigation was begun into all illegal ap- pointments. The hospital was made secure from political sabotage. It was a triumph for the few who had carried the lonely burden of a city's conscience.

Why should a religious leader get involved in such knock-down political conflicts? Shouldn't a rabbi or minister content himself with pulpit pronouncements and leave political action for others?

"While I hold the firm conviction that ministers should never engage in *partisan* political activities," the rabbi wrote in his fascinating autobiography,* I also cherish the un-wavering belief that, where iniquity runs rampant, where depraved and selfish men prey upon a community, it is not only the right but also the compelling duty of the minister to lead in the movement to eradicate such evil powers from his community. If one holds the fearless, God-intoxicated prophets of Israel as his human ideal as I do, one is im-pelled by his conscience to enter the fray with all the courage and strength he can summon."

Mayerberg was born in 1892 in Goldsboro, North Caro-lina, and grew up under the powerful influence of his father who served as rabbi in Goldsboro for nearly forty years. While still a small boy, Samuel nourished the dream of following in his father's footsteps, a rabbi in Israel. The Mayerbergs were a close family. Indeed, on the fateful September day in 1908 when the rabbi and his frightened 16-year-old son set off for Cincinnati to enroll the youth in Hebrew Union College, it was the first time Sam had ever been separated from his twin brother for so much as an hour in all his life.

After his ordination, Rabbi Mayerberg and his bride moved to Detroit where the young clergyman garnered valuable congregational experience as assistant to the dis-tinguished Rabbi Leo Franklin. Later, Mayerberg served

---

* *Chronicle of an American Crusader,* Samuel S. Mayerberg, Bloch, New York, 1944.

in Dayton, Ohio. In both communities he demonstrated his keen interest in community affairs and took a vigorous part in issues involving prison reform, improvement of mental institutions, academic freedom, capital punishment, and interfaith relations.

But all seemed prelude to Mayerberg's call to Temple B'nai Jehudah in Kansas City in 1928 and to the drama which unfolded in 1932 when Rabbi Mayerberg took on one of the most arrogant political machines in America. Speaking before the Government Study Club of Kansas City, Rabbi Mayerberg spelled out in vivid detail the alliance between the city administration and the underworld which held Kansas City by the throat. He charged that the city manager was violating the City Charter and that public funds were being misused. He demanded that the city manager be thrown out of office, that Kansas City recapture the spirit of the charter and clean up the Pendergast mess. The response was overwhelming. Ministers, leading citizens, professional men and women, and community organizations rallied around the rabbi, hungry for leadership and direction. The influential *Kansas City Star* backed Mayerberg to the hilt. The fight was on.

It was an uphill and perilous struggle. Before it was over, attempts were made to bribe the rabbi, his telephones were tapped by the mobsters, he was threatened repeatedly, and he was shot at in a blood-chilling but abortive act of desperation. Mayerberg was compelled to use a bullet-proof car, to be accompanied constantly by bodyguards acting upon orders of the governor, and to keep a loaded gun under his bed at night. It was a fierce, grim, and crucial contest. For years, the furious struggle to smash the machine raged. There were times when Rabbi Mayerberg had almost as much trouble from frightened Jews as he had from the mobsters and venal politicians.

Finally, the fight was won. Several crooked politicians and election officials were sent to jail. Tom Pendergast himself was shipped to Leavenworth for income tax evasion. And, in 1940, under the leadership of the Clean-Up Committee, with a broom as its symbol, the people of Kansas City swept out the machine and, by a vast majority, voted in a reform mayor and new city council. Fear and intimidation passed. Kansas City regained its dignity and its self-respect as a city. And Mayerberg stood over the community, thereafter, jealous of his beloved city's virtue and ready to do battle whenever it was threatened.

So stormy a career as Rabbi Mayerberg's is bound to provoke controversy. Not a few, even of Mayerberg's friends and admirers, have raised questions about some of his actions. For example, it has been suggested that, when a rabbi plunges into a bitter and protracted political controversy in the community, the inevitable divisions and conflicts set in motion within the congregation may, at some point, endanger the congregation itself. Moreover, the record indicates that, in the kind of political crisis into which Mayerberg was catapulted, the line between partisan and non-partisan necessarily becomes blurred. Even Mayerberg, opposed in principle to clergymen being involved in partisan politics, occasionally found himself impelled to mount the political stump for certain candidates and certain parties.

Moreover, an even more fundamental question arises: In facing a problem such as civic corruption, should a rabbi act as an individual clergyman, with all his great personal power, or should he seek to lead the great body of laymen of his own congregation into action? The latter is most difficult, requiring as it does patient education and steady leadership of a congregation which invariably includes its conservative and cautious elements. How change a society whose vested interests line the pews? Perhaps it is revealing that, in his most recent community fight, Rabbi Mayerberg had the staunch support and cooperation of his temple's Social Action Committee. Far from believing that the minister has a monopoly on social justice, Rabbi Mayerberg is enthusiastic about the social action movement which links rabbi and laymen in the holy task of building a better world.

Mayerberg is an institution in Kansas City. Next to the mayor, he is perhaps the number one citizen. His views are hungrily sought by the newspaper, radio, television. When non-Jews seek the help or voice of the Jewish community, Mayerberg automatically comes to mind. From Harry Truman to the eager lad in the Methodist youth group, Sam Mayerberg has earned adulation and admiration.

There are many paradoxes in Mayerberg's personality. A fiery warrior against corruption, he is universally accepted as an unusually warm and considerate gentleman. A focus of public interest and, therefore, of the spotlight of publicity, Mayerberg is neither a publicity seeker nor an egotist. As the voice of Kansas City Jewry, Mayerberg, undoubtedly, has stirred some ill-concealed pique in a few other rabbis and Jewish leaders who accept his preeminence only grudgingly.

Critics of Mayerberg sometimes say he is worshipped by non-Jews, beloved by Jews, and tolerated by his own congregation. This seems unfair. His congregation, tested under fire as few others have been, not only survived recurrent ordeals. The congregation may well have grown under trial to a stronger faith and a keener appreciation of the demands of prophetic Judaism. Somebody once said that God will not look us over for medals and ribbons but for our well-earned scars. Both Mayerberg and B'nai Jehudah can wear their scars with prideful honor.

When Dr. Mayerberg announced that he would retire in 1960, the *Kansas City Star* bespoke the warm sentiment of the community, Jewish and non-Jewish: "In the temple, he has been a builder and an inspiration. In the community, he has often stood as a civic conscience against corruption in government. To forces that have tried to maintain corruption or destroy good government, he has been a voice that could not be turned off. He has gone into the lion's den and asked questions that demanded answers."

Looking back on his long career, Rabbi Mayerberg expresses no regrets. "I can't quite figure out why a tranquil and peace-loving man like me should have become involved in so many hard fights. But they have really been worth while." Then, with a slight weariness in his voice but a glint in his eyes which belied the words, "Personally, I hope I have had my last fight because I would like a little peace before I die."

Abraham Cronbach

"VOICE IN THE WILDERNESS"

THE APPOINTMENT was for 2:00 P.M. at the Hebrew Union College. Dr. Abraham Cronbach, who had spent more than thirty years as professor of Social Studies there, was standing in the lobby of the Administration Building, waiting for this writer at 1:55. He was never known to be late. A slender man, with a wan but friendly smile and a thin ascetic face which seemed almost to reflect light, he extended his hand for a brief handshake. He spoke in a soft, high voice and so slowly that every word seemed carefully measured. He appeared to be a mild, almost Victorian, old gentleman, bearing his seventy-five years with graceful dignity. It was difficult to realize that this man had been a petrel of the American rabbinate, a controversial figure in some of the bitter controversies on the American scene and, for half a century, a Great Dissenter in both the Jewish and the general community.

Abraham Cronbach was born in Indianapolis in 1882. He was the second child of middle-aged parents. His mother was very dear to him and his childhood memories are filled with her warm, loving image. Blessed with an amazing photographic memory, he still recalls objects and scenes he knew in his father's dry goods store when he was a tot of only three. Abraham was an introspective boy, with a precocious and mystic conception of both God and the devil (he thought the devil was responsible for the smoke from the manhole in the street). A Jew in an overwhelmingly Christian neighborhood, where anti-Semitism and extreme poverty were frequent companions, Abraham took an inordinate pleasure from Sabbath candle-lighting and the Passover Seder at home. To him, the hymns which he learned in religious school were not merely songs; they were deep sources of comfort, affording a measure of security when he was plagued, as he often was, by fears and insecurities.

The depression of 1893-1894 left a deep impression on the tender-minded Jewish youngster. The memory of able-bodied men and women rummaging in garbage piles for food for their children, of diphtheria signs blossoming on almost every door in the neighborhood, of soup lines, and of hatred festering in the slum like a hopeless disease—these left their mark on the impressionable boy. A singular and lonely lad, given to playing the violin and poring over fat tomes on religion and science while other youngsters in the neighborhood were playing ball, Abraham drew upon his inner resources and found comfort and inspiration in his religious faith.

While still in high school, the young Cronbach cast off his childhood dream of becoming a lawyer and announced to his startled parents that he now planned to be a rabbi. His father fumed in opposition. Mrs. Messing, the wife of the rabbi and a friend of the Cronbachs, sought to allay the family fears with a prediction, "Don't worry. He's not smart enough to be a rabbi. A professor maybe, but not a rabbi." A generation later, when Cronbach was called to be the first occupant of the chair of Jewish Social Studies at the Hebrew Union College, he dispatched a telegram to his mother, announcing simply, "Mrs. Messing was right."

Cronbach was ordained in 1906. Although he was valedictorian of his class, he had strong feelings of inadequacy about his ability to meet the challenge of the rabbinate. In a sense, he never really conquered this tendency to doubt and deprecate his own ability, particularly his ability to preach. That the congregation would not come to listen to him, and would be bored and unmoved when they did, was a specter that constantly haunted the young rabbi.

Cronbach's first congregation was Temple Beth El in South Bend, Indiana. One of the multitude of famous Cronbachian legends stems from this period of his ministry. According to this legend, a heavy blizzard struck South Bend one Friday evening. The newspapers issued solemn warnings to the people of the community to stay at home. Police herded people off the streets. Despite the weather and these warnings, Cronbach plowed through the snow to the temple and, promptly on schedule, conducted Friday evening religious services. His congregation consisted only of the sexton who lived on the premises of the synagogue. Rabbi Cronbach preached a sermon, wished the "congregation" a Good Shabos and thrashed his way through the waist-high snow back to his boarding house. This rigid adherence to schedules has always been characteristic of Dr. Cronbach as rabbi, as teacher, and as man.

If the pulpit of Temple Beth El, South Bend, Indiana, did not give off sparks of prophetic eloquence, it did begin to set the direction of Rabbi Cronbach's thinking about his own rabbinate. Here Cronbach discarded the idea that rituals and ceremonies contribute to morals. Here, he came to reject textual preaching and mechanical recitations of the prayer book, preferring instead the simplicity of spontaneous prayer as the heart prompts. But, above all else, it was in South Bend that Cronbach began to identify his conceptions of Judaism with service to humanity—not in lofty and utopian sermons but in his own daily, time-consuming labor for the underprivileged, the sickly, the victims of social and economic cruelty in a burgeoning American society.

In 1915, Cronbach was invited to New York by Rabbi Stephen Wise to serve as his associate on the staff of the Free Synagogue. Although Rabbi Wise and the Free Synagogue were deeply dedicated to the concepts of social service and social justice which animated Dr. Cronbach, the personal relationship was not a happy one. Characteristically, Cronbach, looking backward, blames only himself for the fact that Wise asked him to resign after only two years. Wise was a great and masterful preacher, Cronbach recalls, "and I couldn't draw flies." Of deeper significance was a fundamental personality conflict. Two more unlikely associates cannot be imagined.

In his almost painfully revealing autobiography published in the *American Jewish Archives* of April, 1959, Cronbach recalled the following incident:

"A consecration hour was requested by the confirmation class of the Free Synagogue. We held it on a Saturday morning, Confirmation coming the next day. A fervently devout spirit prevailed. Unsuspected holiness and beauty were disclosed by those opened hearts. At the height of the impressiveness, Stephen Wise entered the room. He motioned me not to yield to him, but to continue leading. Attentively he listened to the children. Then, as if he were himself one of the children, America's foremost Jew shared with us his thoughts. He spoke simply and briefly. He said that, between God and him, there was a barrier, a thick wall which he was unable to penetrate. The sense of God's presence was the blessed experience of others. Much as he desired it, the experience was not his.

"How well I understood him! God is near the hearts of the lowly, but to be lowly is, for some of us, impossible. Some of us have duties by which lowliness is precluded. The boon of humility was not consonant with Stephen Wise's gigantic work. His mission in life did not permit him to experience the divine. But that did not exclude him from our devotion. The love which emanated from those youthful souls embraced many. Our great leader came, by all means, within its folds."

While Cronbach's experience at the Free Synagogue was not an unmixed joy, he never lost the friendship of Wise. When Cronbach married Rose Hentel, a teacher at the Free Synagogue, Wise officiated. Six years later, when the Cronbachs adopted a daughter, it was with Dr. Wise's generous help.

The next stop in the Cronbach odyssey of ecclesiastical frustration was Akron, Ohio, where the rabbi's growing sense of personal inadequacy as a preacher was reinforced by a feeling that his iconoclastic views would lead to inevitable collisions with whatever congregation he might serve. Cronbach and his bride came to Akron in 1917. An absolute and passionate pacifist, the rabbi faced the full-throated cry of World War 1 hysteria. Unlike Rabbi Stephen Wise, whose prior pacifism shattered under the impact of World War 1 and who became an ardent champion of the War to Save Democracy, Cronbach refused to yield up his conviction that war, by its very nature, is evil. Knowing the mood of the country as it was reflected in his congregation, he did not seek to impose his pacifist views from the pulpit. But, on the other hand, he would not and did not stoop to currying favor with his congregation by emitting the kind of war whoops which patriotism seemed to demand from the pulpit. His silence was eloquent, and its significance was not lost upon his people.

The end of the war did not solve the problem of Cronbach's constitutional unwillingness to run with the crowd, his stubborn and infuriating impulse to cut against the grain of public opinion. Post-war America rang with feverish alarm about the Bolsheviks; Attorney-General Palmer scoured the land for "subversives," who usually turned out to be socialists or just plain liberal dissenters; and the American people were seized by a fit of anxiety about the "Bolshevik menace" which arose from the Russian Revolution. Foreshadowing the McCarthy madness which was to follow World War II, patriotism was equated with a series of emotion-laden slogans and the American people had no patience for calm and dispassionate analysis—and, God forbid—for dissent. In this setting, on April 24, 1919, Rabbi Cronbach mounted the pulpit and preached a sermon entitled "Bolshevism—Bane or Blessing?" He sought to bring to the congregants an objective analysis of the negative and positive potentialities in the Russian Revolution and appealed to the people to think for themselves and not to make final judgments before much more was known about the seething developments in the Soviet Union. The resultant explosion almost tore the roof off Temple Israel.

When the dust settled, Rabbi Cronbach was condemned from pillar to post. The Board censured him. An emergency meeting was called to consider his expulsion. Although the Board, after a bitter debate, voted to retain the rabbi, it was common knowledge that his days in this pulpit were numbered. Rabbi Cronbach, choosing to spare the congregation and himself further anguish, submitted the following letter of resignation which cut him off permanently from "the regular ministry":

> While highly appreciative of the honor conferred upon me in my reelection to the pulpit of Temple Israel, I am obliged to announce my

withdrawal not only from this pulpit but from the regular Jewish ministry altogether, after the expiration of my present term on October 15.

The reason is that my views on public questions are such as to render the average pulpit position no longer tenable. My recent discourse on Bolshevism and the subsequent censuring I received from the Board of Trustees are only an example of what I believe bound to recur in the future and to recur with even greater tension and friction, so long as I am placed where I shall be required to discourse on the questions of the day and where, at the same time, I shall be required to hold paramount considerations other than those of conscience.

I wish to state, with utmost emphasis, that this reason and this reason only prompts me to this step. Personal considerations are involved in no way whatsoever. The members of Temple Israel have been, beyond my deserts, indulgent toward me and kind to me and mine. Friendships acquired while in the service of the temple will always be remembered and cherished.

For the next three years, Rabbi Cronbach devoted himself to the chaplaincy in prison and hospital installations. He developed strong convictions about the futility of the prison system. Even after he ceased to be a full-time chaplain, his interest in prisoners did not wane. He did not hestitate to befriend Nathan Leopold, the Jew who, with Richard Loeb, had committed what Meyer Levin called "the crime of the century." His contact with prisons and prisoners buttressed his prior detestation of revenge and retribution and made of him a strong opponent of capital punishment and of our entire prison system. If Cronbach had the power, he would destroy all jails and prisons, which he regards as instruments of societal vengeance which corrupt both the prisoners and society itself, and he would confine law-breakers to new institutions for psychological treatment and social retraining.

In 1922 Cronbach was invited to join the faculty of Hebrew Union College as Professor of Jewish Social Studies. Although he entered this new phase of his career with his usual diffident internal *debate* as to his own competence, and though he continued to question his own effectiveness to the very end of his long teaching career, there is little doubt that it was in teaching that Abraham Cronbach made his supreme mark. Hundreds of student rabbis felt the imprint of a rare and sensitive mind, a meticulous love for truth, a sympathy deep and all-pervasive, and a contagious prophetic zeal which evoked a hunger for social justice in the hearts of the future leaders of Israel. One of those young men whom Cronbach helped to shape, Rabbi Jacob Weinstein, wrote of Cronbach in celebrating the professor's 10th anniversary at the College:

"Cronbach is the faithful teacher of values that abide. There are not a few of us who are not yet nihilists or cynics because of him. Our fight for right and justice, whether within or without the synagogue, may have been determined by our chromosomes, but we know that once when it seemed forgotten or futile, Cronbach fanned it into flame again. It has not brought us to the ease of fat places surely, but it has given a quickening energy to our muscles and an abiding strength to our being."

It would be inaccurate to give the impression, however, that Professor Cronbach was always the idol of the students and that the student body annually beat a path to his classroom. Not for Cronbach the silver-throated eloquence, the flashing repartee, and the winsome manner. Indeed, he was always acutely troubled by the knowledge that many stu-

dents were repelled by his exactness, by the outward sever-
ity of his demeanor, and his Cronbachian penchant for self-
flagellation. Nor were his social views always palatable,
either to the students or to the College Board. Destiny
seemed to have fitted Cronbach for a role of goad and gad-
fly, whose mission it was to challenge and shake precon-
ceived ideas, to stimulate fresh thinking, and to disturb
complacency. This has never been a popular role.

After a brief collision with the College Board over his
part in organizing the Jewish Peace Fellowship, a pacifist
society, Cronbach touched off a new furor in 1935. Facing
the frightening menace of Hitlerism abroad, the Jewish
community of America was gripped by a fearful anxiety.
Stephen Wise and others sounded the call of alarm, sum-
moning America to stand up to the awesome threat of
Nazism. American Jewry was preoccupied not only by the
possibilities of extermination facing their coreligionists in
Europe, but also by the spreading poison of anti-Semitic
hatred being brewed by Father Coughlin and by Nazi front
groups in America.

It was at this moment that Professor Cronbach initiated
discussions with representatives of the American Friends
Service Committee about the possibility of bringing together a group of Jewish leaders and a group of Nazi sym-
pathizers to discuss their concerns and their fears. Similarly,
Cronbach appealed to his colleagues and students to join
with him in some Jewish "act of magnanimity" in the hope
that such a step might moderate the hostility which the
Nazis had so clearly evidenced against the Jews. In the face
of bitter condemnation and ridicule, Cronbach insisted that
the Jewish community could not help their fellow Jews by
an attitude of hatred and revenge. Specifically, Cronbach
proposed that a fund be collected in the United States to be
sent to the Nazis of Austria, who were being "persecuted"

by Chancellor Dollfuss and his government. It is a tribute
to Cronbach's logical power that a number of persons in
Cincinnati and elsewhere did respond to his request. Some,
even though they declined to participate in the fund, blamed
their refusal not on the rightness of Cronbach's point of
view, but on their own limitations and weaknesses. His, they
felt, was the true universal religious point of view!

But his was a voice in the wilderness. To some, he was a
hopeless quixotic, who thought he could turn the heart of a
Nazi with love. For the Hebrew Union College, he was a
public relations problem which, in the eyes of the Board,
was too serious to be overlooked in the name of academic
freedom. Cronbach was asked to desist from this project,
and he did, although never doubting that his unpopular
advocacy was nonetheless the wisest course. His heart was
heavy with the suffering of German Jews; Cronbach wore
a "yellow badge" as a mark of his compassion.

Indeed, the grim tragedy which befell 6,000,000 Jews
struck Rabbi Cronbach as an ironic confirmation of his
belief in the futility of meeting hatred with hatred. In 1946,
he wrote the following letter to the presidents of major
Jewish organizations in America:

> If one has a wish, the least that one can do for
> the fulfilment of that wish is to communicate
> it to someone who may possess the power of ful-
> filment, even while realizing how remote fulfil-
> ment may be. My wish relates to those Nazi and
> Nazi-dominated officials who are being brought
> to trial and who will be brought to trial for the
> cruelties perpetrated against the Jews. This is my
> wish: that the Jews might beseech clemency for
> their tormentors and the slayers of their people.
> I can fancy organized Jewry represented at the
> trials by someone authorized to speak as follows:

We Jews have suffered inordinately. Neither our own tragic history nor that of any other people contains any precedent to the afflictions which we have lately undergone.

All that we Jews crave is surcease of our sufferings. We have no wish to inflict sufferings upon others. All that we ask is that Jews all over the world be guaranteed freedom, equality, and opportunity and that they be forever shielded against anti-Semitism.

We seek human rights not only for Jews. We seek them for all men everywhere. To seek them for the Jews alone would be self-defeating as well as ignoble.

The unspeakable miseries which have come upon the world follow a certain pattern with dismal uniformity, the pattern, namely, of retaliation—retaliation for grievances real or imaginary. That vicious circle of retaliation and counter-retaliation must be broken. Otherwise there is no hope for the world. We Jews hereby offer to break that vicious circle. Organized into associations officially represented here, we urge clemency for these defendants.

I shall not protract this letter with any "arguments" in favor of my proposal. How such an act might impress the world, you will surmise for yourself. I will only add that organized Jewry must include not only the American Jewish Congress, the American Jewish Committee, and the American Jewish Conference, to whose heads I am sending this letter. It must also include our brethren in the afflicted countries. They who have been the chief sufferers must, of course, be heeded.

I am not using my printed stationery for this letter, because that stationery contains the name

of the Hebrew Union College. Neither at the
Hebrew Union College nor anywhere else have I,
as yet, found anyone who seconds my proposal.
I do not anticipate that your own reaction will be
favorable. However, in writing to you, to Mr.
Monsky, and to Judge Proskauer, I take the one
and only step which I have power to take. I need
not reprove myself for neglecting to do the one
and only thing which I was able to do.

It is needless to add that, once again, the agonized plea of
Cronbach fell upon deaf ears. One or two of the Jewish
leaders did not even deign to acknowledge his appeal.

Advancing age never stilled the rabbi's restless zeal for
causes he deemed to be good. An opponent of Jewish
nationalism, he associated himself with the American Council for Judaism with full knowledge that most of his colleagues viewed that organization as an ignoble monstrosity.

Writing in his Autobiography, Cronbach makes the following comment about his membership in the Council for
Judaism:

"The type of person attracted to the American Council
for Judaism is, on the whole, the fully Americanized type
such as I served while I was in the pulpit. Still, when I discovered that the American Council for Judaism stressed
religious objectives less than it did its anti-Zionism, I might,
like all the other rabbis, with exceedingly few exceptions,
have withdrawn from the organization. But, by that time,
the Council was under fire, and I do not forsake my friends
when they are in trouble. Even allowing that the wish is
proverbially father to the thought, I think I now perceive
in the Council some changes in the direction of my desire."

But perhaps none of the iconoclastic notions previously
alluded to thrust Cronbach into the fierce maelstrom of public controversy as did his role in the Rosenberg case. There

was every possible reason for any considered person to stay
out of it. The nation was in a panic, partly through artificial
stimulation by the arch-demagogue Joseph McCarthy who
used anti-Communism as a bludgeon to destroy public figures he didn't like; and partly, through the shocking revela-
tions of Communist espionage in important levels of
American government. Moreover, Julius and Ethel Rosenberg were found guilty, after a long and exhaustive judicial
process, of the grave crime of espionage. There can be
little doubt that the American people, as a whole, were
persuaded of the guilt of the Rosenbergs—and wanted them
to be executed. Moreover, American Communists sought
to exploit the Rosenberg Case as an American Dreyfus Case
by embarking upon an immense and world-wide propaganda campaign designed to portray the Rosenbergs as the
innocent victims of a calculated frame-up by "capitalistic
war-mongers." In short, the Rosenberg Case was a porcu-
pine; wherever one might touch it, one would draw blood.
"Therefore," says the Bible, "the prudent doth keep silent
at such a time." But Abraham Cronbach, who can perhaps
be taxed with many faults including those of innocence and
uptopianism and arbitrariness, cannot fairly be taxed with
prudence when his conscience is touched.

Cronbach became an officer of the Committee to Secure
Justice for the Rosenbergs. Organized after the sentencing
of the Rosenbergs, the committee was widely condemned
as a creature of the Communists. It appealed for clemency
for the Rosenbergs. Cronbach, who could accept no man's
party line, was motivated by his abhorrence of capital
punishment. To him, the possibility that society could cold-
bloodedly destroy these persons, and especially a woman,
was monstrous and totally unacceptable. On June 16, 1953,
Cronbach was part of a delegation of clergymen which
called upon President Eisenhower, pleading for clemency.

When the President expressed the view that the full power
of the law should be applied, Rabbi Cronbach invoked the
blessings of God's mercy and justice upon him. The long
and tormented struggle was for naught. The Rosenbergs
were executed on June 20, 1953. Cronbach, at their funeral,
put this postscript on the mournful Rosenberg case:

"The eyes of all the world are on this sorrowful gathering. Millions of people are convinced that Julius and Ethel
Rosenberg were innocent. Other millions have held that,
even if they were guilty, their punishment was excessive.
Still other millions believe that the punishment was just.

"To those who maintain that the punishment was just, I
should like to say a few words. It is an ancient Jewish maxim
that if, after a law has been violated, the violator has been
punished, the violation is to be regarded as canceled. The
defendant ceases to be a defendant. Matters become as if the
violation never occurred. That Jewish maxim is so noble
and so worthy that it ought to be adopted by people everywhere. According to that maxim, Julius and Ethel Rosenberg are now innocent—innocent even if judged from the
harshest point of view. So much for those who think that the
punishment was just.

"For the rest of us, this is a day of bitter reverse. We
toiled and sacrificed and dared in order to prevent this
calamity, but our efforts were in vain. We were defeated.
And yet there is a sense in which we were *not* defeated. We
were defeated juridically but we were *not* defeated spirit-
ually. We succeeded in being true to our finest selves. We
succeeded as regards fidelity to our ideals of mercy, justice,
and courage. The able attorney, to whom you have just
listened, did not win his case. But he triumphed as regards
devotion, industry, and resourcefulness.

"Tasks still remain. One of them is that of discovering
and publishing the truth. The entire truth about this dread-

ful happening has not yet been revealed. There are questions which have not been answered. Perhaps, when the truth has been discovered, all the world will deem Julius and Ethel Rosenberg to have been guiltless. The truth should be sought and made known.

"Another task is that of binding up the wounds—comforting the bereaved, succoring the needy. The dead are beyond our reach. But the living must be solaced and aided.

"There is yet another task, and this is the most difficult of all. We should avoid hatred, rancor, and retaliation. Well worth heeding are those ancient Jewish words: 'Thou shalt take no revenge. Thou shalt bear no grudge. . . . Thou shalt not hate thy brother in thy heart.' Though the judges and the executive rendered a verdict which broke our hearts, we must remember that they did the right as they understood the right.* Our own conception of the right was, of course, far different from theirs. Still, we should not hate. We should not be vindictive. Hatred killed Julius and Ethel Rosenberg. Vindictiveness destroyed this young man and woman. We who achieved a spiritual triumph when we struggled to avert this tragedy—let us not now succumb to spiritual defeat.

"Finally, we who befriended the Rosenbergs should show the entire world that we are loyal among the loyal in our allegiance to America. Let us give our detractors not a scintilla of an excuse for impugning the caliber of our citizenship. Let us make it unmistakably clear that we cannot possibly gain by anything through which America is injured. We gain if America gains. We lose if America loses. Our citizenship should stand beyond reproach. These things we must do if we would bring about a brighter day for our America and a happier time for all humanity."

---

* Mutterings of disapproval were heard from some members of the audience at this and several other points in Cronbach's sermon.

Inevitably, Cronbach has been subjected to public attack. Like the late Rabbis Wise and Magnes, Cronbach has felt the lash of Congressional investigating committees. The report of the House Un-American Activities on the Rosenberg Case listed Abraham Cronbach as a "Communist sympathizer." The *Cincinnati Times-Star* spread the attack on its front page. Cronbach was not surprised by the attack, and he took comfort in the knowledge that many of the outstanding figures in American life had been subjected in recent years to the same brand of character assassination. But he was troubled by the anguish which the charges brought his wife. He promptly issued a statement to the press which said, in part:

"In my early childhood, at the public school's morning exercises, we children used to sing a hymn containing the lines":

> When the wretched meet mine eye,
> Let them find a helper nigh.

"Those lines made upon me a profound impression. Years later that impression was powerfully reinforced by such passages as 'Seek justice, relieve the oppressed' in Isaiah 1:17 and by the bidding, 'To do justly, and to love mercy, and to walk humbly' in Micah 6:8. It was these humanitarian ideals that placed me among the 1,074 individuals, the 134 organizations, and the 23 publications which receive mention—with very few exceptions, unfavorable mention—in *Trial by Treason.*

"For many years I have belonged to the American League to Abolish Capital Punishment. Repeatedly, either alone or with others, I have petitioned the authorities to commute sentences of death. I have done this invariably when the doomed person has been a woman. The execution of a woman is, to me, the supreme horror. In the case of the

Rosenbergs, it seemed fairly obvious that our country had nothing to lose by substituting imprisonment. On any of the others convicted of atomic crimes, the death penalty was not imposed. The newspapers repeatedly carried the assertion—which no one has ever denied—that if the Rosenbergs would confess, the sentence of death would be commuted.

"When, accordingly, I was asked to join the movement to obtain clemency for the Rosenbergs, I dared not say 'No.' To have said 'No' would have been recreance to my most earnest religious commitments. I would have been one who preaches but does not practice. I would have brought scorn upon religion as another example of a religionist who, despite all the fine talk, is deaf to the demands of righteousness. When I was asked to come to the aid of the Rosenbergs, I had to say 'Yes.' There was no other choice.

"I could fill only a fraction of the calls to address meetings. When I did attend those meetings, I heard many utterances of which I disapproved. I soon began to question the advisability of the entire procedure. Today, after a lapse of more than three years, I fear that those meetings did the Rosenbergs more harm than good. Perhaps without those meetings the chances for clemency would have been ampler.

"Yet, despite much that went against my grain, I did not, at any time, either in public or in private, hear any friend of the Rosenbergs voice Communism or voice subversion. I have never in my life met anyone or heard anyone who has urged subversion. If I had, I would surely not have tarried in that person's presence. For what possible interest can I have in my country's injury? What possible temptation can I feel? If America is harmed, do I not have everything to lose and absolutely nothing to gain? I am not only an advocate of non-violence; I am also a protagonist of law observance and law enforcement. Unlike some people—and some highly honored people—I do not recognize any 'law above the law.' "

Benjamin Franklin once said, "Behold the turtle. He makes no progress until he sticks his neck out." The characteristic posture of Cronbach, throughout a long and fascinating life, is that of standing erect with neck outstretched and exposed. Why? Does he conceive of himself as a rebel, a dissenter, an iconoclast? "Yes," he told me. "Indeed, I like to believe that I was named after Abraham, the first and greatest iconoclast who smashed his father's idols. But," he smiled, "I must confess that the truth is I was named after the town drunkard, whose name happened to be Abraham. My mother had had a dream about this man in which he asked that the baby be named after him, and she complied."

Cronbach was asked to look back upon the long and multi-faceted panorama of his life and select what he now regards as the most important thing he ever did. He answered instantly. "The greatest moment in my life was when my wife and I adopted a baby. And the noblest moment of my life came on the train ride from New York to Cincinnati when my wife handed me the infant and I gave her the milk bottle."

In a symbolic sense, Cronbach adopted thousands of Jewish youngsters, and they gave him a deep satisfaction which he regards with awe. Since 1939, Cronbach has served each summer as revered teacher and elder statesman of the faculty at regional and national institutes of Reform Jewish youngsters associated in the National Federation of Temple Youth. During this period, thousands of eager young Jews have been exposed to the searching brilliance of his mind and have taken from him a tender sensitivity to human suffering and injustice. Saturday afternoon at institute is reserved for a voluntary session in the outdoor chapel at which Rabbi Cronbach tells a "Bible story." No one can remember an occasion on which any Instituter not in the infirmary did not attend this session. For forty-five minutes to an hour, Cronbach strides up and down, imitates each character of whom he speaks, unfolds a stirring story. Sometimes the plot hews closely to the Bible text; sometimes the text is just the springboard for an imaginative leap into the depths of human psychology. But always the story is full of meaning and reality for the entranced listeners. That he is beloved by these youngsters is to him a completely "unanticipated and inexplicable" mystery. Few gestures have been so meaningful to Cronbach as the creation by the youngsters of the National Federation of Temple Youth of a Cronbach Chapel at the Leo Baeck School in Haifa, Israel.

What message would Cronbach convey if, through some magic, his words could be heard by all the peoples of the world? "Freedom," he replied. "Freedom. Live and let live. Learn to respect differences. Let Catholics be Catholic. Let Protestants be Protestant. Let Orthodox Jews be Orthodox. Let Ethical Culture be Ethical Culture. Curb your harshness and antagonisms. Let mutualism and cooperation flourish. Let religion forsake bankruptcy by practicing the love and justice it professes. As individuals and as nations, let us differ amiably. Freedom means more than an end to persecution; it means also an end to animosity. Freedom means love and respect for every creature of God, even for our enemy."

Herbert
Lehman

PUBLIC SERVANT

Iₙ 1959 a revolt erupted within the ranks of the Democratic Party of New York City against Carmine De Sapio, the leader of Tammany Hall. The uphill struggle was a bitter one, pitting the idealism of energetic young amateurs and a few battle-scarred veterans against the formidable political savvy and intrenched power of one of the nation's shrewdest bosses. One of the most tireless of the insurgents seemed to bob up all over the city, speaking from a sound-truck uptown, addressing a fervent rally in the Village, exhorting his fellow voters on television programs, whipping off letters to the newspapers, and guiding his troops from the headquarters at the Biltmore Hotel. His central thesis was: the Democratic Party needs "new blood." The vigorous warrior, the "young elder statesman," was Herbert H. Lehman. His age was 81.

This hectic activity is characteristic of Herbert Lehman who has spent a long life in the thick of the fight for liberal ideals. Few American Jews have contributed so much to America. His long career has been studded with paradoxes. Son of a Confederate veteran who was a close friend of

Jefferson Davis, Lehman is today a symbol of those civil rights which are repugnant to the South. The very epitome of the New Yorker, Lehman became a specialist in farm policy and a staunch supporter of the small farmer. Wealthy partner in a conservative Wall Street banking firm, Lehman identified himself with that militant program of social welfare which came to be known as the New Deal and the Fair Deal.

Moreover, Lehman's character and personality are far removed from those qualities usually associated with flourishing politicians. As the *New Republic* said, commenting upon his decision to withdraw from public office: "The career of Herbert Henry Lehman refutes the assumption that to get ahead in American politics one must have a taste for gab, glamour, or graft. As an orator, Senator Lehman is pedestrian; as a personality, he is charcoal gray; as a public official, stringently honest. Yet he has been one of New York's greatest vote-getters. His decision not to run for the U.S. Senate last year is like his entire public life, evidence of supreme integrity, for at 78, Lehman would have been obliged not only to expend his full energies in a grueling campaign, but once elected, to have served without reserve for six more years. The Upper Chamber has not been, for him, a *pied-à-terre*, to be visited occasionally for the purpose of recording a vote. He is that exceptional politician—humane, hard-working, intelligent, and capable of reelection."

Herbert Lehman was born in New York City on March 28, 1879. He was the youngest of eight children born to Mayer and Babette (Newgass) Lehman. His father was a German immigrant who had settled in Montgomery, Alabama, where he developed a thriving cotton business. Mayer Lehman also invested successfully in a variety of southern businesses, including Alabama iron, southern railroads, and

Florida land development. Mayer Lehman sold cotton to the Confederacy during the Civil War and, when northern troops swept into Montgomery at war's end, his warehouses were brimming with cotton. Rather than permit the cotton to fall into the hands of the North, the Confederacy burned the remaining cotton. Lehman, like so many other southern businessmen, was almost wiped out. After the war, Mayer was sent to New York as a Confederate Commissioner to arrange an exchange of Civil War prisoners. Shortly thereafter, he did something highly unusual for a Confederate partisan: he brought his family to New York and founded a business (Lehman Brothers) in the big Yankee metropolis.

Young Herbert was strongly influenced by his father. Having come to the United States to escape German reaction, Mayer Lehman could not and would not forget the precariousness of his liberty. As he prospered in New York City and his family flourished in the gracious style and unostentatious wealth of their brownstone in Manhattan's East 60's, Mayer instilled in his children the most rigorous sense of social responsibility, moral probity, and personal honor. When Herbert was only six, his father would take him on regular visits to the charity wards of Mount Sinai Hospital. Later, while Herbert received his preparatory education at Dr. Sach's Collegiate Institute, his father and a beloved teacher, Frank Irwin, would take him through the grim jungle of the East Side slums. In these trips, the boy was shown his first glimpse of human suffering. He never forgot these experiences. Burned into his adolescent mind was a determination that such misery must not be tolerated.

Young Herbert received his religious training from Temple Emanu-El, New York City. Later, he attended Williams College in Williamstown, Massachusetts, from which he received the B.A. Degree in 1899. Although rather shy, Herbert was immensely popular in his student days, making a deep impression upon his teachers and fellow students for sincerity and competence. His ambition was public service. He dreamed of some day going to Washington to hold an elective office, but his phantasy revolved around the House of Representatives and never the Senate.

Upon his graduation, Herbert applied his energy to redeem a boyhood pledge he had made to himself. He entered welfare work at the Henry Street Settlement. There he led a boys' club, helping deprived youngsters to express their potentialities. Quietly, he extended financial assistance to several of the youngsters—assistance which, in many cases, continued for many years. At Henry Street, he developed a close relationship with Lillian Wald, the founder of the Settlement, whom he revered and to whose work he was constantly devoted.

His business career opened with J. Spencer Turner Company, a textile manufacturing firm located in Manhattan. Lehman began at a salary of $5.00 a week; by 1906, he had risen to the vice-presidency of the firm. In 1908, he left to assume a partnership in the family's banking business. Herbert Lehman was a good businessman but the evidences of public need, the challenge of public service, drew him repeatedly from the routine of a lucrative and well-established business.

When World War 1 broke out, Lehman threw himself into the task of rescuing persecuted and distressed Jews in Europe. He devoted himself to the work of the Joint Distribution Committee and directed the collection and disbursement of $75,000,000 for the relief of Jewish war sufferers in Europe and Palestine. Immense as this responsibility was, it was only a preview of the staggering dimensions of the relief and rescue program which Lehman would head a generation later.

Lehman became a civilian assistant to Franklin Delano Roosevelt, then Assistant Secretary of the U.S. Navy. In August, 1917, he received a commission as captain in the army; two years later, he was a colonel, working with General George W. Goethals in supervising the purchase, storage, and distribution of material for the American Expeditionary Forces. When the war ended, he was appointed special assistant to Newton D. Baker, Secretary of War, and he served as member of the Contract Adjustment and War Department Claims Board. For his war service, he received the Distinguished Service Medal. In his honor, the main street in Poneviej, Lithuania, was named Colonel Herbert H. Lehman Street.

After the war, Lehman resumed his business career with Lehman Brothers. From 1924 to 1927, he served on a mediation committee in the garment industry, helping to adjust labor disputes. In 1926 he was named chairman of a citizens' committee for Alfred E. Smith's election as governor of New York. Through his efficient and skilful work as labor mediator, Lehman had caught the eye of Smith. When the governor became a candidate for the Presidency in 1928, he sought ways to strengthen his support from New York and, in seeking the strongest state ticket, urged Lehman to run for the lieutenant-governorship, alongside Franklin Delano Roosevelt who was bidding for the governor's office of the Empire State. Roosevelt and Lehman squeaked in, though Smith lost New York State and the election to Herbert Hoover.

Lehman was an eminently successful lieutenant-governor, who gave considerable strength to Roosevelt in the administration of the state. Roosevelt called him "my good right arm." Lehman's wide business experience and his close association with labor and philanthropic groups, coupled with his prodigious energy, made it possible for the governor to delegate significant responsibilities to his lieutenant. For example, Lehman personally conducted intensive investigations of the shameful conditions of New York State mental hospitals, on the basis of which he developed and put into practice a program of long-range improvement and expansion.

At one time in 1929, while Lehman was serving as acting governor in the absence from the state of Governor Roosevelt, a riot broke out in the State Prison in Auburn. The warden had been seized by desperate convicts who threatened to kill him unless they were released. Several guards were killed in the riot, and the rampaging prisoners set fire to some of the prison buildings. Lehman was confronted with a harrowing decision. He ordered the state police and New York national guardsmen to storm the prison, free the warden, and restore law and order. But, characteristically, Lehman was not content with a mere restoration of surface peace. He initiated a searching study of New York prisons and followed through with far-reaching changes in the parole and probation system.

In 1929 Lehman again demonstrated the moral courage and integrity which distinguished him as a rare breed of politician. The economic collapse had hit New York a crushing blow. One of the many financial institutions which lay in ruins was the City Trust Company. Thousands of small depositors were hurt, losing virtually their entire savings overnight. An investigation of this situation ultimately sent the State Superintendent of Banks to prison. But Lehman's deeper concern was for the depositors who were the innocent victims. The lieutenant-governor summoned together a group of bankers and persuaded them to put up a fund of $6,000,000 and take over the assets of City Trust. In time, every depositor recovered his money, dollar for dollar. Herbert Lehman personally had poured a million dollars into the corporation. He did not recover any of these funds. Undoubtedly, he never expected that he would.

In 1930, Roosevelt and Lehman were reelected. When Roosevelt in 1932 became a candidate for the Presidency, Lehman ran for governor and won by a whopping plurality of 849,000 votes. He was reelected three times and became the most successful vote-getter in New York history. The major headache of his administration was financing. He inherited a state deficit of $100,000,000; when he left office in 1942, the deficit had been erased and a surplus existed. And this in spite of a broad-gauged and progressive program of social welfare legislation! The governor improved and enlarged a program of unemployment insurance that became a model for other states to follow. He created a social security plan which was later emulated by the federal government. He created the first public housing program in any state of the Union.

Like Roosevelt in Washington, Lehman was forging in Albany an impressive program of social legislation and human welfare. He was a strong supporter of the New Deal, but he was never a mere "rubber stamp." He demonstrated his independence many times, perhaps most dramatically in his opposition to F.D.R.'s "court-packing" proposal. In foreign policy, Lehman was among the first persons in public life to sound the warning against Hitlerism. Herbert Lehman was an early and persuasive advocate of all-out aid to Great Britain when World War II burst in 1939.

Political pundits are at a loss to understand fully the mystery of Lehman's immense appeal to the voters. In physical appearance, he is squat, sturdy, bald, and attired in the conservative garb of a Wall Street banker. His language is austere, if not dull, and he has frequently been compared, even by his admirers, with Calvin Coolidge. His speeches have never been known to set anyone or anything on fire. The *New Yorker* magazine,* in a profile of the then

---

* *New Yorker* magazine, May 2, 1936.

No Senator worked harder than Lehman. He rarely missed a committee meeting and had virtually a perfect attendance in the Senate. His daily routine began at 9:00 A.M., when he would arrive at his office in the Senate Office Building. Seldom did he go home until late in the evening. Lunch, invariably, was taken at his desk. Lehman maintained the largest and busiest staff in the Senate. His staff handled an average of 5,000 letters, including an average of fifteen speaking invitations for the Senator, every week. Moreover, Lehman always placed his staff and office at the disposal of other liberal Senators from both sides of the aisle, to whom he was one of the acknowledged leaders in the fight for civil rights, fair immigration policy, and other progressive measures.

Senator Lehman joined "the greatest legislative body in the world" at a time when its reputation was more than slightly tarnished. Reaction was riding high throughout the nation. In the Senate, such Neanderthal reactionaries as Pat McCarran and Joseph McCarthy had, through their entrenchment in major committees, secured positions of vast power in the Senate and in the country at large. The blight of conformity afflicted both the Senate and public opinion generally; unpopular, dissenting views were automatically identified with subversion or worse. Moreover, a freshman Senator, in the tradition of the august upper body, is supposed to be seen but not heard. Herbert Lehman was both seen and heard, although his words were those of dissent. Quickly, Senator Lehman established himself as the conscience of the Senate—the man who had the courage to speak and vote the convictions of his heart, however unpopular these actions were known to be at the time. Lehman emerged as a soft-spoken but fearless champion of unpopular causes.

At the end of his first year in the Senate, Lehman was

faced with the question of how to vote on the McCarran
Internal Security Act which had been sold to the Senate
and the American people as a powerful weapon to smash
the Communist conspiracy. In an atmosphere in which
virtually any measure advertised as "anti-Communist"
would find a quick sanction, Lehman stood alongside a
small band of courageous Senators who vainly fought the
bill as an invasion of traditional American civil liberties.
Senator Lehman was the only one of the seven Senators
voting against the bill who was running for relection. Said
Lehman, "My conscience will be easier, though I realize
that my political prospects will be more difficult. I shall cast
my vote for the liberties of our people."

The mild and gentlemanly Lehman found himself tan-
gling with such alley-fighters as Joe McCarthy, Bill Jenner,
Jim Eastland, as well as Pat McCarran. Most of his fellow
Senators looked on in fascination but detachment or
cheered him on in the privacy of the cloakroom. When
Jenner was busily rewriting the history of our China
policy, in order to make General Marshall a villain and
President Roosevelt something worse, Lehman sharply challenged the Indiana Senator, reading into the record the eye-
witness reports of such China experts as Joseph Alsop and
others. Similarly, Lehman did battle with Senator Eastland
during the latter's campaign to intimidate the *New York
Times*. Nor did Lehman shrink from combat with Douglas
MacArthur when the general appeared to misrepresent his
own role at the Yalta Conference. Lehman was the first to
denounce the antics of Roy Cohn and G. David Schine,
feckless members of Senator McCarthy's staff, in their
flame-throwing march through Europe. And, when panic
possessed the Senate in the wake of tense developments in
the Far East, Lehman was one of the three Senators who
dared to vote against a blank-check resolution authorizing

the President to go to war in defense of Quemoy or Matsu.

In general, Lehman went along with the Fair Deal, but he dissented on two major issues. He disagreed with the Truman proposal for a compulsory health insurance program; Lehman searched for a compromise which, in his view, would not limit the independence of the doctor or patient. He also opposed the Brannan Plan but supported a farm-price support, along with medical care for rural areas, extension of old-age benefits to farm workers, rural electrification and rural telephone cooperatives.

Lehman's shining hours came when, breasting the strong drift of reaction, he stood his ground for liberal policies and moral principles. An illustration was his futile but plucky struggle against the McCarran-Walter Immigration Act which was adopted in 1952, over President Truman's veto. Lehman—more than any other American—never ceased working and organizing and speaking and writing to expose the "American Nuremberg law" and to sensitize the American people to the need to eliminate the national origins quota system.

No member of the United States Senate was a more implacable foe of Senator McCarthy and the poisonous brew of mccarthyism. At a time when most members of Congress had run for cover, when many were yellow out of fear of being called "Red" by the mccarthyites, Lehman kept up a withering indictment against the spreading threats to civil liberties. He described mccarthyism as follows:

"Let us look more closely at mccarthyism. Let us analyze the characteristics of those who blindly follow the doctrine, the tell-tale marks identifying them—marks which, by no great coincidence, are also those of the Communists:

"1. They use and abuse the Constitutional protections for the free exchange of ideas but seek to deny these protections to all others.

"2. They insist that they and they alone possess the power to determine what is right for everybody.

"3. They appeal to feeling and passion, never to reason; they don't persuade, they threaten.

"4. They understand only dictation and domination, never cooperation and deliberation.

"5. They are completely intolerant of opposition or division, identifying all opposition as heresy, which they would stamp out by threat and terror.

"6. They use and justify the use of any means to achieve their particular ends . . . ends which they consider absolute and unchangeable. Without scruple or compunction they ride roughshod over truth, honor, dignity, and integrity.

"7. They fear and distrust new or foreign people and new or foreign ideas; they believe in iron curtains and isolation.

"8. They drape themselves in the cloak of patriotism but cynically destroy the soul and spirit of the nation whose name they invoke.

"9. They avow respect for religion but stamp ruthlessly underfoot all standards of morality; they threaten to subject to their inquisition even the clergy and the ministry.

"10. They are, in short, the arrogant and absolute who sit in solemn judgment on the loyalty and morality of the fellow citizens, all humbled by the sheer effrontery of such usurpation of conscience and of God.

"This is the decalogue of their characteristics."

Certainly, one of the most mild-mannered of Senators—and already an old man—Lehman refused to join his many colleagues who would flee the Senate floor in distaste when Senator McCarthy began to speak. Lehman preferred to stay and fight. Once Senator McCarthy, in the course of a typically slippery and violent accusation, flourished a document which he said would prove the truth of his charges.

Lehman interrupted to ask McCarthy to read the paper aloud. No, McCarthy replied, he could not possibly do that. But he would show it to the junior Senator from New York and permit him to read it for himself. Lehman quickly walked over to the Wisconsin demagogue and thrust out his hand. Reddening, McCarthy spluttered—but failed to show the document.

In June, 1954, Lehman joined with Senator Flanders in a move to deprive McCarthy of his committee chairmanship. Later, Senator Lehman added his vote to the Senate censure which represented the beginning of the end for the notorious McCarthy.

The cause of civil rights was especially close to the heart of Herbert Lehman. In the Senate, he was a fervid supporter of fair employment practices legislation, anti-poll tax, anti-lynching, and any other measures designed to advance human rights. Recognizing that the undemocratic cloture rule which makes possible a filibuster in which southern Senators usually killed any significant civil rights measure, Lehman pioneered in the fight for a change in the Senate rules in order to make certain that majority rule will prevail. In the eyes of southern segregationists and Ku Kluxers, the name Herbert Lehman is still a red flag which means civil rights and equality for all Americans.

Upon the occasion of his 75th birthday, the *New York Times* observed that Lehman had had brilliant careers in business, philanthropy, and government. Said the *Times*, "To all that he has done he has brought a keen intelligence, a humane spirit, and an urgent sense of responsibility."

Throughout his long career, Lehman has maintained an active association with a host of Jewish organizations. He is a universal Jew, concerned with the entire Jewish community. He has been showered with honorary degrees by several Jewish academic institutions. He has been honored by virtually every national Jewish body. In all this, he has been deeply aware that "America is a nation born of a great ideal and as long as the nation survives, that ideal must and will be cherished and preserved." Within that framework, he believes, "Jewish history teaches that spiritual ideals, in a people, as well as in an individual, give strength and endurance transcending material wealth and power."

Accepting the award of the institutions of Reform Judaism as their choice for Jewry's "Man of the Century," Lehman struck the note which illuminated the sources of his idealism and vision and faith:

"Our mission is to fight for freedom, human dignity, and the rights of free men, not only for ourselves, but for all who are denied their enjoyment and protection anywhere. Our mission is to be a messenger of peace to all the peoples and to all the nations of the world. Our mission is to advance and defend the cause of justice and brotherhood among the nations, among all peoples, and at home. Our mission is to assist the persecuted and the down-trodden anywhere in the world, wherever they are in need or in danger.

"These are some of the causes to which we must dedicate our efforts if we would keep faith with the imperative ethics of our faith. Today, as never before, there is need for our dedication to these causes, and to the fulfilment of the mission I have attempted to define. The forces of danger, and indeed of evil in the world, were never more threatening. The basic values of our faith, the ethical causes to which we are dedicated, and indeed, Western civilization as we know it, stand in deadly peril. Yet today, instead of the total and crusading mobilization of all the energies and resources which are urgently required to meet these dangers, there is a general public atmosphere of apathy, complacency, disunion, and disinterest. On many fronts at home and abroad the forces of repression, fear, and ignorance are gaining the upper hand.

"I do not speak these words carelessly. I prefer optimism to pessimism. I am not a spokesman or advocate of despair. Yet we would deceive ourselves, and dangerously so, if we refrained from looking the facts in the face. Although there are some fronts on which we have made progress, I believe that in the over-all struggle for justice, peace, and human dignity, lately we have not been gaining ground, but losing it.

"I believe that what is mainly lacking from the spirit of these times, in the United States and in other free countries of the world, is a true sense of purpose and direction. We do not really know where we are going, or why. The protection of the status quo has become a major public force and motive. Conformity and avoidance of controversy are widely hailed and accepted. Theoretically, the public favors some changes at home and abroad, but is generally unwilling to exert any real effort, make any real sacrifice, or take any real risks to bring such changes about. Of course, it is easy to say this. How do we do something about it? How do we make our purpose prevail? How do we reinvigorate moral purpose in a frightened, fearful, and escapist world?

"Here is a challenge, if ever there was one, to our faith and to all faiths. Fear has crept in where faith ought to be. Let us resolve to overcome that fear."

The Path
Ahead

W<small>E HAVE</small> met . . . giants, men and women who left
their marks upon society. They were a mixed and
colorful group, so different one from the other, each consumed by private passions and separate life goals. But if they
were all giants, they had something in common. What was
it? What made them giants?

Our giants shared a number of characteristics which must
be understood in any attempt to evaluate their effect upon
American Jewry, upon American life in general, upon
society as a whole.

In the first place, every one of the giants was a critic of
society. They never hesitated to point the spotlight at any
evil, any injustice, any cruelty or inhumanity and, in the
name of decency, demand change. They were obsessed with
the justice of the causes they espoused, and they braved
every form of opposition, in the fulfilment of what they felt
to be their duty.

And this was their second common characteristic: they
did more than talk. These giants were men and women of
action. When they protested against evil, they proposed
improvements and fought for them. They were doers. They
acted in legislative halls and in other political arenas; they
acted in the economic world; they acted in local affairs, in

national affairs, in international affairs, wherever each of
them felt the need to respond to evil and to correct it.

Of course, all our giants were Jews. They expressed in
their lives deeply-rooted Jewish values and Jewish convictions, however faint in several of them was a consciousness
of a Jewish heritage. This is a broad and perhaps dangerous
generalization to make, and it requires justification where a
few of our giants are concerned. For the range of religious
concern and Jewish commitment among our giants was
wide, stretching from deeply-committed rabbis and laymen
to those who never set foot in a synagogue and even reviled
religious sentiment. Nevertheless, every one of our giants
was influenced by Judaism and Jewish values.

For they shared yet another characteristic, and a basic one
it was. They were either born in Europe or were the children of immigrants. They were close to Europe both in time
and space. They knew from their earliest childhood of a
Jewish life which was all-embracing and vital, or they ab-
sorbed their parents' memories of such a Jewish life in
Russia and Poland, in Hungary and Germany. They could
call themselves anti-religious or indifferent to Judaism; but
the consciousness and the memory were there, and they
played their role. There was a uniquely Jewish quality to
their passion for justice and their determination to achieve it.

One more characteristic of our giants must be noted: the
era in which they lived. These men and women were mostly
products of the later nineteenth century. The liberal ideals,
stifled in Germany in 1848, found expression in several of
our giants in America. It was an age of rugged individualism
in America, deeply influenced by radical Protestantism,
radical French political and economic philosophy, nourished
and flourishing in the fertile, free soil of frontier America.
Our giants represented the rich fruition of a happy marriage
between Jews, turning their backs on the persecutions and

disabilities of the Old World, and wide-open America rearing its free institutions in part upon the foundations of the Bible itself. Rampant rugged individualism resulted in social conditions which provided our giants with the stuff of their social protest and social action. Because they, too, were individual giants, products of their time and milieu, they went about their tasks as individuals who were, for the most part, bigger and better known than the organizations with which they may have associated themselves.

Most of our giants are gone; those who survive are now elderly men. Where are their successors? Are new giants arising? If not, why not?

The age of the individual giant is apparently over. Life, including Jewish life in America, has become too complex. Whether for good or ill, ours is the age of organizations. In our bewilderingly ramified world, no individual can achieve broad social change without the resources of organizations. This truth applies to every kind of cause and every kind of group—including Jewry. The day has passed when a Simon Wolf could presume to confer with Presidents on behalf of *all* the Jews, when a Stephen Wise could gain the ear of a nation with prophetic words and deeds, when a Louis Marshall could arrogate to himself spokesmanship for the whole Jewish community. The giants are gone, and their like will probably not be seen again.

The nearest approximations we can see now are the leaders of our giant organizations. The greatest Jewish leaders in America today are part and parcel of the central movements of Jewish life, entrusted with leadership by more-or-less democratic agencies. There are many agencies in the American Jewish community, hundreds of them, a network covering every possible concern, every possible exigency in the life of Jews and of the American people. To the extent that they are aware of the problems and the causes, American Jews turn to these agencies for leadership. For self-defense and for civil rights, they turn to the Anti-Defamation League, the American Jewish Committee, the American Jewish Congress, and increasingly to local Jewish community councils. For aid to immigrants, they turn to the United HIAS. For overseas relief, they turn to the United Jewish Appeal, its beneficiary agencies, local welfare funds. So it goes in every sphere of Jewish activity and Jewish concern. Distinguished Jewish leaders there are, but they are inseparable from their organizations and movements in Jewish life.

The giants are gone; the Jewish community is increasingly organized and, by and large, increasingly democratic. Many of the causes which moved the giants are gone, too. For example, several of our giants devoted their life's work to the realization of the ancient dream of Zionism—Israel reborn. In our age, the miracle fulfilled itself and the world witnesses, for the first time in 2000 years, a Jewish State. The American Zionist movement, its chariots long tied to the nationalist hope, has continued to sputter on. But, at bottom, it has become a sterile movement, overtaken by history. This is not to say that all of the more deeply-based aspirations of Zionism have been realized. They have not. But the Zionist movement has not yet succeeded in re-defining its roles and functions in deepening the spiritual and cultural kinship between the Jewish people of the Diaspora and the Jews of Israel.

Another cause, dear to the hearts of Henrietta Szold and of Albert Einstein, has loomed ever larger on the horizon until it now casts a baleful gloom over the future of Israel itself. Miss Szold warned that the Jewish state would be judged, in a large measure, by the moral imagination with which it links itself in brotherhood to the Arab peoples. It is bitterly true that the infant Jewish state was almost strangled by the invading Arab nations who held forth, not a hand, but a sword. It is equally true that Israel has pleaded for peace and that its Arab neighbors have returned blood-thirsty pledges to drive the Israelis into the sea. But none of this absolves Israel from its sacred responsibility to pursue peace despite all rebuffs; to extend full equality to its Arab citizens; and to assume, as Israel is increasingly doing, its moral burden to contribute, financially and otherwise, to the easing of the tragic plight of the Arab refugees. The incredible progress of Israel, beset by challenges which stagger the imagination, will end in ashes unless somehow Israel finds a way to come to terms with its neighbors.

The bright socialist vision, which once flamed in the liberal and the labor movements and animated several of our giants, has also dimmed against the background of swiftly-changing world events. Many of the great evils associated with capitalism have proved, in America, to be susceptible of solution within the framework of a free economy. Free enterprise has been tempered with the brakes of the welfare state; indeed, many of the social welfare goals of Lillian Wald have now been taken up as governmental responsibilities. Socialism came to England but it proved not to be the panacea which liberal sentimentality had anticipated. New questions arose: Does a planned economy perforce impinge at some point upon the liberties of the citizen? Is security a higher value than freedom?

And Soviet Communism, spuriously characterizing itself as socialist, has held before the world a harsh reminder that liberty cannot survive the all-powerful, all-planning, all-pervading state. Jewish socialism—and American socialism in general—virtually disappeared as the old planks of the socialist platform have, one by one, been incorporated into the foundation of a mixed economy, providing economic vitality, strong labor movements and ever-increasing social security for the American people. The American economy is far from the millennium; but neither has it proved incapable of righting many of the wrongs which liberals of another generation regarded as inherent and incurable.

Pacifism was another cause precious to several of our giants. Although the pacifist movement was always numerically a small one, it garnered the hearts of many of America's finest spirits, Christians and Jews alike. But the pacifist movement in general was dashed to bits under the hammer blows of our violent generation. Jewish pacifism in particular was exploded by Hitler. Israel's resistance to aggression and its wide-spread acclaim around the world tended to confirm the growing Jewish acceptance of self-defense and resistance to evil. There are still a few Jewish pacifists and a Jewish pacifist organization, but they are lacking in influence. Paradoxically, at a time when men are asking, as never before, fundamental questions about mankind's inability to survive another war, the convictions of pacifists and the philosophy of pacifism are nearly abandoned in American society.

Yes, the causes have changed; some have been lost in the shuffle of events; but new ones constantly emerge. What are these changing issues of our own day?

First and foremost, the paramount challenge on the agenda of mankind: human survival in a nuclear age. How the world aches for the voices which can speak to the conscience of mankind on the immorality of a nuclear death-race in a darkly divided world! Albert Schweitzer has stood as a lonely watchman in the night. Now and then the pope has sounded a vigorous voice. The Quakers have continued to bear witness to the religious duty of peace-making. It would be too much, however, to say that in our time Jews serve as a "light unto the nations" in translating Isaiah's Peace Vision into the realities of this aching world. Would our giants be silent in the face of atomic testing and the stock-pilings of ICBM's, the shabby alliances with corrupt and feudal regimes, the abject surrender to politicians and generals of the very destiny of mankind, the sheer physical hunger of most of the people of the world? Here, if anywhere, the world awaits leadership which can rise above political and military stratagems and speak to one mankind under God.

We live in the midst of a racial revolution—in America and throughout the world. The dark-skinned peoples, who make up most of mankind, are no longer content with the patronage of their white benefactors. This revolution has confronted America with a testing challenge—and a glorious opportunity to vindicate its heritage of equality. The task has fallen to this generation to undo the wrongs of the past. The last decade has seen swift progress in breaking through more and more barriers of segregation and discrimination. But it has also seen violence and terror and stark cruelty. The decision of the U. S. Supreme Court in May, 1954, calling for desegregation of the public schools, has ushered in a new era for America. Our leadership of the free world will depend, in large part, upon how we respond to this challenge. Jews must play their proud part in this historic transition. One need not indulge in speculation to know, from the whole tenor of their lives, with what intensity our giants would have entered the fray to continue the battle which—for Jews—has raged 3,000 years since Egypt.

Nor would our giants have hesitated to come to the aid of their fellow Jews in all lands. Would they have kept silent, for one moment, against the monstrous cultural and religious genocide which Soviet tyranny has inflicted upon 3,000,000 Jews, stamping out every semblance of Jewish spiritual identity? One can hear the blasts of a Stephen Wise, the cold indignation of a Louis Brandeis, crying out in protest. And, recalling the fury with which several giants brought about the abrogation of the infamous treaty with Russia because of the exclusion of American Jews, can one imagine for a moment that the giants would accept with equanimity the current treaty between the United States and Saudi Arabia, which infringes upon the citizenship of American citizens who happen to be Jewish? One wonders how long this ignoble provision would stand if all the men and women of this book were living now and training the fury of their moral outrage upon the conscience of the American people. The giants knew the value of anger, and they would not be content to let the bland lead the bland.

A thorny issue, whose character has changed markedly over the past few decades, is that of maintaining the American principle of separation of church and state. The giants embraced this principle as the heart of the American experiment, knowing it was the key to religious liberty in this land. In recent years, however, there has emerged in America a mounting impatience with the Jeffersonian concept of a wall of separation between church and state. Powerful influences have been brought to bear to drive holes and wedges into the wall. Particularly is this true in connection with American public schools, which have been subjected to heavy pressures to introduce various religious programs. These include Bible reading, released time programs, prayers, holiday observances, "moral and spiritual values," and a host of similar practices. In the view of the Jewish community, these sectarian programs in public schools threaten the principle of separation of church and state under which both religion and the state have flourished free; jeopardize the integrity of public education; and create divisiveness and community discord. Most of the "giants" were religious men and women and several had bitter memories of the

religious persecutions of the Old World. Like most contemporary Jews, they would have insisted that religion is
vital—and that it belongs in the home, the church, and the
synagogue, and not in the public school.

The issues, which might have aroused our giants were
they living today, are innumerable. Would they have sought
to eliminate the moral abomination of capital punishment?
Would they have awakened the slumbering public to the
gross failure of the American prison system? Would they
have appealed for a new sensitivity to ethics in the market-
place? Would they have condemned the meanness and
cruelty perpetrated in America in the name of an hysterical
and primitive anti-Communism? Would they have demanded the abolition of the unworthy McCarran-Walter
immigration act and pleaded for a more humane policy, in
keeping with American traditions of welcome? Would they
have stirred the American people to intensify our efforts to
aid the mentally ill, to eliminate slums, to improve our
schools, to protect the dignity of the aged, to extend our
medical and technical know-how to all the corners of the
world? We do not know what banners they would have
raised. We only know this: they would not have been innocent bystanders to the drama of society. They would
have lashed out at the apathy and detachment of the good
people. They would have entered the arena and they would
have dirtied their hands in the very substance of life.

We have dealt with giants thus far, and we have posited
the thesis that our giants have been and will continue to be
succeeded, in large measure, by American Jewish organizations. But what have either the giants or the organizations
to do with the 5,250,000 Jews of America? Did the giants
represent them with or without their knowledge? Hardly.
The overwhelming majority of the Jews of America knew
of their giants only as names in the newspapers, and most of

them couldn't have cared less. Even today, the majority of
the Jews in the United States do not belong to most of their
organizations, know little or nothing of their purposes and
functions.

Then what of the ordinary Jew? Has the ethical distinctiveness of the Jew dissipated in the free air of America?
Or are there group values characteristic of American Jewry?
One can look at society at almost any point and some Jewish distinctiveness is evident. Juvenile delinquency is an
alarming problem in America; but the number of Jewish
delinquents is infinitesimal. Alcoholism is a growing problem
in America; yet there have been fascinating studies to determine why alcoholism is almost non-existent among Jews.
Divorce has mushroomed in America, dissolving one marriage in three; but Jewish family life continues secure and
stable. There are laments in every community about the
low level of giving to charity and United Funds; yet Jews
contribute five times as much to Jewish philanthropies as all
Americans together give to the Red Cross. In 1958 Jews
contributed $200,000,000 to overseas relief and local Jewish
causes, with perhaps an additional $600,000,000 for the con-
struction of new religious edifices.

More and more Americans are encouraged to go to college; Jews, representing only 3 per cent of the total population, contribute 8 per cent of the nation's college graduates.
A recent study in Washington, D. C., revealed that 41 per
cent of the Jewish adults there have attended a college or
post-graduate school. Much such data can be adduced.
These differences can be explained only in terms of the per-
sisting values of the Jewish group: the sanctity of marriage,
the importance of the Jewish home, reverence for learning,
continuing group cohesiveness.

The group difference shows up on many levels. At the
height of the McCarthy madness in America, a public

opinion poll was conducted on attitudes toward Senator McCarthy. The results were startling. Some 56 per cent of the Catholics polled indicated a favorable response to McCarthy; similarly with 49 per cent of the Protestants. But 85 per cent of the Jews condemned McCarthy as a menace. How account for such a striking disparity? Samuel Lubell, astute student of political behavior, suggested that Jews tended to associate the power-drunk Senator with Hitler and other tyrants of their history. It may also be that the respect for learning and the tolerance of differing views, which are imbedded in the Jewish religious tradition, had their effects. We will seek to explore this at a later point.

The distinctive attitudes of American Jews also reflect themselves sharply in voting behavior. While some Jewish leaders tremble at the very words, "Jewish voting bloc"— and indeed there is no such thing if one means by that a deliverable Jewish vote—there is no gainsaying the fact that Jews as a group do reveal some very decided voting characteristics. In his *The Political Behavior of American Jews*,* Professor Lawrence Fuchs points out that American Jews have tended to vote "liberal-international" and, in the past twenty-five years, have given anywhere from 70 per cent to 90 per cent of their votes to the New Deal and Fair Deal and the Democratic Party. Why? While acknowledging such factors as psychological insecurity, Fuchs points emphatically to the love of learning and the hunger for ts'doko (righteousness), which are at the apex of the Jewish religious value system, and which Jews tended to associate with Roosevelt, Truman, and Stevenson.

Scratch any liberal and forward-looking movement in the United States and one finds Jewish participation far disproportionate to the 3 per cent of the population which

---

* *The Political Behavior of American Jews*, Lawrence Fuchs, Free Press, Glencoe, Ill., 1956.

some 5,000,000 Jews constitute in America. One may use the struggle for Negro rights as an example. Rabbi Stephen Wise was one of the founders of the NAACP; Arthur Springarn, its current president, is a Jew. Mr. Kivie Kaplan, its stalwart volunteer and fund-raiser and Board member, is a Jew. Jewish organizations have always been acknowledged leaders in the civil rights movement, and national Jewish organizations have been no less diligent in defending the rights of Negroes than of Jews. Morris Milgram, pioneering builder of interracial housing, is Jewish. State-wide and city campaigns for Fair Employment Practices laws, fair education, and fair housing programs are frequently mobilized and spearheaded by Jewish community relations agencies. Check public opinion polls in the South on the attitudes toward segregation: Jews are sharply distinguishable in the liberality of their racial views from their white Christian brethren. And no figures on the American scene are more symbolic of civil rights than Herbert Lehman and Senator Jacob Javits.

Or note the nation-wide campaigns to alert the American people to the racist and inhumane nature of American immigration policy. While this effort involves Protestant, Catholic, and Jewish agencies alike, no knowledgeable observer would pretend that the Jewish community has not played a leading role in exposing the national origins quota system and the McCarran-Walter Immigration Act as blots on the American conscience. Similarly, a recent poll indicated that Jews are more interested in international affairs than any other group in America. Liberal and literate magazines find a high proportion of their readers are Jews: 20 per cent of the subscribers to the liberal magazine, the *Reporter*, and 18 per cent of the readers of *Harpers* are Jews.

Jewish leadership can be traced in the fight against capital punishment, against censorship, campaigns to achieve fairer security programs, to ratify the Genocide Convention, to promote the U.N. and to secure an international Human Rights treaty, better education, improved housing, expanded mental health facilities, etc., etc. Our purpose is not to canonize the American Jew and to wrap him with halos. Such canonization is both un-Jewish and premature, as we will see later. Moreover, much of the above can be interpreted as enlightened self-interest and reflex action in response to an inner psychological insecurity. In addition, Jews are obviously more secure in an open, liberal, democratic society. But it *is* fair to say that, whatever the reasons, Jews represent a healthy ferment in American society, that they are goads to the national conscience, and that they are frequently nudniks (Yiddish for badgerers) for principle. America would lose a measure of its élan if it lost its Jewish community.

What historical reflexes, if you will, make the Jew stand out in these ways? Whence comes this special antenna which has made the Jew recoil against social injustice? Many answers have already been hinted at. The Jew has been history's prime victim, and thus Jews are sensitive to the under-dog. Anti-Semitism can only be fought successfully by combating discrimination against all peoples, and thus Jewish security is interwoven with the preservation of a free society in which all people can express their fullest potentialities, without distinction as to race, color, or creed. There are many other possible answers. But we cannot, finally, deal with the Jew without considering the unique religious faith which made him what he is.

Judaism did not merely give the world the idea of one God—but of a God of Justice whom man could serve only through righteous living. Judaism differed radically from the primitive religions which preceded it. Likewise it differed —and still differs—from its daughter faith, Christianity.

Christianity is preoccupied with saving the individual soul through faith; Judaism is concerned with saving mankind through acts of lovingkindness and justice. Christianity emphasizes belief; Judaism emphasizes a way of life. Christianity has a strong concern with the hereafter; Judaism is intoxicated with this earth and this life. Christianity, holding man to be tainted with original sin, has a decided strain of asceticism; Judaism, holding man to be born good, bids him to enjoy his life "for life is good." Christianity says, Thy will be done; Judaism sees man as co-partner with God in building His Kingdom here on earth.

Israel became a "peculiar" people through the covenant established at Mt. Sinai between God and the Jewish people. What was the meaning of the covenant? It meant that Israel pledged itself, for all time, to live the moral laws of God and to teach them to all mankind: to be just, humane, loyal, and compassionate. It meant that the task of the Jew was to be a servant of God, to strive for the elimination of social evil and man's inhumanity to man. There are those, including some Jews, who denounce the "covenant" concept as presumptuous. Perhaps. But there can be no doubt that this sense of bearing the yoke of God, of being a "holy people," has much to do with the miraculous stubbornness with which Jews have sustained themselves and their messianic dream through centuries of persecution.

In Judaism, the relations between man and man were actually placed on a higher level than those between man and God. Wrongs committed by man against God can be atoned for on the Day of Atonement, but transgressions by man against man can be forgiven only when the injustice is remedied. Belief in God is significant for the Jew only as that belief is transmuted into righteous action. The rabbis attribute to God the following revealing words: "Would that they had forsaken Me but remembered My Commandments." The deed, rather than the creed, is exalted in Jewish tradition. Judaism is essentially a summons to social action.

Jewish ethics flowered in an ever-growing body of law. The principles and practices of Judaism, as they unfolded through the centuries, expressed themselves in *mitsvos:* commandments, both ethical and ritual. These commandments set the Jewish people apart, and they helped to perpetuate the moral purpose which was the mission of the Jew. The holiness of the Sabbath, the rights of the alien and the widow, the wages of the hireling, the need for avoidance of slander and gossip, the care to be taken with weights and measures, the importance of ts'doko, concern for the orphan and the prisoner—these and hundreds of other practical ethical concerns were the very substance of Judaism and Jewish law. The Jewish religion permeated every aspect of daily living, infusing the most ordinary detail of family and business relations with a touch of the Divine.

Are Jews among the leaders in the fight for civil rights for all? It should not be surprising. Judaism first gave the world the concept that every human being is sacred because he is created in the image of God. A famous Midrashic legend asks why God created one man, Adam. The rabbis answer that man was created one, and made out of the dust of the four corners of the earth, so that no one in the future could ever say to his fellow, "My fathers were greater than your fathers." The Jewish tradition rejects racial distinctions. "Are ye not as the Ethiopians unto Me?" God demands of the Israelites. At Passover, and frequently throughout the year, Jews are enjoined to "know the heart of the stranger, for thou wert strangers in Egypt." In contrast to other ancient peoples who suffered the ignominy of slavery, the Jewish people never sought to repress or minimize the bitter memory. They glorified it. It became a constant reminder that God intended all men to be free.

If it is true, as asserted earlier, that Jews traditionally abhor censorship and have respect for differing views, is this also not to be expected? In the Jewish value-stance, learning is a prime value. Ignorance is virtually the ultimate sin. Even in the shabby medieval ghettos of Europe, where Jews suffered severe physical and social disabilities, Jewish learning was an island in a sea of gentile illiteracy. For Jews, the People of the Book, have maintained a profound reverence for study, for literature, for intellectuality, for the labor of the mind. Censorship is regarded as profanation of the mind. Throughout history, the Jewish people have been the victims of suppression: the Talmud was suppressed here, the Bible there, the Scrolls of the Torah somewhere else.

But, in Jewish tradition, free speech was cherished. "These and those may be the words of the Living God," said the rabbis, insisting on respect for honest differences and opinions. The assertion of unpopular opinions illumines the Bible. The prophet Nathan denouncing King David for having stolen Bathsheba from her husband, Elijah excoriating King Ahab for his evil-doings, Job talking back to God —these are but a few of the many examples of fiercely unpopular opinion freely and openly expressed, with no question of the right of self-expression. The Talmud itself is a sea of opinions, majority and minority, each accorded the honor of inclusion in the Sacred Writings. The schools of Hillel and Shammai differed sharply in most of their interpretations of the law; the Talmud includes them both and in detail. Recent studies of the *shtetl*, Jewish ghettos in Europe, confirm the respect for differing views in these tightly-knit Jewish communities. This tender solicitude for free expression, this sensitive respect for differences, has, without any doubt, left its mark upon Jews of our age. In a sense, Jews were against mccarthyism thousands of years before Mc-Carthy.

No fair-minded person can fail to be struck by the ethical power of the Jewish heritage. But what guarantee is there that any part of this heritage will continue to shape the lives and attitudes of future generations of American Jews? That is the rub. There can be no guarantee. And the tragedy is that, here in America, where Jews have become the freest and the most prosperous Jewish community in the history of the world, where the pluralistic culture encourages the projection of group values, where a mighty network of Jewish institutions has been reared—that *here* Jewish distinctiveness may be buried. Jewish values are not preserved in the stars; they are maintained, or they die. In Russia today, it has been contended by Soviet spokesmen, Jews do not care about their religion; like all Russians, they care more about "sputniks" than religion. This may be so. For Jewish life there has been crushed under the hammer of Soviet repression. But if Jewish values perish in America, it will not be through governmental pressures. Separation of church and state is one of the brightest jewels in the crown of American liberties. If Jewish values succumb in America, it will be through acculturation and assimilation.

There are danger signals. The great banners which have rallied American Jews in the past have been Zionism, anti-defamation, and philanthropy. Each of these has been essential, and each has rendered a vast service to the Jewish community. But no one of them, nor all of them together, can assure the perpetuation of the Jewish ideals which stretch back to the original Jewish giants of history. Acculturation has already bitten deeply into Jewish life in America. Could it be otherwise—for a Jewish community establishing itself amidst an overwhelmingly Protestant Christian culture? Some young, sensitive Jews have abandoned their Jewish heritage to seek the buried treasure in socialism, science, Communism, political reform, psychiatry, one world, or Zen Buddhism. Of these, many have returned, some chastened and wiser. But, "personally I am not religious" has become a telling motif of millions of American Jews. With all the religious revival and sharp increase in synagogue attendance and new building, Jews still indicate the least interest in religion and have the poorest record of "church" attendance of any religious group in American life. Herberg has said that Jews are serious about religion, without taking religion seriously. Can Jewish values endure without the heart of the Jewish faith? Is Jewishness without Judaism worth the effort to maintain? Can nostalgia for Jewish foods, Jewish jokes, Yiddish phrases, and Jewish folk customs sustain the flesh and blood of Jewish ethics?

What does all this mean? It may mean that Jews are enjoying a residual legacy, that they are the unwitting heirs of a tradition whose fructifying force continues to color their unconscious attitudes and their values. But that force is being diluted—washed out in the comfort, the suburbia, the social striving, the success-worship, and the middle-class acquisitiveness in which American culture is enmeshed. It is still there, inexplicable and strangely persistent, even among Jews who have consciously rejected their Jewishness. But for how long before it becomes an atavism and a proud memory? Jewish ethical standards arose out of the historical experience of the Jewish people and out of the total religious regimen which Jews, until recently, observed without question. Somebody has described this residual legacy as akin to one's going into a room which has been heated overnight but where the heat has now been turned off. The warmth continues for a period. But, sooner or later, the room will become cold unless the occupant supplies his own heat. Perhaps this is the current situation of American Jewry.

There has already been a decline in Jewish ethical practice. Despite the facts cited earlier indicating a low rate of alcoholism, divorce, and juvenile delinquency among Jews, it is also significant that these figures are now on the rise. It is no longer a source of wonderment to observe a Jewish group riotously drunk; or a bunch of Jewish youngsters, looking for trouble. We have the spectacle—once inconceivable and still unusual—of Jewish hunters, casually shooting animals and birds just for pleasure. Historically, Jewish ethics touched upon every detail of business dealings; no business decision, however minor, was devoid of religious obligation. In our time, business is largely divorced from religion and "business is business" signifies the accepted exemption of business practice from ethical judgment. Jews are probably no worse than non-Jews in business practice— but they are probably no better, either. The bitter fruit of acculturation is the desire of Jews to be like everybody else, only more so. This is human and understandable, but it is a bold departure from the haunting Jewish guide: "What does the Lord require of me?"

Increasingly, American Jews have become native-born (about 80 per cent) and middle-class and have imbibed the values of middle-class America: conformist, complacent, acquisitive, with success and money the gods to be worshipped. The suggestion that Jews are different, and should strive to maintain their difference, is anathema to millions of Jews. One result is that Jews, like everybody else, are subject to the crassest prejudices and values of the general culture. The near-pathological yearning to be accepted by the non-Jews, to be like the non-Jews, explains much about the failure of most southern Jews to speak up for the rights of their Negro neighbors. While southern Jews feel differently about civil rights than their white Christian neighbors (in their secret hearts, Jews know segregation is wrong), there are a few Jews who have joined White Citizens Councils to demonstrate their kinship with their neighbors; others who have sought to silence their rabbis and national Jewish bodies on the racial issues; and many others who have lapsed into guilty silence and moral neutrality on the greatest moral issue of our time.

And even among northern Jews, many of whom have fled from the central city and have settled in the illusory security of their homogenized white ghettos to escape the "invasion" of non-whites, there is an increasing tendency to accept the ugly stereotypes about Negroes and Puerto Ricans which poison the atmosphere. Is not this inevitable? Perhaps so. But what a tragic and heartbreaking irony if the Jewish principles which survived the agonies of martyrdom through the centuries should be thoughtlessly yielded up by Jews who are free to be Jews but unwilling to be different!

And what of the future? This generation has been moved and shaped by the Depression, by the profound experience of Hitlerism and the destruction of 6,000,000 Jews, and the stirring rebirth of modern Israel. These events have slowed Jewish alienation, deepened Jewish identification, and renewed the sources of Jewish inspiration and liberalism. But what of the children who didn't live through these shaking events? One can be encouraged by the obvious truth of the so-called Hansen's Law that the third generation tends to accept what the second generation rejected; that the grandchildren of immigrant families tend to sympathize with the ways of the grandparents. But recent studies of the ethical values of Jewish youngsters give grounds for pause, if not concern.

A study by Rabbi Jerome Davidson,* in 1958, indicated that Jewish youngsters exemplify virtually the same blandness and lack of passion in the face of social evil which has

---

* *The Religious Attitudes of Reform Jewish Youth*, Jerome K. Davidson, Union of American Hebrew Congregations, New York, 1959.

been decried in American youth generally. If the moral sensitivity languishes, what good is it if Jewish children accept themselves as Jews and readily identify themselves with Jewish life? If Judaism becomes to them an aspect of social conformity—they have their "church" too—then survival will be an empty achievement. Survival for what?

While the dangers are real, the total picture is far from being a bleak one, and there are bright spangles of promise on the horizon. American Jews are identifying with the Jewish community. They are no longer stultified by fear of anti-Semitism. They are returning to the synagogue. And they are, increasingly, eager to learn more about their faith and its meaning. Many are hungry for enduring values. These are not small matters, for the key to the survival of Jewish identity and ethical values is Judaism. The nuclear institution, above all others, is the synagogue, which must assure the continued spiritual nourishment of the Jewish community.

To applaud the reemergence of the synagogue in America is not to blink at the fact that the synagogue in America—Reform, Conservative, and Orthodox—as presently functioning—is frequently an inadequate vessel to hold so rich a wine as the Jewish tradition. The number of Jews to whom religious services are spiritual experiences is small—and this is true of Orthodox, Conservative, and Reform congregations. Most Jews attend services irregularly, usually on the High Holy Days and, perhaps, at Yiskor (memorial) services. Prayer has become a lost art for most American Jews. What draws Jews to their synagogues in America seem to be: the desire to give their children "a little Jewish education"; to have a place to go to services during the High Holy Days, and social pressures, including the desire to belong, to relate to other Jews, and to identify with the community. Only 1.8 per cent of the Jews responding to a questionnaire-study by Rabbi Albert Gordon* gave as their reason for joining a synagogue that, "I am religious."

The synagogue is the repository of the totality of Jewish life, and should be the exemplar of all that is noblest in the Jewish tradition. But the synagogue itself is subject to secularization, class snobbishness, and materialistic pretentiousness. Too many Jews confuse the new building, the membership campaign, the bazaar, and the theater party—the means—with the purposes of the synagogue. Too many Jews believe that Judaism is an occasional thing which one acts out, prayer book in hand, within the four walls of the temple. To too many Jews, the synagogue has become a kind of air-conditioned shrine where one goes, lightly and pleasantly, to pay obeisance to a proud Jewish past which expired some 2,000 or 3,000 years ago. To too many Jews, the synagogue—and Judaism itself—has become irrelevant to life. These are strong criticisms, and many of the devoted rabbis and laymen of American synagogues—of all denominational groups—will not only echo them but add their own more damning indictments. And many Christians will acknowledge that their churches face the same kinds of problems. Be that as it may. We are left with this: the synagogue, with all its limitations in current practice, is nonetheless the most viable and hopeful instrumentality for the survival of a meaningful Jewish life in America. Its potential is vast. If the Jewish community fails to realize this potential, creative Jewish survival in America is a question mark.

Then what is the purpose of the synagogue? It is no less than the purpose of Judaism itself: to deepen the quality of the life of the Jew, to enrich it with study and with Torah, and to strive tirelessly to bring about God's Kingdom on earth. Many Jewish religious leaders are reaching out, in imaginative programming, toward these high goals. These

---

* *Jews in Suburbia*, Albert I. Gordon, Beacon Press, Boston, 1959.

programs include a new emphasis on adult education, without which educating the young is ultimately a futile task. They include religious camping and retreats for young people as well as adults. They include experimentation with more intensive Jewish education, even including day schools. They include creative religious services, using the power of poetry, drama, music, and the dance. They include a fresh appreciation of Jewish culture and literature. They include a new dimension of reciprocal relationships between American Jewry and Israel. They draw upon modern techniques, including television, films, audio-visual techniques, psychological tools. All these are in responses to a growing restlessness among American Jews, a hunger for positive values and for a faith which will be satisfying to them in a sick world in which all lesser gods have failed.

One thing more is needed. The synagogue in America must inspire ethical sensitivity and social action, else it prove false to the inner compulsion of the Jewish faith. Within the past few years, the synagogue has, finally, begun to redeem its moral heritage. Spearheaded by the Reform Jewish movement, under the dynamic leadership of Rabbi Maurice N. Eisendrath, president of the Union, a synagogue social action movement has developed in all three branches of Judaism. Responding to the stimulus of the national Jewish religious bodies, synagogues all over the country are setting up Social Action Committees to study social problems, and to bring to bear upon the American community the ethical insights of the Jewish faith. It is ironic that Protestant and Catholic church bodies had long before developed such social action programs.

Reform, Conservative, and Orthodox bodies have established a high degree of cooperation among themselves and with Jewish civic bodies through the National Community Relations Advisory Council and the Synagogue Council of

America, coordinating bodies for the Jewish community. Increasingly, the American synagogue is demonstrating that it not merely stands in a community, it stands for something —and that something is the eternal Jewish ethic of a living Judaism. Thanks in part to social action, the irrelevancy of the synagogue may be overcome. And the gap between preachment and practice, which repelled so many sensitive and intelligent Jews, may gradually be narrowed. Moreover, synagogue Social Action Committees are cooperating with Christian church bodies in joint enterprises aimed at shared social objectives—meaningful brotherhood in action which stands in sharp contrast to the bland hypocrisy of "Brotherhood Week."

In our time in America, anti-Semitism is at a low ebb. For the first time in centuries, Jews are able to go beyond self-defense and self-protection and project their ideals into the life of the general community. Judaism has much to say about world peace, family relations, segregation, religious liberty, capital punishment, economic justice, and the host of social problems which afflict America and the world. America, which is grounded on the Judaic-Christian heritage, is in dire need of the best spiritual and moral insights which each group possesses. In this, the synagogue has a role to play of no small significance.

Religious ethics has been the genius of the Jewish people. This legacy has not been vouchsafed to the rabbis alone. Every Jew, whether he wishes it or not, is heir to the tradition. But the tradition itself can be sustained only *if* the American synagogue can rise to the needs—and the opportunities—of our generation. If Jews can banish the fat complacency and peace-of-mind smugness which clings to many synagogues like incense and, instead, make the temple a powerhouse of Jewish learning and ethical action; if Judaism is presented as an affirmative commitment to a way

of living and not as a timid and bloodless form of Jewish
"church-going"; if synagogues pioneer in a Judaism which
is not easy and comfortable but lean and hard; if synagogue
programs are built not around magicians, beefsteak dinners,
rummage sales, and theater parties, but are rooted deeply in
Judaism in all its blazing power and glory; if Jews once
more rejoice in their distinctiveness and express their ethical
values not merely by the words of their lips but by the work
of their hands—then the future of American Jewry will be
neither Orwellian nor millennial. It will bear the seeds of
promise of a better Jewish community and a better world.

For is this not the destiny of the Jew? To pick up the
weighty burden and the ancient task passed down from
hand to hand through 110 generations; to be a peculiar people, a servant of God, and a giant of justice in order to

Make the right to go forth unto the nations.
To break not the bruised reed
Nor the dimly burning wick to quench;
To make the right to go forth according to the truth;
To fail not nor be crushed
Till we have set the right in the earth;
To be a light to the nations,
To open the blind eyes,
To bring forth the prisoner from the dungeon,
And them that sit in darkness from the prison house.